YEATS THE P

YEATS THE POET
The Measures of Difference

Edward Larrissy

HARVESTER
WHEATSHEAF

New York   London   Toronto   Sydney   Tokyo   Singapore

First published 1994 by
Harvester Wheatsheaf
Campus 400, Maylands Avenue
Hemel Hempstead
Hertfordshire, HP2 7EZ
A division of
Simon & Schuster International Group

Typeset in 10/12pt Plantin
by Dorwyn Ltd, Rowlands Castle, Hants

Transferred to digital print on demand, 2002
Printed and bound by Antony Rowe Ltd, Eastbourne

British Library Cataloguing in Publication Data

A catalogue record for this book is available from
the British Library

ISBN 0–7450–1629–4

1 2 3 4 5   98 97 96 95 94

For Jocelyn Ferguson

Do m'shùilean-sa bu tu Deirdre . . .
(Sorley Maclean)

CONTENTS

LIST OF FIGURES

ACKNOWLEDGEMENTS

One of my chief debts is to the late Professor Richard Ellmann, the most genial of men, and, as is acknowledged by all, the best of scholars. But my debt is incurred for insight into particular topics at a stage when I had not meditated this book: he never encountered my hobby-horses and bears no responsibility for the eccentricities to be found here.

I am grateful also to the members of the English graduate seminars of the Universities of Cambridge and Southampton, who made helpful comments when I read drafts of chapters to them; and to the three referees who made detailed comments on, and criticisms of, an early version of the complete book.

I must also acknowledge the kindness and efficiency of the staffs of the Bodleian Library; Warwick University Library and its photographic department; and the photographic department at Thames and Hudson. It is by kind permission of Thames and Hudson, and of Dr Joscelyn Godwin, that I am able to reproduce plates from his book on Robert Fludd. Pauline Wilson of Warwick University Computing Services was also unfailingly helpful and patient.

Finally, this book would never have been completed without the patience and encouragement of my editor, Jackie Jones.

TEXTUAL NOTE AND ACKNOWLEDGEMENT

I am grateful to the Macmillan Press of London and Basingstoke, to the Macmillan Publishing Company of New York, and to

Michael Yeats for permission to quote from W. B. Yeats, *The Poems: A New Edition*, ed. Richard J. Finneran (London, Basingstoke and New York, 1983; 2nd rev. edn 1989). Quotations from Yeats's poetry normally cite this edition: the reference is to *P*, followed by the page number. The text and page numbers for poems are exactly the same as in the widely available *The Collected Poems of W. B. Yeats: a new edition*, 2nd edn, ed. Richard J. Finneran (New York, 1989, London and Basingstoke, 1991).

Excerpts from Yeats's poems are reprinted with permission of Macmillan Publishing Company from *The Poems of W. B. Yeats: A New Edition*, edited by Richard Finneran. Copyright 1919, 1924 by Macmillan Publishing Company, renewed 1947, 1952 by Bertha Georgie Yeats.

Excerpts from Yeats's prose are reprinted with the permission of Macmillan Publishing Company from *Essays and Introductions* by W. B. Yeats. © Mrs W. B. Yeats 1961; from *The Letters of W. B. Yeats*, edited by Alan Wade. Copyright 1953, 1954, and renewed 1982 by Anne Butler Yeats; from *Memoirs of W. B. Yeats*, edited by Denis Donoghue. Copyright © 1972 by Michael Butler Yeats and Anne Yeats; from *Explorations* by W. B. Yeats. © Mrs W. B. Yeats 1962; from *A Vision* by W. B. Yeats. Copyright 1937 by W. B. Yeats, renewed 1965 by Bertha Georgie Yeats and Anne Butler Yeats; and from *Mythologies*, by W. B. Yeats. © Mrs W. B. Yeats 1959.

LIST OF ABBREVIATIONS

Au   *Autobiographies* (London, 1955, 1970 reprint).
AVA   *A Critical Edition of W. B. Yeats's* A Vision (*1925*), ed.
          George Mills Harper and Walter Kelly Hood
          (Basingstoke and London, 1978).
AVB   W. B. Yeats, *A Vision* (London, 1937).
CL, I   *The Collected Letters of W. B. Yeats*, ed. John Kelly and
          Eric Domville, Vol. I, *1865–1895* (Oxford, 1986).
E&I   W. B. Yeats, *Essays and Introductions* (London, 1961).
Ex   W. B. Yeats, *Explorations*, selected by Mrs W. B. Yeats
          (London, 1962).
FFTI   W. B. Yeats (ed.), *Fairy and Folk Tales of Ireland*,
          foreword by Kathleen Raine (London, 1979). First
          published as *Fairy and Folk Tales of the Irish Peasantry*
          (London, 1888) and *Irish Fairy Tales* (London, 1892).
L   *The Letters of W. B. Yeats*, ed. Allan Wade (London,
          1954).
M   W. B. Yeats, *Mythologies* (London, 1959).
Mem   W. B. Yeats, *Memoirs*, ed. Denis Donoghue (London
          and Basingstoke, 1972).
P   W. B. Yeats, *The Poems: A new edition*, ed. Richard J.
          Finneran, 2nd edn (London and Basingstoke, 1989).
UP, I   *Uncollected Prose by W. B. Yeats*, ed. John P. Frayne, Vol.
          I (London, 1970).
UP, II *Uncollected Prose by W. B. Yeats*, ed. John P. Frayne and
          Colton Johnson, Vol. II (London and Basingstoke, 1975).

VP   *The Variorum Edition of the Poems of W. B. Yeats*, ed.
Peter Allt and Russel K. Alspach (New York, 1957; rev.
1966).

VPl   *The Variorum Edition of the Plays of W. B. Yeats*, ed.
Russel K. Alspach (London, 1966).

VSR   *The Secret Rose, Stories by W. B. Yeats: A variorum edition*,
ed. Phillip L. Marcus, Warwick Gould and Michael J.
Sidnell (Ithaca, N.Y. and London, 1981).

1

INTRODUCTION: MATTER AND METHODOLOGY

This book seeks to examine the interaction between Yeats's divided Anglo-Irish inheritance and his aesthetic. The latter comprises the central questions of his poetry, for it would be no more misleading than most generalisations to say that art is his subject. That Yeats's aesthetic exhibits his characteristic doubleness is well known, and the fact has been the subject of a valuable recent book.[1] But I hope that I shall be able to shed fresh light on this topic by considering it with the aid of concepts of difference derived from contemporary literary theory (including deconstruction) and through an investigation of some key elements in his divided Anglo-Irish identity. By this I do not refer only or chiefly to Yeats's sense of the value of Georgian Ireland and 'the people of Burke and of Grattan', but rather to certain institutions and attitudes of the Anglo-Irish in the nineteenth century, especially as these bear on Celticism. It is not a new thought that Yeats considered himself fitted by birth – better fitted than his Catholic social inferiors – to be the purveyor and translator of an exotic Celtic quality and an ancient wisdom, through the medium of poetic norms he perhaps understandably thought of as largely 'English' in character, or at least categorisable in relation to the norms of the English tradition. I realise that this is a formulation which will not please everybody; but I hope that I can show that in his early work Yeats thinks of 'measure' in relation (though not exclusively) to an English, modern or cosmopolitan mode; an affinity with the 'immeasurable', by contrast, he sees as ancient and Celtic. I mean 'English' to go with 'modern' here, for Seamus Deane has reminded us that for Yeats, the special quality of the Irish was maintained to the degree that 'they had remained loyal to those old beliefs and that old eloquence which had formerly characterized the seventeenth-century English'.[2] These sentiments are distant cousins of 'dissociation of sensibility', and they imply that 'The Curse of Cromwell' descended on both islands. W. J. McCormack reminds us of this fact when he prints a version of 'A General Introduction for my Work' in which Yeats quotes a stanza from the 'Cromwell' poem, which is full of echoes from the Gaelic, as a testimony to the Irish bitterness he feels towards England. But Yeats goes on, in a typical reversion on his first thought:

> Then I remind myself that though mine is the first English marriage I know of in the direct line, all my family names are English, and that I owe my soul to Shakespeare, to Spenser and to Blake, perhaps to William Morris, and to the English language in which I think, speak and write, that everything I love has come to me through English; my hatred tortures me with love, my love with hate.[3]

I shall not attempt to convey here the subtlety of McCormack's commentary, but simply observe that the Cromwellian malady came from England and, despite appearances, did most lasting damage there. Yeats was conscious that alienation had infected the modern English poets from whom he had learnt, and that implied self-conscious 'measure'. The ancient Irish poets had managed a measure less self-conscious because in touch with the 'unmeasured' ('To Ireland in the Coming Times'). By the time he came to write 'The Statues' this attitude and this use of terms had changed, of course, in ways which are themselves worth noting. But my starting-point and point of reference will be Yeats's early conviction that the Anglo-Irish poet could mediate felicitously between Celtic qualities, which might on their own be too dishevelled and wandering, and English or modern ones which might become so measured as to be merely mechanical. But complexity attends these matters and conditions my use of terms, so I should like to take this opportunity of outlining in advance 'what is most difficult'.

I DIFFERENCE

I have already declared both an indebtedness to deconstruction and an interest in Yeats's cultural identity: both of these areas of concern lead to the word 'difference'. Many would regard this as a strange marriage. Yet such an overlap is not uncommon in this late age of theory. Nevertheless, one can almost hear that useful old jest: What is the difference between difference and *différance*, and what difference does it make? Certainly the overlap can create confusion, for both interpreter and reader. As Michèle Barrett remarks, with respect to the use of the word in feminist criticism, it is surprising 'what can be fitted into this capacious hold-all of a concept' and not always clear what is 'the meaning of the term in different contexts'.[4] She goes on to abstract from this confusion what she takes to be intelligible usages in feminist criticism: (1) sexual difference; (2) difference in Saussurean linguistics and methodologies derived from them, including deconstruction; and (3) the recognition, or experience, of sexual difference.[5] She has also a further and unrelated worry, and this is simply that deconstruction is unable or unwilling to offer adequate accounts of the relationship between power and discourse.[6] In broad terms, the following chapters offer accounts of, and relationships between, cultural difference and *différance*. I hope that the awareness of culture here offered is sufficiently sensitive to relationships of power.

The foregoing paragraphs assume what is frequently and understandably assumed: that the Anglo-Irish identity is self-consciously divided and alienated, and that Yeats's quest for Unity of Being has to be seen as conditioned by this fact even as it seeks to overcome the malady. 'Difference' in my title, therefore, draws on the way in which this word may refer to problems of identity; but it does so with reference to the cultural forms amidst which Yeats lived. Yet I do mean the word to comprise also those phenomena of language and signification that Derrida denotes by the word *différance* – deferral and differentiality – and I do find some of the terms in which he discusses these phenomena useful in my own analyses. As in my book on Blake, then, I find that a divided inheritance brings with it divided discourses and may entail an acute self-consciousness about the way in which language and form lead away from unity even as they struggle to encompass it.[7] And as in that book, I find a number of specifically Derridean concepts, such as that of the *hymen*, illuminating in analysing certain images ('the red-rose bordered hem' and 'the broken wall' in Yeats) which are the sites for an exploration of ambivalence about the sign: an ambivalence that recognises difference and deferral even as it attributes plenitude of meaning. Crazy Jane's assertion that 'nothing can be sole or whole/That has not been rent', which represents some of Yeats's most daring thinking, can fruitfully be seen in the same light. In analysing such images I am following at least two tendencies which have for long been leading away from the old orthodoxy of practical criticism: one is the Yale-deconstructionist tendency to interrogate images and, of course, words and phrases, in terms of fields within the poem which tend either more towards unity or more towards the subversion of unity and to correlate their findings with thematic elements which tend in either of these two directions. The other tendency is the cultural critic's readiness to include what used to be thought of as 'external' to the poem. In any case, Yeats's poetry has a strong propositional content, even when some of the propositions he makes disagree with others in the same volume. It is not possible to prescind what Yeats thought he was asserting at any one time from questions about form and imagery. But in this respect he only illustrates a more or less general condition of texts, and thus of criticism. As Theodor Wolpers says, writing in a recent collection called *The Return of Thematic Criticism*:

> Of course, the relation between motifs and themes and their mutual contributions to the total 'meaning' of a work may be very complex. But as with all aesthetic phenomena, abstraction and concretion are only two sides of the same coin. Every motif can be turned into a theme or given thematic dimensions if emphasized and generalized appropriately. And each abstract theme can be made a motif if adequately particularized.[8]

Nevertheless, it would be vicious to ignore or relegate the striking formal and linguistic exemplifications of *différance* in Yeats's work. These have been the subject of some ground-breaking recent studies. Hazard Adams, in *The Book of Yeats's Poems*, builds on and differs from Hugh Kenner's contention that Yeats was trying to write 'The Sacred Book of the Arts'.[9] Like Kenner, Adams notes the careful placing of poems within books and the self-consciousness about the juxtaposition of consecutive books.

But Adams emphasises the dynamic, divided and shiftingly anti-thetical character of Yeats's Book.[10] In the same spirit, the following pages will advert to Yeats's ambivalence about the Book and to some of the textual effects of that ambivalence.

Among these effects one may note in particular the construction of a book as a series of deferrals and quotations which veers away from some lost original plenitude. Warwick Gould, starting from the recognition that the first version of *A Vision* uses framing devices suggested by the *Arabian Nights*, reaches the conclusion that *A Vision*, considered as a project encompassing the two versions, is 'a series of provisional statements'.[11] Although my book is chiefly concerned with the poetry, it will be necessary to consider Yeats's occult writings. In any case, the character of the latter provides a suggestive analogy with, and a strong reminder of the nature of, some of the poems. For these also evince a self-reflexive interest in writing. A case in point: Stan Smith has done for Yeats what Paul de Man did for Shelley in terms of 'the structure of forgetting'.[12] In 'The Tower' Smith finds 'double forgetting', a 'curtailing of the fiction in the course of its repetition' and 'perpetual unfinishedness of the narrated subject'.[13]

One of the ways in which Yeats's books differ from the image of the Sacred Book is in their foregrounding of conflict, of contrary ideas and attitudes, of 'antinomies': we move from 'Sailing to Byzantium', where the soul copes with the decay of the body by clapping its hands and preparing to turn into a mechanical bird, to the next poem, 'The Tower', where the speaker cries out in anguish and desperation against the process of ageing. We move from one truth to its 'counter-truth'. Yeats takes from Blake, and from the occult and alchemical tradition, the notion of 'contraries', and with it the idea, to be found in *The Marriage of Heaven and Hell*, that 'Without contraries is no progression'.[14] An energetic investment in contrary positions, all the while adopting, in his mature phase, a strong poetic voice, is in some ways a curious enterprise. Yeats might say, with Dr Jekyll, in a novel that attracted the attention of Madame Blavatsky, 'I was in no sense a hypocrite; both sides of me were in deadly earnest.'[15] As a principle of writing, this offers a limited analogy with aspects of postmodernism: Ashbery's voices, for instance, often sententious and authoritative, but detached from notions of objective truth. This view of Yeats makes me sympathetic to the work of Joseph Adams, who closely analyses the syntax of the poems, finding in them the cultivation of an undecidability which belongs to the realm of difference.[16] Yet, as David Pierce astutely remarks, 'The idea of endless play . . . needs further attention, for it is not absolutely certain that this leads to "difference": it could be incorporated into a Platonic theory or into Yeats's belief that he needed to hammer his thoughts into unity.'[17] I would put it the other way round, though: it is not certain that 'difference' leads to 'endless' play. For my sad part, I am not sure what 'endless' play would look like. I am quite certain that Yeats does not resemble it. 'Limited difference' may sound like a banal joke, but the phrase has a certain usefulness. And 'measured difference' will be a term I shall use on occasion, and which I hope to be able to invest with a particular sense. But to put it in general terms, Yeats adopts contrary positions, but they are chosen from a finite and closely related series derived from his Anglo-Irish inheritance and the aesthetic debates which, for him, were intertwined with it.

Nevertheless, Adams makes a good practical point about the behaviour of syntax in a number of Yeats's poems: that is to say, he gives a detailed account of the way contraries are at work even within individual poems (let alone as between poem and poem) underneath the superficial effect of unity provided by the strong voice. A similar thought has been expressed, with non-technical trenchancy, by Robin Skelton in his book *Celtic Contraries*:

> Yeats deliberately played literary and anti-literary, rhetori-
> cal and vulgar, ways of speech off against one another. The
> result was often a poem that seemed to be spoken by a
> man who was at once an aristocrat and a peasant, a high
> priest and the man next door, a man, in other words,
> capable of many viewpoints, many perspectives.[18]

I offer below some parallel observations, especially about parts of *The Green Helmet* volume. At the same time, I think that the energy Yeats invests in procuring the effect of the strong voice is itself worthy of study and comment. Such an approach is not at all at odds with that of Adams and others, who find 'difference' within the poems. The strong voice is one of Yeats's gestures at unity, a unity attempted out of what defeats unity. That strength is given priority over logic or coherence. As R. B. Kershner says, reading Yeats is like listening to 'a speaker who uses the artifices of rhetoric . . . in ways that continually frustrate a reader's desire for syntactic logic'.[19] This is the effect that Adams refers to as *The Masks of Syntax*. Variety of registers and rhetorical force: it is a combination most obviously to be found, among Yeats's forebears, in Byron, whom I assume to be a very important influence.

But despite all these thoughts about *différance* it will already, perhaps, be clear, from my initial remarks about cultural history, that I must be chary of referring to my account as deconstructionist. This is not because of the element of historical description in it as such: in my opinion those who think Derrida implacably rules out every activity under this heading have misunderstood Derrida. The point is partly that too much weight is here given to reconstructing Yeats's texts as historical phenomena. But it is also that at least in his later poetry Yeats is, in a sense, writing about aspects of deconstruction. He is still taking up firm positions of various kinds, but he seems already to be aware of some of the possibilities addressed by Derrida. I would venture that this is scarcely surprising: Derrida is a post-Romantic philosopher in the tradition of Nietzsche and Heidegger, some of whose more adventurous deconstructions are performed on (or guided by?) Mallarmé. These facts seem to me to help to explain why deconstruction has expended so much energy on Romantic and post-Romantic texts. In any case, Yeats prevents the critic everywhere; and this is true even in the case of his notorious political contradictions – which is not to say that they do not exist. Although in principle I assume the value of concepts such as 'the unconscious of the text', it is hard to deploy them economically and in strength when dealing with Yeats. It is cleaner and more fruitful to concentrate on the poems, bracketing out questions that probe intention: with respect to these the clanking machinery of theoretical knowingness is at best otiose in Yeats's case.

But it is now time to outline some of the assumptions about the Irish cultural milieu that guide my study, and to indicate briefly how these operate in tandem with notions of difference.

II THE ANGLO-IRISH TRIAD

Yeats, I have suggested, thought that it was desirable to mediate between 'Celtic' and 'English' qualities. He saw himself as effecting this in poetry. In *Autobiographies*, besides striking descriptions of the Anglo-Irish consciousness of internal division, one finds revealing suggestions of the Anglo-Irish capacity for mediation. Thus in *Reveries over Childhood and Youth* (1914) Yeats dreams of imposing the 'right image' on the 'soft wax' of the Irish condition:

> O'Leary had once said to me, 'Neither Ireland nor England knows the good from the bad in any art, but Ireland unlike England does not hate the good when it is pointed out to her'. I began to plot and scheme how one might seal with the right image the soft wax before it began to harden. I had noticed that Irish Catholics among whom had been born so many political martyrs had not the good taste, the household courtesy and decency of the Protestant Ireland I had known, yet Protestant Ireland seemed to think of nothing but getting on in the world. I thought we might bring the halves together if we had a national literature that made Ireland beautiful in the memory, and yet had been freed from provincialism by an exacting criticism, a European pose. (*Au* 102)

Notice the contemplative distance from Ireland achieved by the word 'memory', and the inclusion of the word 'European' in a series that also offers England, 'courtesy' and Protestantism.

In a passage from *The Trembling of the Veil* (1922) Yeats identifies himself with Ireland in a less complicated way, offering the opposed terms of looseness and measure simply as qualities which in Ireland might enter into a fruitful dialogue with each other:

> If we were, as I had dreaded, declamatory, loose, and bragging, we were but the better fitted – that declared and measured – to create unyielding personality, manner at once cold and passionate, daring long-premeditated act; and if bitter beyond all the people of the world, we might yet lie – that too declared and measured – nearest the honeycomb. (*Au* 207)

But 'bitterness' is itself a word that, in the 1920s, is implicated in Yeats's ambivalence about Ireland. In a letter to Lady Gregory, written from Rapallo in February 1928, he speaks of how *The Tower* (1928), a volume which began with a renunciation of Ireland in 'Sailing to Byzantium' (composed 1926), astonished him 'by its bitterness' (*L* 738). But 'bitterness' is also an Irish quality which has infected him, as he tells Olivia Shakespear in another letter of the same period: 'Once out of Irish bitterness I can find some measure of sweetness and of light . . .' (*L* 737). There is distance and intimacy again.

In Yeats's early thinking there is a homology between the position of the Anglo-Irish caste, with regard to Ireland and England, and that of the poet, with regard to the infinite and the finite. True poetry and the true poet are deemed to lie at the boundary between the infinite and this world: this boundary is marked by difference, but flames with a significance imparted by the touch of eternity. This triad, with poetry as the middle term, is no mere background to the work, but woven into its texture and themes. I acknowledge a broad debt to the thinking of Lucien Goldmann for my way of analysing this concept; but I do not offer the same detail of socio-economic grounding for the homology, being content to see its persuasiveness for Yeats and thus its interest for the interpreter of Anglo-Irish experience. Indeed, this book is 'middlingly' theoretical, somewhat in the spirit of Hartman's description of Lionel Trilling as a Middle Man between historical and textual concerns. It thus mirrors its interpretation of its subject, whom it sees in terms of an analogous mediation. The three Parts of this book can be seen as a textual embodiment of both the interpretation and its methodological basis.

Yeats does not occupy the middle point of the triad simply because there is nowhere else to go, or even because from this position he could best combine measure and passion. As I have suggested, he also believed there were certain intrinsic inherited advantages for one of his background in encouraging a new Unity of Culture in Ireland. To be specific, I follow Elizabeth Cullingford and Roy Foster in finding far more than merely suggestive the following two facts: that Freemasonry was an all-pervading institution of Irish Protestantism; and that the Golden Dawn was a quasi-Masonic organisation.[20] Foster, in his important Chatterton Lecture 'Protestant Magic' (1989), discusses the characteristic Ascendancy interest in the occult and its links with Anglo-Irish Gothic fiction and neo-Gothic 'Big Houses'.[21] He thus unveils a fertile context not only for Yeats's magical activities, but also for his spiritualist investigations and his purchase of Ballylee Castle. Most significantly, Foster's lecture convincingly suggests that 'the Irish Ascendancy occultist' felt capable of exercising a mediating and unifying role.[22] That role was further enhanced, in my opinion, because Irish Protestants felt that they had a readier access than their Catholic compatriots to the spirit of the Celtic Church and thus, indirectly, to the finer aspects of Celtic paganism and Druidism. They might also approach the findings of Gaelic scholarship, to which they greatly contributed, free of the prejudice and censorship they were always ready to perceive as native to the Catholic priesthood. Yeats at first, then, enters into the matter of Ireland as into a possession, albeit not with a complete sense of security, and for that feeling of identity with his subject-matter, the Rose, in its fullness and expressive flowering, is an apt emblem. Nevertheless, it is very clearly an emblem of mediation: between infinite and finite, spirit and flesh, passion and measure.

From the point at which Yeats came to see the poetry of his early period as decadent and imprecise, these concepts of boundary and mediation undergo various adventures and transmutations which are amongst the chief subjects of this book. The most interesting adventure is that whereby the boundary moves from its median position and takes instead the function of an external bound. Along with the tendency for this to happen goes the tendency for Yeats to consolidate his specifically Anglo-Irish tradition and identity as differentiating him from the Catholic tradition. The voice of the people of Burke and of Grattan through Yeats adopts the part of external criticism and chastisement. This figure merges with the image of the Platonist scholar in his lonely tower and with the occult investigator who is slightly reminiscent of those characters of Anglo-Irish Gothic: Le Fanu's Dr Martin Hesselius or Bram Stoker's Van Helsing. This strong margin to Yeats's interpretation of Ireland can be seen as a notable case of making a virtue out of marginalisation. Characteristically, though, even this move is subject to ambivalence and contrary views: Yeats is often concerned to impose a firm outline around experience, invoking certain neo-Platonic conceptions of form; but at other times, he is anxious lest in doing so, and in doing it in a scholarly and sometimes 'geometric' spirit, he might be courting a world of death, the mere husk and outline of the Tree of Life, an image with which he was familiar from the Lurianic Kabbalah. He is indebted to his master, Blake, for the concepts of 'outline' and 'bound' through which he sometimes attempted to solve his problems, but related images such as the veil, the wall, the mirror and the book may also become focuses for the recognition and the misrecognition of *différance*.

One way of decoding such movements in Yeats's work is to examine images and ideas that offer hints of a structure parallel to the one I have offered of the poet as mediator and then instructor of the Celtic. Two important trains of imagery which do this are those provided by Orientalism, and by the idea of Woman. That Ireland possessed oriental qualities, and even origins, is a notion of great date, but one that becomes prevalent from the late eighteenth century onwards.[23] Yeats is not the first Anglo-Irish poet to be fascinated by or to exploit the Oriental: Moore, Darley, Ferguson and Mangan did so too. And Yeats's own interest has certainly not gone unrecorded.[24] He could see himself either as mediating oriental qualities and dispositions in a facilitative way, or, when readiest to identify with the 'harsh geometry' of *A Vision*, as offering a codification and measure of an oriental wisdom best felt upon the pulses or 'embodied'. But what sort of Orientals are we talking about? For the Oriental was a capacious category, capable of covering, and suggesting a similarity between, all kinds of things from Morocco to Kyoto – via Byzantium. Edward Said puts, in useful general terms, the contradictory state of affairs which obtained, noting:

> how strongly the general character ascribed to things Oriental could withstand both the rhetorical and the existential force of obvious exceptions. It is as if, on the one hand, a bin called 'Oriental' existed into which all the authoritative, anonymous, and traditional Western attitudes to the East were dumped unthinkingly, while on the other, true to the anecdotal tradition of storytelling, one could nevertheless tell of experiences with or in the Orient that had little to do with the generally serviceable bin.[25]

There was, of course, much confusion and darkness in the bin. A pertinent instance mentioned by Said is to be found in one of Yeats's favourite novels, Balzac's *La Peau de chagrin*, 'where the fateful talisman's Arabic script is described as Sanskrit'.[26] Not only simple clarity, but attention to the way Yeats plays out his own contradictions, necessitate the discrimination of Orientalisms, to paraphrase Lovejoy; or at least, of Orientals. Fortunately, Yeats can be seen to repeat some of the discriminations made by previous Romantic writers, and, where he does not repeat them, to play a comparable game of oppositions within the broad field of the East.

John Barrell has offered an extraordinarily astute record of the oppositions discerned by one Romantic writer in his *The Infection of Thomas De Quincey*, and his analysis has much to offer the student of Yeats.[27]

Barrell begins, in the spirit of Said's remarks, by pointing to the 'miscellaneous oriental soup' in the works of De Quincey and other writers and by explaining that oriental objects could serve as 'blank screens on which could be projected whatever it was that the inhabitants of Europe, individually or collectively, wanted to displace, and to represent as other to themselves'.[28] In the case of Yeats, who moved in the freer atmosphere of *fin-de-siècle* syncretism and occultism, this could be rephrased to include sameness alongside otherness. And the displacements and representations are those of the Celtic and – what is often in various ways distinct in Yeats's mind – Irishness. Barrell proceeds to note sets of binary oppositions within the oriental soup, which may vary in content according to the identifications and displacements required by a particular argument. Thus, in the Romantic period, the Greeks could be oriental, because of their incorporation in the Ottoman Empire. But clearly the Classical Hellenes were occidental opponents of the Asiatic Persians. Yet even the Persians could, on the other hand, be seen as 'a common friend against some horrid enemy from the infinite deserts of Asia'.[29] Similar games can be played with Byzantium.[30] And, most piquantly, even Muslim nations 'should not be seen as in all respects exhaustively and irrevocably antagonistic' towards Christian ones. One might find common cause with Ottomans, Arabs and Moors:

> To these peoples, and to European Christendom, we might apply the collective name *Frankistan*, to differentiate them from the peoples of southern and eastern Asia, whether the effeminate 'Mohammedans' of Bengal, or the 'Hindoos' and Buddhists, for example, with their 'foul', 'monstrous idolatries', and (especially) the 'pollution' of 'Hindoo polytheism'.[31]

Again, it must be stressed that Yeats does not share the sense of monotheist superiority. Yet it is clear that he uses a shifting series of oppositions, according to need. Thus Byzantium can be occidental with respect to Asiatic vagueness, but oriental with respect to Western reason. Moorish and Arab culture possesses an oriental capacity to live close to passion, but unlike the Buddhists they share the Western propensity to measure, as evidenced in the invented Arabic origins of the concept of gyres. Japanese culture may seem antithetical: ancestors, aristocracy, warriors, swords, discipline. But its reverence for Buddha's emptiness aligns it more with a cast of mind Yeats found quintessentially primary and Asiatic. Perhaps the most central opposition is that which sees, in Arabic and Moorish culture, on the one side, a passionate and fiery temperament, and on the other, a propensity for occult science and geometry. Byron was not alone when, in his dedication of *The Corsair* to Thomas Moore, he compared the Irish and the oriental temperament; and on the other hand, it is clear that Yeats sees his own occult science as exhibiting a congruence between Druidical magic and oriental occultism. This opposition, then, might be used to displace into terms of oriental imagery a parallel contrast between Irish spontaneity and directness on the one hand, and the Anglo-Irish occult science of that spontaneity and directness on the other. In general, descriptions of more or less 'oriental' qualities might affix themselves to certain Celtic characteristics, or to more specifically Gaelic Irish ones, or to Anglo-Irish ones.

The same is true of certain 'feminine' qualities. Renan had followers who agreed with him that the Celts were an 'essentially feminine race', and Yeats was in many ways one of them.[32] The Rose is the site of a mingling of feminine and masculine, but being a rose it symbolises the fact that such mingling occurs by courtesy of what in Yeats's early period is seen as a feminine principle of Eternal Beauty, and a feminine matrix of incarnation. In this principle are blended echoes of Maud Gonne, of the Gaelic personification of Ireland, of the faery woman, and of the 1890s figure of the Occult Mother, as Diana Basham calls her.[33] Not surprisingly, when Yeats reconstitutes himself in a more avowedly Anglo-Irish mould, the strong voice he adopts is seen as 'masculine'. But Yeats, like Oisin according to the original subtitle of *The Wanderings*, had met 'a Demon' (*VP 1*), although he was never sure that he had been '*Trapped*' by her. He could, of course, become a learned interpreter of woman's mediumistic contact with the demonic (again like the Anglo-Irish Gothic investigator) construing his wife's automatic writing. But perhaps this was the trap: through the perverse half-proffer and then refusal of Maud Gonne's demonic enticement to be driven into the stiff husk or shell or outline of demonic science. Yeats's work is haunted by the notion of a

Faustian bargain with the demonic, for bargains may occur across boundaries, as in the tales of the faery changelings. But the entice-ment and the science also belong to Ireland, for she may indeed be a 'terrible beauty'.

Does Yeats ever relax the stiff antinomies that mark his middle years? To a degree, I think. The later pages of this book tell how, in his later work, there may be found an increasing tendency to cele-brate the mingling of contrariety in our profane flesh. Part of this involves the well-known identification with the feminine, as in 'A Woman Young and Old'. But part of it in the end involves also a new and unexpected assumption of Irish identity so strong that it can privilege the later Gaelic tradition which was usurped by his own ancestors, while attempting to link it with those ancestors themselves. Boundaries break and mingle, and with some unex-pected consequences. But this is to anticipate too much. The first task is to delineate the ways in which Yeats's historical position provides the materials for, and structures the handling of, his pre-sentation of Irish mythology and sensibility. The first part of this book, then, because it is proposing certain historical theses in rela-tion to initial assumptions of Yeats which are then subject to revi-sion and transmutation, is longer than the later parts, even though it does not address a larger body of poetry.

Part One

The Matrix

2

MATRIX AND MEAN

I

'**H**is mind, like the minds of so many students of these hidden things, was always running on Masonry and discovering it in strange places.' (*E&I* 34). Thus Yeats on an 'evoker of spirits' in his essay on 'Magic' (1901). And he could speak with authority, being also a student of hidden things, who belonged to the quasi-Masonic Order of the Golden Dawn. But Freemasonry was also a pervasive institution of the Irish Ascendancy. These facts, taken together, point to an important way in which Yeats felt he was socially and temperamentally fitted to take possession of the matter of Ireland and transmit it into a future where she would be free.

Freemasonry in the British Isles has almost entirely Protestant associations. In Ireland, by the mid-nineteenth century, its membership was most likely to be Church of Ireland. The Orange Order was founded by Anglicans, but probably always included Presbyterians.[1] While this was sectarian in outlook, the Freemasons liked to think that they were not. A recent cultural history of Ireland has this to say:

> Among the most enduring of the secret societies was the Freemasons, who became prominent among free-thinking sections first of the British and Irish and then of the European nobility. Among their members was James, 1st Duke

of Leinster, whose Duchess wished to install Rousseau as tutor to their children. By the end of the century the egalitarian overtones in masonry had encouraged its spread through society and, at least in Ulster, it began to be regarded as a possible alleviator of sectarian bitterness.[2]

Yeats was born into a caste and a family with strong Masonic connections. And although by his day the 'egalitarian overtones' had been moderated, the sense of being a rational mean between sectarian extremes persisted. This fact makes a contribution towards Yeats's sense of his capacity to mediate between Irish extremes in general. But so also does the supposed character of Freemasonry, as of Rosicrucianism, for their mystical doctrines were supposed to derive from the Orient, a location which, as we have seen, was thought throughout the nineteenth century to have strong associations with the Celtic, with Ireland, and more especially with Ancient Ireland, and her temper and wisdom.

The connections of Yeats's family with Freemasonry are well attested, if not well known. His favourite uncle, George Pollexfen, who had copied the Golden Dawn instruction manuals and used to discuss astrology with him, died on 26 September 1910. His sister Lily wrote of the clutter that evoked Pollexfen's peculiar mixture of interests:

> All about in the [upstairs] room are pictures and photographs of race horses and yearlings, and then the interests of his later years, books on astrology, symbolism and such. His masonic orders all are there – and all in perfect order.[3]

These last items, and the Golden Dawn manuals (but not the pictures of race horses), were left to Yeats. At George Pollexfen's funeral the Masons packed the little Protestant church: Yeats's letter to Lady Gregory about the occasion is worth a thousand statistics on the prevalence of Freemasonry:

> The funeral was very touching – the church full of the working people, Catholics who had never been in a Protestant church before . . . . The Masons (there were 80 of them) had their own service and one by one threw acacia leaves into the grave with the traditional Masonic goodbye 'Alas my brother so mote it be.' Then there came two who

threw each a white rose, and that was because they and he
were 'Priori Masons', a high degree of Masonry. (*L* 553)

It is intriguing to speculate on the associations these grave
Masons might have felt with the emblem of the white rose. Ian
Fletcher publishes his researches on 'The White Rose Rebudded:
Neo-Jacobitism in the 1890's'.[4] He does this not because he be-
lieves there is any intrinsic link between Yeats's secret rose and this
one, but by way of defining more closely one area of 1890s sen-
sibility. But the link may be real. By a paradox which looks especi-
ally acute from an Irish perspective, there are indeed historical links
between Freemasonry and Jacobitism.[5] If they survived into the
1890s one may at least surmise that they would have buttressed the
haughty Ascendancy sense of being above sectarian extremes, for it
is not conceivable that crypto-Catholic Jacobitism is the kind we
are talking about. At the same time, however, Nationalists them-
selves were strongly aware of the Jacobite roots of their cause in
general, and of some fine patriotic songs and poems in particular.[6]
Yeats's contact, the Fenian and editor of the *Boston Pilot*, John
Boyle O'Reilly (1844–90; see *CL*, I, 20n), was the author of a
poem called 'A White Rose':

> The red rose whispers of passion
> And the white rose breathes of love;
> O, the red rose is a falcon,
> And the white rose is a dove.
>
> But I send you a cream-white rosebud,
> With a flush on its petal tips;
> For the love that is purest and sweetest
> Has a kiss of desire on the lips.[7]

Given O'Reilly's knowledge and background one may feel that the
sense in which he is offering himself includes the offer of a meto-
nymy for the political cause which had transported him to an Aus-
tralian penal colony for three years.

There is no evidence that Yeats was ever a Freemason in the
sense of belonging to a Lodge that called itself Masonic.[8] Things
are complicated by the fact that one might acquire a charter from
'an irregular Masonic rite, meaning one that was not recognised
by either the German or British Grand Lodges'.[9] On this point,

19

while the Yeatses were in Oxford in the 1920s his wife, George, signed a declaration of intent to join 'The Honourable Fraternity of Ancient Masonry', having been proposed by Marion J. Halsey, the Grand Master. Sorority might have been a more appropriate word. And indeed, a woman Mason is a most unusual person. But whatever the eccentricity of this Oxford Lodge, the terminology associated with it shows that it sought to be orthodox in Masonic terms.[10]

But of course, there is something triflingly pedantic about the question as applied to Yeats. For he was, in a substantial sense, a member of 'an irregular Masonic rite': to wit, the Order of the Golden Dawn.[11] In virtue of this fact Elizabeth Cullingford very properly calls him 'a "speculative" Mason'.[12] While everyone knows the story of how Yeats denied to Maud Gonne that the Golden Dawn was Masonic, her subsequent departure from the organisation on the grounds that it was, reveals both his motives and her well-informed conviction:[13] well-informed because she too was Anglo-Irish. And the story of Claude Cane earlier in her book shows how easy it would have been to acquire the information.[14] Yeats also tells the story, in a letter of 1898 to Lady Gregory, of how he was disgusted by stage-Irish mockery at a Masonic concert he attended with his uncle (*L* 304; *Au* 409). But it is interesting that he was there, for it shows a context.

Maud Gonne thought she recognised 'Masonic Emblems' in the Golden Dawn.[15] Despite the meticulous documentation of its history, it will be worth rehearsing some of the facts that bears on this question. The written materials for the 'G. D. of the Outer' were contained in cypher manuscripts purportedly discovered by a clergyman, the Reverend A. F. A. Woodford on a bookstall in London in 1884. He is supposed then to have taken them to Dr William Robert Woodman and Dr William Wynn Westcott, who were officers in the Societas Rosicruciana in Anglia, to which Edward Bulwer-Lytton had belonged. It was an elite society comprising only Master Masons, presumably comparable to those 'Priori Masons' who threw white roses into George Pollexfen's grave. The textual evidence about these manuscripts, however,

> suggests that Westcott organised a series of faked documents in order to give the impression that the Hermetic Order of the Golden Dawn derived its authority and status from an enigmatic German source.[16]

Not only Woodman and Westcott were Masons, but also the notorious MacGregor Mathers, who played an important, though not exemplary, role in the Golden Dawn.

Yeats was not alone even among the Anglo-Irish intelligentsia in feeling the attractions of his tribal cult. Oscar Wilde, like his father, was a Mason. And although there was probably a degree of levity in his appreciation of the costume of the Apollo Lodge in Oxford, this seems to have been outweighed by a genuinely serious and committed attitude to the organisation.[17] In any case, he was raised to the eighteenth degree in the Apollo Rose-Croix Chapter, which was High Church (and thus, by the way, probably not inimical to Jacobitism and white roses).[18] There he learned that the Rose Croix 'dealt explicitly with Christ's death and resurrection and offered a ritualized progress towards illumination and a communion rite'.[19] There is much truth in the suggestion that many Anglo-Irish writers are ambivalently haunted by the power of the Catholic faith professed by their social inferiors. Both Yeats and Wilde, in their different ways, seem at times to be supplying a deficiency which is measured by Catholicism. One of the chief differences was that Wilde was ready to toy with and eventually succumb to the Catholic Church, while Yeats's attitude to official Catholicism always contained a large quota of mistrust and a sense of superiority. In Wilde's case, both the relationship and the Anglo-Irish bent for factitious unity may be illustrated from the emblem on the title page of his *Poems*, 'designed on his instructions, which showed a papal tiara above a Masonic rose, both enclosed in an egg-shaped oval along the sides of which, is printed the rubric, "*Sub hoc signo vinces* . . ."' [20] For Yeats, however, the Golden Dawn was a superior surrogate which might help him also to unity. W. J. McCormack's words about Sheridan Le Fanu offer distant but substantial analogies with this aspect of Yeats: 'The Swedenborgian world, and indeed other symbolic systems in his fiction (the Great House, relations between the sexes, crime, and innocence), strive towards the reconciliation of opposites'.[21] It might be amusing to note what the Yeatsian equivalent of 'crime' is. 'The Vision of Evil', perhaps? But even that jest may contain an insight.

The superiority of the Golden Dawn lay in the fact that Yeats was able to connect its truths not only with those of the Druids, but also with those embodied in one of the most characteristic institutions of his own caste. So characteristic, in fact, that when Sir

Samuel Ferguson, in his 'Dialogue Between the Head and the Heart of an Irish Protestant', considers the possibility of affiliating himself to Irish Nationalism, he expresses the question in terms derived from Masonry, asking 'whether an Anglo-Irishman ought not to apprentice himself to "the craft and mystery" of mass agitation *à la* O'Connell'.[22] It would not be too great an exaggeration to claim that Yeats strove to imbue Irish Nationalism with a sense of craft and mystery. Or, as he himself puts it in 'What is "Popular Poetry"?' (1901): 'I learned from the people themselves . . . that they cannot separate the idea of an art or craft from the idea of a cult with ancient technicalities and mysteries' (*E&I* 10). The people, if they had known them, might not have relished the associations of Yeats's 'craft' and 'mystery'. And a stanza from Croker's *Popular Songs of Ireland* points to the enduring association of Freemasonry with oppressive Protestantism in the minds of the people:

> Bad cess to that robber, old Cromwell, and to all his
>   long battering train,
> Who rolled over here like a porpoise, in two or three
>   hookers, from Spain!
> And because that he was a Freemason, he mounted a
>   battering-ram,
> And he loaded it up of dumb-powder, which in at its
>   mouth he did cram.[23]

Of course, the association of Cromwell and Freemasonry is absurd, and Yeats would have found it so. Indeed, for him that is part of the point.

II

Yeats's outlook was conditioned by another, and more visible, Ascendancy institution: the Church of Ireland itself. Not, of course, that he maintained respect for 'the simple-minded religion' of his childhood, or would have felt any associations with Protestant practice that were sweeter than 'chloride of lime' (*E&I* 428). Rather, the Church of Ireland offered the model of a way of conceiving oneself as more Irish than the Irish. This solution, unlikely as it might seem, was an attractive one to the Anglo-Irish in what few would deny was a colonial predicament of a kind, perhaps because there were so few other candidates for a solution. That Yeats felt the predicament as strongly as any, many pages in the *Autobiographies* attest. The situation of the colonist had been plangently expressed by Sir Samuel Ferguson in his 'Mesgedra':

> For thou, for them, alas! nor History has
> Nor even Tradition; and the Man aspires
> To link his present with his Country's past,
> And live anew in knowledge of his sires;
>
> No rootless colonist of an alien earth,
> Proud but of patient lungs and pliant limb,
> A stranger in the land that gave him birth,
> The land a stranger to itself and him.[24]

As Vivian Mercier has pointed out, there were two ways in which the Anglo-Irish intelligentsia in the nineteenth century could hope to feel connected with ancient Irish roots: one through scholarship in the Irish language; the other through 'determined efforts to link the post-Reformation Church of Ireland with the pre-Norman Celtic Church of St Patrick and his successors'.[25] The latter way offered extensive roots in the spirit of the Celtic past, especially, I shall claim, with Druidism.

It had been evangelical Protestant zeal, rather than a sense of rootlessness, which had first, in the early eighteenth century, led clerics of the Church of Ireland, and, for that matter, Presbyterian ministers, to promote the learning of Irish with the hope of making some progress among the Gaelic-speaking peasantry.[26] But the tradition of Gaelic scholarship for its own sake grew among Church of Ireland clergymen, so that in the nineteenth century one finds many of the best scholars of the Irish language numbered among them. This is not a phenomenon of the Gaelic Revival, but pre-dates it. From 1838 there was a Chair of Irish at Trinity.[27] By the time Synge went up it was occupied by the Rev. James Goodman, a native speaker from County Kerry, who was passionate for the recording and playing of Irish pipe music, but, as Synge recorded with dismay, seemed to know nothing, or at least care nothing, about the ancient literature of Ireland, or even about the folk-tales.[28] But earlier Protestant scholar-clergymen had included the Rev. Euseby Cleaver (1826–94), a founder member of the

Ossianic Society, 'an organisation which marked the transition
from antiquarianism to a commitment to the spoken language';
and the Rev. Maxwell Close (1822–1903), a strong defender of the
intrinsic value of Irish studies.[29] In the end such tendencies issued
in a remarkable Church of Ireland organisation: the Cumann
Gaodhalach na h-Eaglaise, formed in 1914 to express 'all those
aspirations for a more intense and real national character in the
church'.[30] But for some Protestant Gaelicists there was a subtle
political tinge to their cultural enthusiasms. T. W. Rolleston, an
influential scholar and interpreter, hoped that the work of the
Gaelic league would undermine the power of the Roman clergy.[31]
The Catholic Church was often seen as a foreign intrusion into a
lost realm of heroic Celtic manliness and pure Celtic Christianity: a
realm in which a Victorian evangelical Protestant could almost feel
at home. For while the poetic spirit of the Celt might be seen as
'essentially feminine', Celtic heroes themselves were a different
matter: 'Great were their acts, their passions, and their sports', in
the words of Thomas D'Arcy McGee.[32]

There is something typically Anglican about the Church of Ire-
land's claim to be 'the Ancient Catholick and Apostolick Church of
Ireland'. But the point is that by this phrase they sought to claim
descent from the Early Irish ('Celtic') Church. The claim itself was
more clearly stated by Bishop Ussher in his *Discourse of the religion
anciently professed by the Irish and British* (1631):

> By such records of the former ages as have come unto my
> hands (either manuscript or printed), the religion pro-
> fessed by the ancient bishops, priests, monks and other
> Christians in this land was for substance the very same
> with that which by public authority is maintained therein,
> against the foreign doctrine brought in thither in latter
> times by the bishop of Rome's followers.[33]

Yeats's outlook was partly conditioned by the prevalent Anglo-
Irish conviction of having a readier access to the spirit of early
Christian Ireland than that which was vouchsafed to priest-ridden
Papists. But it was also conditioned by the feeling that that spirit
itself had preserved some of the best of the spirit of pagan, pre-
Christian Ireland. The poem sometimes known as 'The Rune of St
Patrick', and at other times as 'St Patrick's Hymn Before Tara',
was often taken as evidence of some survival of pre-Christian and

probably Druidic notions.[34] Yeats would undoubtedly have known James Clarence Mangan's translation. The poem addresses 'The God of the elements' and proceeds to imply the identity of God and His creation:

> I place all Heaven with its power,
> And the sun with its brightness,
> And the snow with its whiteness,
> And fire with all the strength it hath,
> And lightning with its rapid wrath,
> And the winds with their swiftness along their path,
> And the sea with its deepness,
> And the rocks with their steepness,
> And the earth with its starkness; –
> All these I place,
> By God's almighty help and grace,
> Between myself and the powers of darkness![35]

The poem of which this is a fragment was compared with what was recognised in the nineteenth century as the oldest fragment of Irish poetry, 'The Mystery of Amergin'. It was with this supposedly pre-Christian fragment that the editors of the influential anthology, *Lyra Celtica* (1896), began their selection:

> I am the wind which breathes upon the sea,
> I am the wave of the ocean,
> I am the murmur of the billows,
> I am the ox of the seven combats,
> I am the vulture upon the rocks,
> I am a beam of the sun,
> I am the fairest of plants,
> I am a wild boar in valour,
> I am a salmon in the water,
> I am a lake in the plain,
> I am a word of science,
> I am the point of the lance of battle,
> I am the God who creates in the head [i.e. of man]
>   the fire [i.e. the thought].

> Who is it who throws light into the meeting on the
>   mountain?

Who announces the ages of the moon [If not I?]
Who teaches the place where couches the sun [If not I?].[36]

This 'strange pantheistic utterance', as William Sharp called it in
his Introduction, was felt to have transmitted its tone to the Celtic
Church.[37] And it was assumed to be a relic of the old Celtic re-
ligion. There were, at any rate, striking parallels in other Celtic
poems. Yeats himself quotes a song from the Scottish Gaelic which
is 'over a bride', but which he relates to the memory of Christ and
of 'old symbolical observances': it identifies the bride with 'the
beam of the sun', the 'pilot star', 'the deer of the hill', and 'the
grace of the sun rising', among other things (*E&I* 9–10). And
Alfred Nutt, in the second volume of *The Voyage of Bran*, which is
devoted to 'The Celtic Doctrine of Re-Birth', gives a translation
from the Welsh of the 'so-called Book of Taliessin', among which
are these characteristic lines: 'I have been a dog; I have been a
stag;/I have been a roebuck on the mountain.'[38]

Of the many texts which might be adduced to show that Druid-
ism and Christianity mingled in Ireland it seems best to quote John
Rhys in his *Lectures on . . . Celtic Heathendom*:

> Irish druidism absorbed a certain amount of Christianity;
> and it would be a problem of considerable difficulty to fix
> on the point where it ceased to be druidism, and from
> which onwards it could be said to be Christianity in any
> restricted sense of that term.[39]

And the relationship might have extended as far as philosophy.
Alfred Nutt quotes de Jubainville as suggesting an influence of
Amergin's poem on the early medieval Irish philosopher, John
Scotus Eriugena.[40] Eriugena was in Yeats's time the subject of
occasional mention by students of neo-Platonism.[41] He also en-
joyed the favour of being mentioned by Huysmans in *Là-Bas*, and
was thus exotic and occult.[42] In 1900 Alice Gardner published her
Studies in John the Scot, which bore on its blue cloth cover a golden
seal of Solomon in the shape of two intersecting equilateral tri-
angles, or 'ternaries' to give them their occult name.[43] This device
refers to Scotus's elaborate doctrine of emanation from and return
to the One, which, though it bears an obvious affinity to those neo-
Platonic ideas from which it was formed, was worked out in such
detail as to encompass even a place for the Great Year in the

scheme.[44] It is intriguing to find an emblem which played such an important part in Golden Dawn rituals given that application to the workings of Time which it also receives in Yeats's *A Vision*.[45] Intriguing, but not necessarily completely surprising, since it was largely accepted in the nineteenth century, and had been since time immemorial, that, in the plain words of Eugene O'Curry, Druidism was 'that form of the Eastern Philosophy or Religion which prevailed in early ages in our own as well as other western nations'.[46] The Eastern philosophy to which he refers is that of the Magi.[47] 'In fact', as P. W. Joyce puts it, 'the Irish druids were magicians, neither more nor less.'[48] Magicians practising Eastern religion and magic in the West, like the speculative Masons of the Golden Dawn. Magicians who, like the poet of craft and mystery, were intermediaries; for as Douglas Hyde notes, the Druid 'was looked upon as an intermediary between man and the invisible power'.[49] So Yeats's sense of being a modern Druid encompassed far more than the mere lines at the end of 'Fergus and the Druid':

> . . . I have been many things –
> A green drop in the surge, a gleam of light
> Upon a sword, a fir-tree on a hill,
> An old slave grinding at a heavy quern,
> A king sitting upon a chair of gold . . .
>
> (P 33)

All Yeats's activities could be seen in relation to the idea of the Druid. That role was one permitted him by his Anglo-Irish birthright, and essentially characterised by the action of the 'intermediary': intermediary between the infinite and the finite, between tradition and the living people. This position offers an analogy with that whereby the Anglo-Irish poet is the mean between the extremes of Celtic immeasurability and the over-exactingness of modern measure.

The following chapter seeks to show how this place of mediation can be figured either as fullness of possession and expression, as in the image of the Rose; or can be subject to the fear that it is in fact a place of alienation and resistance to full expression: a husk, a lifeless shell, a dead book or an empty paradise. In the first case the line of mediation is inflated to suitable fullness. And though deferral is recognised, it leads to unity. In the second case the line becomes a mere outline of departed meaning or a barrier to fullness of meaning.

27

3

THE HAPPY SHELL AND THE SAD SHELL

I

The danger of fixity and the value of process are not, of course, themes new with Yeats, whether handled primarily in relation to signification or to some broader notion of life. Indeed, part of the interest in pursuing the topic of unity and *différance* in Yeats is in seeing how he works his matter in dialogue not only with Blake, but also, for instance, with Keats, Shelley, Coleridge and Browning. As one of the chief topics of Romantic writing, the subject has its relative autonomy for Yeats, and need bear no overt signs of its relationship to the poet's handling of the matter of Ireland. This is the case, for instance, with the early, uncollected verse drama, *The Island of Statues* (1885; *VP* 644–79). In this play, many seek the flower of Joy but are turned into statues: attempting a malign fixity, they reveal a kinship with abstraction. The shepherdess Naschina, however, who is blessed with an empathy with the sources of imaginative life, is able to pluck the flower. But in doing so she falls victim to a fate akin to that of Oisin: gaining immortality, she is alienated from earthly love: those who love her will die.

A slightly later work on the themes of passion and abstraction, the disavowed early verse-drama *Mosada* (*VP* 689–704), has, by contrast, a covert but still obvious relation to the poet and Ireland; for it is on an oriental subject, and, as so often, this permits a displaced handling of Irish or Celtic subjects. The plot concerns a

Moorish girl, Mosada, who lives in a village called Azubia (perhaps Zubia, near Granada) which is in Andalusia (for she mentions the Alpujarras) in the period of the Spanish Inquisition. A venerable and central strand of Orientalism which took for its object the Islamic lands had always included an interest in North Africa and a recognition that Spain had during several centuries been 'oriental'.[1] Yeats's continuing interest in Moorish society is most evident in the 'Leo Africanus' episode. This begins perhaps as early as 1909 and comprises several dramatic seances of 1912–14, an extended piece of automatic writing (1915?), and a number of items in the Automatic Script which forms the basis of *A Vision*.[2] The essential point of the episode is the notion that Leo Africanus, a Moorish traveller who had been enslaved and forcibly converted to Catholicism, but had escaped and returned to Islam, was Yeats's anti-self. All Yeats's uses of Moorish imagery involve complex relations between occultism, Catholicism and disguised representations of the Celtic. *Mosada* is no exception.

Mosada herself is in love with a man she calls Gomez, from whom she is separated, but Moorish astrology has given her the reassurance that she will meet him again before she dies. Furthermore, she will be able to see his present whereabouts if she burns some precious herbs and gazes into the smoke. Her friend, the otherwise friendless lame boy Cola, is present at this ceremony and warns that the 'great monk Ebremar', who is obviously a Grand Inquisitor, says that such magic is a sin (*VP* 692). She is not worried by this warning, but soon two Inquisitors break in and arrest her. She is imprisoned in a dungeon; and, expecting to be burnt at the stake, she takes a slow-acting poison. Ebremar, who, we have learnt, is a stern, zealous and merciless man, enters the dungeon to make Mosada, whose identity he does not yet know, confess her sins before dying. But he recognises her and attempts to revive her, whereupon we recognise him as her former lover, Gomez. His buried passion is revived. But she is in a trance, reliving the day of their parting, and his efforts to break into her dream are useless. She dies, and the little drama moves swiftly to its end.

Mosada's use of magic is 'feminine': that is to say, it is instinctive and untheoretical. Her culture possessed occult science in the shape, for instance, of 'the alchemists of Fez', as Yeats called them in the 'Leo' manuscript.[3] Closer to Spain, though not a Moor, is Ramón Llull, that 'Raymond Lully' who appears in the original

titles of some of the poems in *The Green Helmet and Other Poems*.
For Llull was reputed to have learnt some of his alchemical lore
from the Moors of Majorca. But Mosada, as befits a woman, keeps
her magic close to its sources in dream and its uses in passionate
experience. She is, in fact, more like the subjects of Yeats's Irish
folklore writings and redactions. She is oriental temperament rep-
resenting Irish temperament, as in Byron's reference to the 'feel-
ing' of Ireland's 'daughters' in his dedication of *The Corsair*.

The presence of Ebremar is a reflection of the way in which the
modern Irish people are threatened by the intolerance of the Cath-
olic Church. In this picture of the Inquisition, in fact, one feels
something of the fear natural to an Irish Protestant whose family
hailed from the northern part of the island, indeed, from the tradi-
tional 'northern half'.[4] Sligo is, of course, within the northern
borders of the western province of Connacht, but its population,
among which Protestants formed a good majority, could feel them-
selves to be almost continuous with the significant Protestant
minorities in south Donegal and south-west Fermanagh.[5] Indeed,
Yeats must have felt his sojourns in Sligo as an inhabiting of an
uncertain, permeable boundary between Protestant and Catholic
Ireland; a boundary which permitted him access to good and bad
in both traditions as well as founding on the one hand, alienation,
and on the other, the apparent possibility of mediation between the
two traditions.

Ebremar had taken the wrong road: the wrong road for patrio-
tic Irish Catholics, too. The Catholic priesthood is 'bad theory',
as compared with the 'good practice' of Mosada, woman of the
Moorish people. The absent term, 'good theory', is provided by
the occultist, who in Moorish society is an alchemist and astrol-
oger, and in Irish society, a Rosicrucian who is likely to come
from the Ascendancy. Yet the two types of theorist, as we have
already noted, have a certain kinship which suggests the dangers
of abstraction even for the occultist whose soul is attuned to
Druid lore. If Ebremar's story forcefully presents the idea of a
choice in which life and passion have been abandoned, read in the
context of the whole of Yeats's *oeuvre* it reminds one that the
choice of occult science might itself often appear to him as an
accursed, Faustian compact.[6] In this aspect the choice of the role
of mediator, so far from being the encouragement and flowering
of the best possibilities in Irish culture, seemed rather an empty
shell of acquired and partly alien lore and learning: the line of

mediation was really an inflexible outline on the circumference of life, and not at its centre.

II

The most obvious example of a Faustian choice or bargain in early Yeats is to be found, of course, in *The Countess Cathleen* (*VPl* 1–179), a play which, because of the associations it imparts to this theme, is well worth mentioning in a study chiefly devoted to the poetry. The play's gestation began in February 1889, immediately after the first meeting with Maud Gonne, and the writing was done with her in mind. It is a solecism to confuse the name of Cathleen (or Kathleen in the original version of the play (published 1892)) with the name Cathleen Ni Houlihan, as found in the later play (1902). For the source of the first Cathleen is in the folk-tale 'The Countess Kathleen O'Shea' (*FFTI* 211–14). Yet clearly, The Countess Cathleen is a personification of Ireland, like the more famous Houlihan, who herself belongs to the tradition of the *aisling*, or vision poem, a genre in which the poet beholds the apparition of a woman representing Ireland. The woman may wear the fair aspect of one of the *sidhe*, or occasionally she may be the *Sean Bhean Bhocht* ('Shan Van Vocht', or Poor Old Woman as in *Cathleen Ni Houlihan*). As 'Erionnach' says in *The Poets and Poetry of Munster* (1860):

> We should observe that, in almost all the political compositions of the middle of the last century, Ireland is personified by such endearing names as '*Roisín Dubh*' (Clarence Mangan's '*Dark Rosaleen*'), '*Caitlín Ni Uallacháin*', '*An Chroaibhin Aoibhinn*', &c.[7]

The poem which this note precedes, 'Sile Bheag Ni Chonnollain', celebrates another of these personifications, and, as is normal, she has a fairy look, being like 'nymphs of Faery', and being 'thought a fay' by the speaker.[8] Examples could be multiplied from the same volume or from Daly and Walsh's *Reliques of Irish Jacobite Poetry* (1844), where a fine *aisling* poem by Owen Roe O'Sullivan ('the Red') is quoted. O'Sullivan appears in the original titles of a number of Yeats's poems from *The Wind Among the Reeds*, and provides a precursor conception for Red Hanrahan. The

31

poem in question is 'Ag Taisdiol na Bláirne' ('Strolling Through Blarney') and describes how the vision of a fair maiden interrupts the gloomy thoughts of the speaker concerning foreign domination of Ireland.[9]

Maud Gonne was herself seen by some of the Irish peasantry as 'a woman of the Sidhe who rode into Donegal on a white horse surrounded by birds to bring victory'.[10] She might even personify Ireland.[11] Yeats both responded to and developed this way of seeing her. It was a conception that was to impart to her the notorious and immemorial ambivalence of Faery; and that ambivalence can already be seen in the treatment of famine and the bargain of a soul in *The Countess Cathleen*.

It is a mistake to think that the Great Hunger was the only serious famine to afflict Ireland in the nineteenth century; or that dearth of food was the only want that might reduce the Irish to walking skeletons. Maud Gonne gives an account of an occurrence of famine in which she exerted herself in aid of the populace in north Mayo in 1897.[12] On this occasion she seemed a fairy once again, for a priest told her of the prophecy of 'Brian Ruadh' who went to sleep 'in the fairy wood where none should ever linger' and as a result was able to prophesy 'that there would be a famine and that a woman dressed in green would come and preach the revolt'.[13] The people decided that Maud Gonne was that woman.[14]

In 1897 the famine gave rise to 'famine fever' and this itself might be the cause of death.[15] But the conditions of life among the Irish poor in any case rendered them prone to the depredations of cholera. One of the most appalling occurrences of this had occurred in Sligo in 1832, within the memory, that is, of people well known to Yeats. The most vivid and suggestive record of the plague is given in a letter written by Charlotte Stoker to her son Bram Stoker, author of *Dracula*. It has occasionally been suggested that this account excited the latter's imagination:

> Many were said to be buried alive. One man brought his wife to the hospital on his back and, she being in great agony, he tied a red neck handkerchief tightly around her waist to try and relieve the pain. When he came to the hospital in the evening he heard that she was dead, and lying in the dead house. He sought her body to give it more decent burial than could be given there (the custom was to

dig a large trench, put in forty or fifty corpses without coffins, throw lime on them and cover the grave.) He saw the corner of his red handkerchief under several bodies which he removed, found his wife and saw there was still life in her. He carried her home and she recovered and lived many years . . .
On some days the cholera was more fatal than on others, and on those days we could see a heavy sulphurous cloud hang low over the house, and we heard that birds were found dead on the shores of Lough Gill.[16]

But the prime association of the suffering Irish peasantry with the living dead was created near the origins of their oppressions, in the events recorded and celebrated by Edmund Spenser in *A View of the Present State of Ireland*. It will be worth quoting from this dialogue a few of the well-known words of Irenaeus, themselves quoted at length by Yeats (*E&I* 374), which evoke the extremity of hunger, and the kinship with the grave, to which the Irish had once been reduced in Munster, and which he recommends as an English strategy:

> Out of everie Corner of the woods and glinnes they Came Crepinge forthe vppon their handes for theire leggs Coulde not beare them, they loked like Anotomies of deathe, they spake like ghostes Cryinge out of theire graves, they did eate the dead Carrions, happie wheare they Coulde finde them, Yea and one another sone after, in so muche as the verye carkasses they spared not to scrape out of theire graves.[17]

This was the venerable imagery associated by the end of the nineteenth century with a recurrent condition of the Irish people, a condition for which some members of the Ascendancy felt themselves responsible. In Bram Stoker's story 'The Invisible Giant', which was influenced by his mother's description of the Sligo epidemic, the hero and heroine 'did all they could to help the poor people'.[18] This was what Maud Gonne sought to do, and what had been done by William Middleton's father 'after the great famine': according to Yeats, he 'had attended the sick for weeks, and taken cholera from a man he carried in his arms into his own house and died of it . . .' (*Au* 7–8).

The Countess Cathleen's selling of her own soul to save the starving people figures forth Yeats's fear that spiritual death was to be the result for Maud Gonne; and an irretrievable result, despite the consoling note at the play's ending. Such, at any rate, is a reasonable inference from the famous lines in the third stanza of 'The Circus Animals' Desertion' (*P* 347). But if Maud Gonne was a fairy queen and a personification of Ireland, who went to spiritual death, might she not become a dead fairy queen of Gothic aspect, as Ireland herself might be seen, for instance, in Nora Hopper's lines 'To Sheila ni Gara' (Ireland)?

> Out of the wind and out of the rain,
> Sheila, come to my arms again;
> Close though your grave clothes wrap you round,
> Come from your quiet underground.[19]

In a personification such as this, the woman representing Ireland acquires all the Gothic associations with which the suffering Irish people had occasionally been invested, not least in *The Countess Cathleen* itself:

> TEIGUE They say that now the land is famine-struck.
> The graves are walking.
> MARY What can the hen have heard?
> TEIGUE And that is not the worst; at Tubber-vanach
> A woman met a man with ears spread out,
> And they moved up and down like a bat's wing.
> (*VPl* 5,7)

While this does show Yeats depicting the Irish victims of famine as akin to vampires, it is scarcely enough on its own to establish that the image of the beloved might mingle both with Ireland and with that of the demonic woman of fairy. And if one is to accept the suggestion, one must also accept the irrational tendency in myth and folklore for both opposites and contiguities to merge. This principle, recognised by Frazer and accepted by Freud, was also known to Yeats. In any case, if *The Countess Cathleen* is read alongside *The Wanderings of Oisin* and other early Yeats texts, it points in the direction of such merging. This is important, not for what (if anything) it says about Maud Gonne, but because it shows Yeats conceiving Ireland – through the medium of Maud Gonne, and of traditional symbolisations – as potentially a dangerous vampire who might lead her compassionate adherents into that state of Life-in-Death which had borne the image of the Fatal Woman from Coleridge downwards.

Another instance of mingling and transference of ideas relates to hunger and starvation, which are so frequently used by Yeats as metaphors for desire. In 'The Circus Animals' Desertion' Yeats speaks of being 'starved for the bosom of [Oisin's] fairy bride' (*P* 347), just one line before invoking the 'counter-truth' represented by *The Countess Cathleen*. The juxtaposition, relevant even though occurring so many years afterwards, is of contraries and not of blank opposites: *The Wanderings of Oisin* and *The Countess Cathleen* represent contrary uses of the idea of hunger. Oisin, like his maker, hungers for the fairy bride, but receives a 'vain' – that is, 'empty' – simulacrum of satisfaction. The Countess Cathleen, bewitched by the Irish people, is possessed by a spiritual hunger retrospectively stigmatised by Yeats as 'fanaticism and hate'. She exchanges her soul for the repletion of the people's starved bodies, enacting in that movement the essence of the counter-truth: Oisin's was a spiritual hunger for an emotional satisfaction, which turned out to be empty; Cathleen's was a spiritual hunger for the material satis-faction of others, which turned out to be even emptier. The dream that leads away from the heart is closer to being dead than that which maintains connection with it.

Hunger for the Fatal Woman is bound up with the most urgent questions of the poet's quest for a full meaning, and this could be illustrated from Coleridge or Keats as much as from Yeats himself. Life-in-Death is an image of the hindrance and evacuation of meaning: seeming like one who should offer complete satisfaction of desire, she represents only frustration and deferral, and thus finds her fitting place in the frosty 'Rime' of the Mariner's alienated wanderings. If Yeats could harness this par-ticular Romantic tradition to his sense of the dangers inherent in pursuing the matter of Ireland, that supports the notion that he was anxious about his ability to possess that matter and make it the subject of a poetic utterance which did not bear the effects of alienation. For an unalienated Irish poetry was indeed what he desired to write, embodying 'a mythology that marries' the race 'to rock and hill' (*Au* 194). If, nevertheless, 'the Gaelic muse' remained for him a 'malignant fairy' (*FFTI* 385), this was not merely a matter of 'images of women', but also of images of the frustration and deferral of poetic utterance. But this argument requires more attention to fairies, and especially to *The Wanderings of Oisin*.

III

The spirit that, as the Druids saw, wanders through all things, must not be fixed. And such was also an important part of Blake's message. On the other hand, there is a felicitous kind of acceptance of wandering and contrariety which gives rise to Joy. This acceptance and this Joy, it seems reasonable to infer, are the true preconditions for happy poetic making. This important topic of Joy makes its appearance in *The Island of Statues*, in the early poems later gathered in *Crossways* and in *The Wanderings of Oisin*. And Blake also has a doctrine about the attainment of Joy, which is broadly similar to Yeats's, and is best encapsulated in 'Auguries of Innocence', a poem from the Pickering manuscript which was included, in an eccentrically arranged form, in William Michael Rossetti's Aldine *Blake*:[20]

> Man was made for Joy & Woe
> And when this we rightly know
> Thro the world we safely go
> Joy & Woe are woven fine
> A clothing for the Soul divine
> Under every grief & pine
> Runs a Joy with silken twine[21]

In the spirit, though hardly the manner, of Keats's 'Ode on Melancholy', Blake warns that those who attempt to trap and solidify joy, and avoid all possible occasions of sorrow, are the victims of an insecure and life-denying philosophy – or perhaps one should say temperament – and will end only in a melancholy state neither of joy nor of sorrow. This is the clue to understanding the mistaken and uncomprehending words of Urizen:

> I have sought for a joy without pain
> For a solid without fluctuation
> Why will you die O Eternals?
> Why live in perpetual burnings?[22]

36

They might almost be the words of Patrick to Oisin. What Yeats does is to link the energetic condition of Joy-and-Sorrow with his own way of conceiving this world according to a supposedly Druidical and Brahminical conception of the One as principle of the Many: humanity should not, like Urizen, seek to overleap the Many and go straight for the security of the One: the best way to make contact with the divine is to realise that one must immerse oneself in this world of multiplicity, accepting that it is characterised by mutability, and by Sorrow as well as Joy. This doctrine bears some resemblance to that of Browning, whom Yeats as a young man 'especially' espoused for his 'air of wisdom' (*Au* 81).[23] Indeed, this very aspect of Browning's thought is treated in Yeats's letter to the *Boston Pilot* of 22 February 1890, where the following conversation provides the text:

> 'Mr. Browning, you are a mystic.' 'Yes', he answered, 'but how did you find it out?'
>   To Browning thought was mainly interesting as an expression of life. In life in all its phases he seems to have had the most absorbing interest. . .[24]

Acceptance of mutability and death was also a theme of the occult traditions with which Yeats had come into contact, for they, like Blake, had inherited the alchemical doctrine of contraries.[25]

The connection of these ideas is most obvious in *The Wanderings of Oisin*, where the Druid theme is very explicitly linked to the Urizen theme at the point where the beautiful young man with the sceptre expounds the philosophy of Tír-na-nÓg:

> Joy drowns the twilight in the dew,
> And fills with stars night's purple cup,
> And wakes the sluggard seeds of corn,
> And stirs the young kid's budding horn,
> And makes the infant ferns unwrap,
> And for the peewit paints his cap,
> And rolls along the unwieldy sun,
> And makes the little planets run:
> And if joy were not on the earth,
> There were an end of change and birth,
> And Earth and Heaven and Hell would die,
> And in some gloomy barrow lie

> Folded like a frozen fly;
> Then mock at Death and Time with glances
> And wavering arms and wandering dances.
>
> (*P* 362)

So far, so relatively simple. But the reader may well pause at that gloomy barrow, added in *Poems* (1895) (it had originally been 'some urn funereal'). For a barrow in Ireland, sometimes called a 'liss', would frequently be the home of the *sidhe*, the same that inhabit Tír-na-nÓg, of whom the beautiful young man is one. There need be no problem with that mere fact, and there is no problem with it in Yeats's reference to Caoilte, in 'The Secret Rose', as 'him who drove the gods out of their liss' (*P* 70). But in *Oisin* the liss is unmistakably a barrow. And there lies ambivalence. After all, Oisin himself has forsaken 'change and birth'. Is he then dreaming under a sinister fairy hill, like True Thomas, of whom Yeats had thought after seeing a mysterious light moving with preternatural swiftness up the slopes of Knocknarea (*Au* 78)? Is Oisin being subjected to the notorious perversity of the *sidhe*, specifically of that *Leanhaun Shee* described by Yeats both as 'Gaelic muse' and 'malignant fairy'? This reading might seem to be suggested also by some of the lines that follow:

> But here there is nor law nor rule,
> Nor have hands held a weary tool;
> And here there is nor Change nor Death,
> But only kind and merry breath . . .
>
> (*P* 362–3)

We have been told that the end of 'change and birth' is to lie in a barrow. What difference, aside from the rhetorical, lies between that and the end of change and death? And yet, though Yeats does wish to exploit this sinister ambiguity, it is only to further the point that a life of endless joy is not of 'earth' and is at odds with its true nature. Hence Oisin's longing to return and see his old companions once more. The true condition of humanity is to live in the world of variety, multiplicity, change, and mingled Joy and Sorrow. Above this world, so to speak, is the world of Eternal Joy; below it, a world of grey abstraction, where neither Joy nor Sorrow exists. Neither world is human. But the human world may tend to either extreme. The age of St Patrick, to which Oisin returns, tends more to grey abstraction; the heroic Fenian age more to the world of Eternal Joy.

These will seem unexceptionable comments to many readers of the poem. Yet our argument requires that they be stated baldly so that the relationship of *The Wanderings of Oisin* to what I have called 'The Anglo-Irish Triad' may be clearly perceived. For the position of the poet mediating between Celtic immeasurability and modern abstraction is clearly paralleled here. Furthermore, the perception of these parallel triads provides an illuminating glimpse of the true role of the Other World in Yeats's poem. For the three islands, of 'vain' gaiety, battle and repose – originally of 'The Living', of 'Victories' and of 'Forgetfulness' (*VP* 1, 29, 47) – themselves provide an empty parallel with the cosmic triad of Joy, of Contrariety and of Abstraction, and thus a parallel also with Yeats's diagram of the position of the Anglo-Irish poet. The Other World, then, is like an empty quotation both of the perceptive poet's view of life and of the place of the poet. That one should see the Other World as this kind of empty sign writ large is further suggested by the obviously literary and national character of the poem's subject. For the Ossianic tale was easily the best qualified to convey the message of a centrally Celtic matter, following Macpherson. It was also a choice that allowed the assertion of Ireland's primacy in the development of the Fenian cycle, as against Scotland: a contention which had fired the patriotic pique of a number of Irish antiquarians, for instance, James Hardiman in his *Irish Minstrelsy*.[26] It permitted Yeats to provide a modern version of part of what in itself was regarded as the pre-eminently heroic patriotic cycle, the subject of specialist interest: Michael Comyn's poetic retelling of the story had been twice translated into English in the nineteenth century; there were also other sources Yeats might have consulted; and the chief organised body of Irish antiquarians termed itself the 'Ossianic Society'.[27] Finally, of course, Oisin was the poet of the Fenians, and Yeats was donning his mantle.

The choice of subject was, precisely because of all these facts, intended to assert the poet's unity with Ireland: Oisin is expressly mentioned in the famous lines from *The Trembling of the Veil* about finding 'unity from a mythology that marries [races] to rock and hill' (*Au* 194). But in the end the 'literary' character of the poem is ambivalent. For while it is a plausible aid to Yeats's self-definition as an Irish bard, it also tends to create an effect of remote artifice. For it must be weighed with the ultimate hollowness of the Other

World to which Oisin goes: hollowness in the sense already described: that it is an unearthly copy of Yeats's view of the poet's place in the world. The intensity of this effect is due largely to his own innovations with the material, for in Comyn's version Oisin arrives first at the 'Land of Virtues' and there encounters the giant. But he succeeds in killing it, departs with the fairy enchantress Niamh for Tír-na-nÓg, stays there for three hundred years, and then returns to Ireland for a nostalgic visit.[28] This narrative lacks the uncanniness of Yeats's poem.

And 'uncanny' does seem to me an appropriate word. Following Freud's discussion of Hoffmann's 'The Sandman', with its doublings and its beloved who turns out to be a mechanical doll, this term is often referred to Gothic phenomena such as *Doppelgänger*, Brocken spectres and artificial monsters, as well as to quieter, but no less sinister duplicates and repetitions.[29] In Freud, the ambivalence of what is *umheimlich* lies, at root, in its closeness to what is *heimlich* ('canny, known, home-like' but also 'secret' in a sinister and dangerous sense). A repetition or double may be a fantastic representation of the doubling of the self: it is consoling, narcissistic, and offers an assurance to the ego against the threat of extinction. The uncanny as a doubling that is clearly strange, unknown and other, offers a threat to the ego's security, and one that is the more troubling to the extent that it does so through the medium of what at first looks familiar. In this sense, the uncanny is the return of the repressed. Our nature is threatened in its very home. Freud's point, and one that has been developed by critics of his essay, is that the *Heimlich* and *Unheimlich* merge and interweave.[30] Those critics are thus able to see in Freud's essay a precursor of Lacan's dialectic of the Imaginary and the Symbolic: the Imaginary proffering wholeness, the Symbolic recalling the Ego to the founding breach of castration.

There is no reason whatsoever why the term 'uncanny' should be reserved for representations of human doubles or automata. Since, as Lacan points out, the visual field may be made to offer wholeness of various kinds, particularly through works of art, all works of art cater to narcissism.[31] But for Lacan, all works of art also proffer an estranging and renunciative moment, the taming of the gaze (the *dompte-regard*). It is fair to say that a corollary of this theory is that all art exhibits the dialectic of the uncanny. Therefore, the literature of the uncanny merely becomes a special, self-conscious sub-category of art, and by no means one that is bound to representations of human doubles.

40

The uncanniness of Yeats's poem makes itself especially felt at those crucial moments in each of the three Books when a token or sign of the human world enters the Other World, and precipitates dissatisfaction in Oisin with the island where he is currently sojourning. In Book I the discovery is described thus:

> When one day by the tide I stood,
> I found in that forgetfulness
> Of dreamy foam a staff of wood
> From some dead warrior's broken lance:
> I turned it in my hands; the stains
> Of war were on it, and I wept,
> Remembering how the Fenians stept
> Along the blood-bedabbled plains,
> Equal to good or grievous chance . . .
>
> (P 365)

That the staff comes from a world of contrariety is less worthy of note than the fact that the fragmentary character of the finding is emphasised: not only is it not the complete spear, it is not even the whole haft. As a fragment of the world that suddenly seems more friendly than Tír-na-nÓg, it underscores the alienation of Oisin's present condition. Yet that very fragmentariness makes the world Oisin has left seem alien too, since the staff operates according to a very common form of 'making strange', like a quotation out of context, as do the other similar events in Books II and III. At the same time, its starkly presented quotation of 'reality' serves to suggest both the 'quoted' character of the Happy Isle and its unreality. These moments, then, impart uncanniness to the whole poem. They show both this world and the other as proffering satisfaction and withholding it, and they show Oisin as estranged in both worlds, like the Anglo-Irish identity in Ireland and England, respectively: a substantial though not an easy correspondence.[32] Yet the sense of chill otherness remains more clearly fixed on the fairies' world than on ours, as it does in Yeats's earliest fairy poem, 'The Stolen Child':

> Away with us he's going,
> The solemn-eyed:
> He'll hear no more the lowing
> Of the calves on the warm hillside
> Or the kettle on the hob

Sing peace into his breast,
Or see the brown mice bob
Round and round the oat-meal chest.
For he comes, the human child,
To the waters and the wild
With a faery, hand in hand,
From a world more full of weeping than he can understand.

(*P* 19)

As Declan Kiberd says, the 'vagueness' of the fairies' world is 'no match for the concrete homeliness of feeling with which the poet renders the details of a country kitchen'.[33] 'The Stolen Child' is understandably placed in the section headed 'Changelings' in *Fairy and Folk Tales of the Irish Peasantry (FFTI* 57–9); and the fairies are of the kind Yeats roundly terms 'Kidnappers'.[34]

But the chill imparted by *The Wanderings of Oisin* is more stealthy, even doubtful. And many have noticed that Niamh is in aspect by no means the demonic kidnapper she becomes in 'The Hosting of the Sidhe', composed in 1893 (*P* 55), seeming to be motivated by a love comprising compassion, sympathy and tenderness. Yet the original sub-title of *The Wanderings of Oisin* was *'How a Demon Trapped Him' (VP* 1).

Yeats is here employing a subtle ruse already adopted by Keats in *The Eve of St Agnes*: that of displaying the feminine as unconsciously demonic. For while it might appear to be Porphyro who steals Madeline away, in reality it is she who invokes him with her 'ceremonies' (st. 6). The night is compared to that on which 'Merlin paid his Demon all the monstrous debt' (st. 19) – that is, was entrapped by the witch Viven.[35] And Madeline is moved by Porphyro's singing about a cruel fairy, 'La belle dame sans mercy' (st. 33): these are the 'complainings' she finds so 'dear' (st. 35). They elope when Porphyro has agreed to be her 'vassal' (st. 38). Keats's Madeline, then, offers a subtle version of the uncanny, and has no palpable design upon us but to offer a view of feminine magic.

Yeats's patriotic design is slightly more palpable, and involves Niamh in the question of his relationship to Irish mythology. For in so far as Faery may stand for the whole tradition of Irish mythology and folklore, and for its lure, so may Niamh; and her function as *anima* has to be seen in this light: she represents the possibility of possessing what I have called 'the matter of Ireland'. But in so far as she is subtly uncanny, she simultaneously represents the possibility of not possessing it, of an alienating quest away from reality and identity. A conceivable rebuttal of this point of view would indicate that it is the Ireland of Finn and the Fenians that represents the desired state. Yet it is only necessary to remark that the whole of the Fenian cycle is marked by the irruption of Faery to suggest how problematic such a rebuttal would be. Indeed, the fantastic character of Irish romance is an unanswerable rebuke to those twentieth-century commentators who see the Celtic Twilight as a fabrication, and who base their judgement only on the un- doubtedly spare and exact qualities of the finest Irish medieval poems. The world of the Fenians is on the permeable boundaries of Faery, and this character of it is itself a contributor to Yeats's idea of the 'twilight': a boundary between the world of dreams and the mundane. It is this realm of uncertainty he is constantly explor- ing in different ways.

One way of regarding the malign aspect of a voyage to the Other World is to see it as constituting a movement away from a fluid and permeable boundary, which is at the centre of a triad where the infinite is on one side and the finite on the other, towards a fixed boundary at the edge of the world (the land beyond the wave): a kind of mural of static tableaux. In that case the world comes, ironically, to resemble in its very shape the 'urn funereal' offered by the prince of Faery in the first version as an image of a world without 'change and birth' (*VP* 19, 18): as in Keats's Ode (to which Yeats would later compare *The Wanderings: Ex* 163), it be- comes a series of discrete, intensely worked pictures of life, revolv- ing around a void. The fact that entry into such a world is malign also casts grave doubt, of course, even on its potential participation in the infinite. But just as there is deliberate uncertainty about the character of Niamh, so there is about the Other World: it may only be a condition of imperfect human perception that one cannot be happy there; but on the other hand, perhaps the whole adventure is a trap, the result of malign demonic enticement.

IV

One way of thinking about the codifications of experience I have referred to as a triad is in terms of layers, or levels, broadly similar to Blake's levels of existence: the level of human life may be conceived as a weaving of contradictory warp and woof, implying its dependence on some prior essential truth, as in Shelley's meta-phors of veils; as with Browning, there can be no premature leap over the concrete for the artist: that way lies abstraction and Andrea del Sarto; and the question of the artistic definition of states of existence becomes very pressing. This last point bears on the problem of composing any individual poem. How far does the artist, in defining his subject-matter, approach the malign fixity of abstraction? Yeats does not display on this question the anxiety of Blake, always concerned lest the prophet Los, with his creative tongs, be declining into the priest Urizen, with his compasses for dividing and measuring. Rather, Yeats shows an extreme self-consciousness about the question in his own tendency to present contradictory or contrary states adjacent to each other in the same volume, thus foregrounding the question of definition. These 'self-distrusting methods', as he called them, nevertheless owe much to the example of Blake. And Yeats's evolution of a system out of them is also modelled on Blake. On the other hand, his way with an individual 'mood' is usually more provisional and tentative in feel, more Shelleyan: the very idea of moods, moods governed by the wind and its listlessness, as in *The Wind Among the Reeds*, is sugges-tive of this.

Too stern a way with mood or state of mind might bring about the condition of hardened form of which the 'urn funereal' was an image. Another such emblem is that of the empty and silent shell, like those described in Book I of *The Wanderings of Oisin*:

> . . . a trumpet-twisted shell
> That in immortal silence sleeps
> Dreaming of her own melting hues,
> Her golds, her ambers, and her blues,
> Pierced with soft light the shallowing deeps.
>
> (*P* 359)

The image may not seem malign, but it does comprise hollow silence and an ungenerous sense of the self-appreciation of nacreous beauty.

The use of conflicting versions of the shell image to support con-trary states of mind is to be found in 'The Song of the Happy Shepherd' and 'The Sad Shepherd' (*P* 7–9), from *Crossways*. The titles denote the definition of opposed states of mind, avowing that they come out of Milton's 'L'Allegro' and 'Il Penseroso', via Blake's

'Two Contrary States of the Human Soul'. The songs originally came from the end of *The Island of Statues*, which Yeats called 'an Arcadian play in imitation of Edmund Spenser' (*Au* 92). In so far as they allude to Spenser, they suggest a compromise form of the Celtic or Irish, such as might appeal to an Anglo-Irish poet who discerned in the elder poet an appreciation of the 'hills and woods' where the wandering Irish 'did their shepherding' (*E&I* 373), and fancied that Irish 'rivers and hills' came 'much into his poetry' (*E&I* 360). Yet even in his twenties, when he wrote *The Island of Statues*, he must have had some notion of Spenser's attitude to Irish rebels, even if he was at that time ignorant of his plans for wandering shepherds. A slight distance from the Celtic is also suggested by the phrase 'warring kings', for this alludes to that cliché of British apologists for the imperial role in Ireland: that Britain had intervened in a country which, whatever its early contribution to the preservation of classical civilisation and the spread of Christianity, had descended in the Middle Ages into an anarchy brought about by the incessant strife of warlike kings and chieftains.[36]

None of this adds up to the suggestion that Yeats is promoting a West British line on Ireland, even in so subtle a way; rather it points to a slight reservation. For the quality of feeling espoused and embodied by 'The Happy Shepherd' can in context be seen as 'Celtic': this must be the character of a poem, in a group such as this, which offers a palliative to the ills attending the too serious, too Germanic, too scientific and industrial modern society. Not only Arnold's *Celtic Literature*, but also his 'Scholar Gypsy' consort with each other as allusions in 'The Song of the Happy Shepherd', as perhaps they do in Wilde's 'Pan'.[37] When Yeats asserts the value of words, dreams and Arcady against the 'starry men' of science and materialism, with their 'cloven' hearts, the confidence and the image may owe something to Blake, but the sense both of the problem and the cure is more redolent of Arnold's pastoral lament over the 'strange disease of modern life,/With its sick hurry, its divided aims'. The happy shepherd is offering a Celtic quality which accepts both Joy and Sorrow, after the manner recommended, for instance, in *The Wanderings of Oisin*. It is also a transitional quality, which laments the past but offers a specific against a modern malaise. And it is slightly infected by what it rebukes, formally, politically and philosophically. For all these reasons it seems appropriate that his song should be sad as well as happy, and that the words hummed into the shell should fade 'in ruth'.

Nor does the happy shepherd's advice work for everybody. The sad shepherd, for instance. He does follow the happy shepherd's advice, with the express thought that it will work (*'I will my heavy story tell/ . . . / . . . my ancient burden may depart'* (P 9)). One might object that the sad shepherd is here being his usual sad self, but that the happy shepherd was, by contrast, happy when he spoke. But this is not so. Both are sad when they speak. The nature of the happy shepherd's instructions is quite clear. Some settled disposition of character, then, means that what works for one does not work for the other. The happy shepherd accepts the alternation of Joy and Sorrow, while retaining his essential human loyalty to Joy. The sad shepherd, as if predestined to damnation, has been chosen by Sorrow, rather than choosing Sorrow himself: 'There was a man whom Sorrow named his friend.' And this is not a matter of being fated to assent to certain abstract doctrines. Rather, his whole temperament has been fated to lack that *virtù* which might, with its energy, have overcome, however temporarily, the effects of his sadness, by imparting spontaneous force, melody and joy to his words. So here is a contrary as strongly marked as any delineated in one of Blake's pairs from Innocence and Experience. More so. For there is irony in each of Blake's series: neither Innocence nor Experience represents a final answer. But Yeats does privilege the happy over the sad shepherd: the latter, alas, can never be 'Celtic' enough, no matter how hard he tries.

This pair of poems can serve as a good initial example of how Yeats can be very firm in his demarcation of the boundaries between contrary attitudes or 'moods', however subtle and tentative he may occasionally be in his depiction of a mood itself. The image of the shell, used in two different ways, both underlines the notion of a boundary between states and operates to define in the one case empty form, and in the other a form that, as full as it can be in this world of contrariety, still has to compromise with measure and fixity.

4

HUSKS, WANDERING AND THE NATION

S elf-consciousness about the question of the conflicting claims of form as limitation and form as expressive was a topic which was bound to occur in relation to Blake's figure Urizen in the commentary of the Ellis–Yeats edition, where it is discussed in notably Yeatsian, rather than Blakean terminology:

> Urizen is seen in vision as the primeval priest, or spiritual father, assuming power among the spirits or imaginative moods of Great Eternity, an unimaginative mood by contrast, or rather he desires to be so in order to be a separate self – self-contemplating – and dominate other moods. The Eternals therefore gave him a place in the region of selfishness, of personality, of experience, the North, the iron land that the senses create in the mind, for the land of the South, from which he first came, is mind-created, not merely mind-analysed, and no selfishness is allowed there, no personality that is not merely a means of brotherhood.[1]

Now there can be no doubt that Urizen, as the imposer of bounds or limits, also represents the creation of limiting form at the level of artistic creation. Nor can there be any doubt that he and these activities bear a weight of negative connotation, of which Yeats is here demonstrating his awareness. Yet in doing so he associates Urizen with one quality of which he characteristically approves: personality. Furthermore, Urizen's opponents sound unfortunately 'objective' or 'primary' according to the terminology of *A Vision*. And the fact that Urizen's personality is here seen as ordering the materials of art according to Yeats's usage ('moods') can remind us that, however uncertain Yeats may seem about the relationship between form and subject-matter, he always exhibits a greater confidence in the expressive potential of traditional verse-forms than does Blake. His later assertion, 'Measurement began our might', is a natural development of his practice – and a notably Urizenic remark.

With the problem of form and content, as elsewhere, Yeats is drawn to the idea of a triad: two opposites linked by a mediating term. We find this structure applied, among other things, to poetic creation in the Ellis–Yeats *Blake*:

> This poetic genius or central mood in all things is that which creates all by affinity – worlds no less than religions and philosophies. First, a bodiless mood, and then a surging thought, and last a thing. This triad is universal in mysticism, and corresponds to Father, Son and Holy Spirit.[2]

Despite the fact that this passage describes a progression, it also alludes to the familiar distinction between matter and spirit, and form and content. The triad is congruent with that which describes the place of human existence in the scheme of things: above, the world of immeasurable Joy; beneath, a world of abstraction; and in between, the human world of difference, of mingled Joy and Sorrow. The middle term is really that which best corresponds to the role of the poet, mediating between essential thought and abstract measure.

As for the aim of nurturing Irish unity, Blake also offered clues there: as a true 'poetic genius', he had sought to marry himself mythologically to 'rock and hill'. This was not merely a matter of asking, 'And did those feet in ancient time/Walk upon England's mountains green?' It involved, as in these lines from *Milton*, the living presence of mythological symbols, beings and even new places, in Lambeth and Hounslow:

> From Golgonooza the spiritual Four-fold London eternal
> In immense labours & sorrows, ever building, ever falling,

> Thro Albions four Forests which overspread all the Earth,
> From London Stone to Blackheath east: to Hounslow west:
> To Finchley north: to Norwood south . . .
>
> (*Milton*, pl.6, 1–5)

In writing thus Blake reveals the poet's innate desire to animate the world around, wherever it be. But he could not be content with the mythologies that were at hand. As Yeats says:

> He was a symbolist who had to invent his symbols; and his counties of England, with their correspondence to tribes of Israel, and his mountains and rivers, with their correspondence to parts of a man's body, are arbitrary . . . . Had he been a Catholic of Dante's time he would have been well content with Mary and the angels; or had he been a scholar of our time . . . have gone to Ireland and chosen for his symbols the sacred mountains, along whose sides the peasant still sees enchanted fires, and the divinities which have not faded from the belief, if they have faded from the prayers, of simple hearts; and have spoken without mixing incongruous things because he spoke of things that had been long steeped in emotion; and have been less obscure because a traditional mythology stood on the threshold of his meaning and on the margin of his sacred darkness.
> (*E&I* 114)

The point is not the quite banal one that Blake 'lacked a mythology' *tout court*, for the characteristic remark about Dante implies that the traditional Christian one was available, but nowhere in a form that Blake could have put to authentic use. As with the reference to Shelley's Prometheus, the implication is also that classical mythology is difficult to revive in any but fustian guise. By the same token, then, Yeats's good fortune is not merely that he is pioneering the revival of his national mythology, but that people still believe in it, and in its relationship to local 'rock and hill'. Furthermore, in the spirit of the Romantic paradox whereby both solitary genius and the organic community may equally commend themselves, Yeats ends by according prime value to the poet's ineffable vision. It seems that, after all, the role of the myth is merely to stand on the 'threshold' of the poet's meaning, on the 'margin' of his 'sacred darkness': in Blake's terminology, to provide the 'bound' or 'outward circumference' of vision. The essential difference is that between an outline that is mechanically imposed (classical myth) and one that is organic and expressive (living Irish mythology). But the reason for choosing a living mythology is to ensure a living mode of expression for the original genius. Yeats was not about to acquiesce in the folk, and despite his genuine desire for a common culture, this was not to be one in which the Romantic conception of the poet had withered away, nor, perhaps, one in which the leading role of Anglo-Irish artists and intellectuals was threatened.

II

Yeats's conception of a contrast between living form and external form, his sense of this conception as relevant to the life of both nation and poet, and his indebtedness to Blake in formulating it – all are suggested by the epigraph to his *Crossways* poems: 'The stars are threshed, and the souls are threshed from their husks.' This is attributed to Blake, and is, in fact, a misquotation from 'Vala or the Four Zoas'. The line is given correctly in the Ellis–Yeats edition: 'And all the Nations were threshed out, and the stars threshed from their husks.'[3] This line alludes to certain Kabbalistic ideas which recur in Blake's work in the context of the fall and resurrection of Albion, the ancient or primeval man, who himself (there are good grounds for believing) is modelled on the Kabbalists' 'Adam Kadmon', also a primordial or archetypal man.[4] That the original man contained the stars in his limbs is a notion Blake and the 'Lurianic' Kabbalah shared. The idea was that the light of the godhead narrowed into particular lights emanating from the eyes, mouth, ears and nose of Adam Kadmon: these are the proximate sources of the creation.[5] In writers influenced by this tradition the lights may appear as stars:

> Heavenly Man . . . even after the fall remained a microcosm whose every member corresponds to a constituent part of the visible universe. These limbs are comparable to the stars, while his skin corresponds to the sky, indicating 'secret things and profound mysteries'.[6]

This is the source of Blake's words addressed 'To the Jews' in the Preface to Chapter II of *Jerusalem*: 'You have a tradition, that Man anciently contain'd in his mighty limbs all things in Heaven & Earth.' Blake's next words Yeats would have been inclined to take quite seriously: 'this you received from the Druids.' And finally, Blake expresses the idea of the fall in terms of the star image: 'But now the Starry Heavens are fled from the mighty limbs of Albion.' The idea of the stars, and also the idea of husks and threshing, in Yeats's epigraph to *Crossways*, derive from this description of the fall. But they cannot be fully understood without some account of how the fall will be overcome.

The threshing is an image of the process of restoration by which the stars will shine again in Albion's limbs unimpeded by the results of the fall, the 'husks' of dead, externalised form. But what exactly are these 'husks'? To understand this one has to understand the more remote cause of creation, which consists, according to the Lurianic Kabbalah, in a 'contraction' of the Godhead: 'the existence of the universe is made possible by a process of shrinkage in God.'[7] Thus, 'The first act of all is not an act of revelation but one of limitation.'[8] This act is performed by one of the two major aspects of God: that of Din, or Judgment (the other is Hesed: 'love' or 'mercy'). When God has withdrawn, the world of manifestation appears, as it were, in the space He has left. First to arrive is Adam Kadmon. Then the lights he bears coalesce into the form of ten *Sephiroth*, or spheres: three of these are manifest aspects of God; the lower seven, parts of the world, the number seven deriving from the seven days of creation in Genesis.

But the quality of judgment, responsible for the original contraction, causes the spheres to be provided with 'bowls' or 'vessels', so that they may have bounds.[9] The Kabbalistic tradition had always believed that the quality of judgment became evil when torn away from the opposing one of mercy, and had already developed the notion of evil as akin to the 'bark' of the cosmic tree, or the 'shell' of the nut.[10] This is the source of the Lurianic conception of 'vessels', and ultimately of the 'husk' image in Blake's line. In order to give a real existence and separate identity to the power of evil which has thus been created, divine light rushes into the vessels, and they are shattered: evil remains, separate, as the broken husks of what were once the natural boundaries of the spheres.[11] The burden of the epigraph to *Crossways* as Yeats renders it is that souls are being renewed and their light is growing, at the same time that the dead external husk is removed as part of the same process of renewal. Appropriately enough, the line must have reminded Yeats at some level of its original form in Blake, where it speaks of 'Nations' being threshed, for the renewal of the nation goes hand in hand with the renewal of the poet. But characteristically, in line with the preservation of the Romantic poet's ineffable role, Yeats has rewritten it to speak of 'souls'.

The task for the Nationalist poet, then, as adumbrated by this epigraph, is to find poetic 'vessels' for the spirit of the nation, vessels that will be formed by the shape of that spirit, which will not be the imposition of some artificial form. In 'Poetry and Tradition' Yeats looks back on the aspiration from the disillusionment of 1907. The Romantic Nationalism of John O'Leary seems to have had its day:

> Power passed to small shopkeepers, to clerks, to that very class who had seemed to John O'Leary so ready to bend to the power of others, to men who had risen above the traditions of the countryman, without learning those of cultivated life or even educating themselves, and who because of their poverty, their ignorance, their superstitious piety, are much subject to all kinds of fear. (*E&I* 260)

It is the sentiment of 'September 1913', with its fumbling 'in a greasy till': 'Romantic Ireland's dead and gone,/It's with O'Leary in the grave.' Or as Yeats put it in 1907, thinking of the lost possibilities for art, 'Ireland's great moment had passed, and she had filled no roomy vessels with strong sweet wine, where we have filled our porcelain jars against the coming winter.' Yeats had tried to fill Ireland's 'vessels'. Ireland had failed to live up to the honour conferred upon her. No matter. The poets had filled jars for themselves in any case. In the end, a nation has to prove itself worthy of its great souls. But if it should fail to do so, the artist will work away on his own. The conviction that 'life is greater than the cause' may have 'withered' in Ireland in 1907, but 'we artists, who are the servants not of any cause but of mere naked life . . . became as elsewhere in Europe protesting individual voices' (*E&I* 260). We are defying chronology. Yet the relationship between artist and people, here made explicit, is already discernible in Yeats's earlier work and pronouncements (some of which we shall look at in more detail) and not least in Yeats's suppression of the word 'Nations' and addition of the word 'souls' in the Blake epigraph.

But life, as we have already learnt, is unpredictable and various. Yeats should have been prepared for Ireland's recalcitrance by his

early philosophy, much of which is summed up in the title he gave
to a group of poems in *Poems* (1895), mainly from *The Wanderings
of Oisin: Crossways*. They are indeed early poems, dating from the
mid- to late 1880s. The two most palpable allusions in the title are
to 'pathways' and to the Cross. The former was a word which was
certainly in Yeats's mind: in these poems he had been trying, he
said, 'many pathways'. At an obvious level this refers to the variety
of style and subject-matter in these poems. But at an arcane level,
with which Yeats would have had the greatest familiarity by 1895,
the word was used for 'pathways' on the Sephirotic Tree. The
initiate in the Golden Dawn was encouraged to approach mystical
union with the godhead by ascending the Tree to its crown by
means of the twenty-two 'pathways' which were held to run be-
tween the spheres. This method, which offers some analogies with
the *via affirmativa*, was also known as 'the way of the serpent',
which went 'gyring, spiring to and fro' around the Sephirotic
Tree.[12] The satanic overtones of this image are worth pondering.
There is reason to think that Yeats was conscious of and relished
them.

For the Golden Dawn there were two other means of contact
with the divine which could be described in relation to the Kab-
balistic Tree of Life: one was the 'Way of the Arrow', a direct
ascent up the centre of the Tree, avoiding the tortuous gyring of
the Serpent. It was achieved through sacrifice: the sacrifice, that is,
of immersion in the manifold spheres of existence: those very
spheres of existence through which the Serpent delights to trail his
path. The Way of the Arrow is, therefore, the way of the saint or
ascetic. It is obviously reminiscent of the *via negativa*.

Kathleen Raine identifies as the third 'way' contact with the
divine through the descent of inspiration, of the divine lightning.
She also, correctly I think, identifies this as the way of the Daimon,
citing *Per Amica Silentia Lunae* (*M* 340). Now while it is under-
standable to see a relative distinctness about this mode of union
with divine powers, it is not absolutely distinct from the way of the
Serpent. This seems to me the correct inference to draw from what
Yeats says about the descent of the lightning in an internal Golden
Dawn document:

> We receive power from those who are above us by per-
> mitting the divine lightning of the Supreme to descend
> through our souls and our bodies. The power is for ever

seeking the world, and it comes to a soul and consumes its mortality because the soul has arisen into the path of the lightning, among the sacred leaves.[13]

Now the way of the Serpent is, unlike the way of the Arrow, 'among the sacred leaves'. It seems to me to be a fair inference from this that the lightning will descend, at propitious moments, on those who follow the way of the Serpent: patient and assiduous magical rituals and visualisations, intended to carry the soul along the pathways and through the spheres, will occasionally, for the fortunate initiate, be supplemented by unsought inspirations of the Daimon. These two modes of illumination are supplementary to each other. And indeed, they correspond to the modes that Yeats felt he experienced and could value. Especially, he valued the descent of the lightning. For this reason he chose as his occult name for the Golden Dawn the phrase Demon est Deus Inversus – usually conveyed by its initials D.E.D.I. – which he came across in the first volume of Madame Blavatsky's *Secret Doctrine*, as Allen Grossman has noted.[14] Blavatsky claims that God is the 'synthesis of the whole Universe', in a manner that Yeats would have found congruent with Druidical–Brahminical philosophy, and from this premise she deduces that one cannot divorce Him from evil:[15]

> The ancients understood this so well that their philosophers – now followed by the Kabbalists – defined evil as the lining of God or Good: *Demon est Deus Inversus* being a very old adage. Indeed evil is but an antagonizing blind force in nature; it is *reaction, opposition,* and *contrast* . . .[16]

The relevance of this to the pathways of the Kabbalistic Tree, as conceived by the Golden Dawn, is that the descent of the lightning is indeed the inversion of the Godhead: God descending. And with his knowledge of the Kabbalah, gained from Mathers, and from his background reading to Blake, Yeats would immediately have recognised 'the lining of God or Good' as another way of expressing the 'husk' idea. Grossman concludes that 'reaction' and 'opposition', which are the 'role of the demon' constitute 'the role of the poet in Yeats' fantasy' and that 'this was the identity which occult discourse allowed him at once to assume and conceal.'[17] This is nicely put. But the question of opposition is not merely one of fantasy but also of form. Not that it is easy to formulate the relationship between the husk idea and Yeats's conception of form, since it is the subject of a profound ambivalence.

Had there been a direct and uncomplicated translation of Kabbalistic ideas into Yeats's work, one might have expected the 'husk' symbol to be unambiguously evil in his own terms. And the epigraph to *Crossways* does suggest the importance of winnowing away the husk to reach the inner light. Yet it is undoubtedly true that Yeats is attracted to the idea of oppositional evil, partly because of a whole nineteenth-century tradition going back to Blake's *Marriage of Heaven and Hell*, with its proclamation that 'Opposition is True Friendship', and its Proverbs of Hell. He would have recognised the influence of these Proverbs on the aphorisms at the beginning of Wilde's *Dorian Gray*, and have seen the 'style' and the 'mask' proclaimed in the latter as aesthetic versions of the oppositional outline, or husk. His choice of the Demon title is also related to this affinity. For the Hebrew word conveying the idea of 'shells' or 'husks' – *Kelipoth*, *Klippoth* or *Qlippoth* – is also used for, and translated as, 'Demons'. Yet he could not but be sensitive to the less attractive implication of this symbol: that it represented the imposition of lifeless and inexpressive form: the implication, in fact, that Blake throws into relief in the figure of Urizen. On the other hand, in so far as the demonic is associated with fidelity to the saving energy and imagination which should in the end restore lost light to humanity, it may also be associated with Christ. This is the chief implication of the reference to the Christian symbol in the title *Crossways*. Life suffers in action in the world (or the Tree of Life). In doing so it encounters contrariety: 'That shaping joy has kept [Cleopatra's] sorrow pure . . . for the nobleness of the arts is in the mingling of contraries . . . and its red rose opens at the meeting of the two beams of the cross, and at the trysting-place of mortal and immortal, time and eternity' (*E&I* 255). The ultimate contrary is that which defines the line between time and eternity. Art is created there. The poem becomes a tissue of meanings determined by the shape of the line marking the boundary between time and eternity. This conception is thus another way of conceiving the 'good outline' which defines the vital work of art. The line also runs through the poet's mind. This is why the artist must suffer, like Coleridge (whom Yeats cites) and so many post-Romantic poets, the fate of the *poète maudit*: 'for he who lives in eternity endures a rending of the structures of the mind, a crucifixion of the intellectual body' (*E&I* 128). There need be no contradiction between the satanic and Christian overtones of these symbols. Yeats, like Blake in *The Marriage of Heaven and Hell* and 'The Everlasting Gospel', was capable of comparing Christ, as Promethean rebel against a timid tyrant God, with the sublime conception of Satan. Indeed, Christ can be compared with all wounded and sacrificed gods, including The Hanged Man of the Tarot. The wicked pack of cards played an important part in Golden Dawn symbolism and visualisations because of the theory that it embodied symbols of the Kabbalistic spheres and pathways. The Hanged Man is upside down: *deus inversus* again.

It must be stressed, however, that the idea of husk and externality could have decidedly negative implications for Yeats. A fragmentary manuscript from before 1896, containing matter which fed into *The Shadowy Waters*, shows Yeats introducing an old man figure reminiscent of Urizen, who displays a 'globe of crystal', which represents 'realistic art'.[18] This is the world in the mirror, as in 'The Two Trees', or even the world as mirror, since it is a globe. In a sense, then, it is the essence of all husks, for we may also assume that a crystal globe is a type of empty shell.

The ambivalence expressed in all this, as with Blake, rests on a mistrust of the possible reductionism of form, combined with a sense that no artistic creation is possible without some limitation. Such limitation had better play the role of creative definition: vital, demonic in the best sense. Yet might not even this dynamism be incapable, in the world of Time, of avoiding the habits which turn form into treasonous and deadly formulation? For on the other hand, Yeats does aspire to the 'immeasurable', to a part of what is comprised in Blake's 'Infinite'. Indeed, such an aspiration is supposed to be quintessentially Celtic, and constitutes part of his claim to come under that description himself. Thus, Hyde's *Love Songs of Connacht* 'express this emotional nature [of the Irish Celt] in its most extreme form . . . they seem to be continually straining to express a something which lies beyond the possibility of expression, some vague, immeasurable emotion' (*UP*, I, 377). The Celts, and other peoples whose lives and mythologies were still close to nature, 'had not our thoughts of weight and measure' (*E&I* 178).

Yeats's problem in *Crossways* is encapsulated in the epigraph. It is to find forms for the immeasurable that will be sufficiently marked to provide him with an incisive outline without giving the impression that the immeasurable can be measured. We must now turn again to the poems to see how he fares.

One of the first things one notices about this group of poems is its variety of style and subject-matter. The Arcadian contraries of the shepherd poems; 'Indian' verse-drama in 'Anashuya and Vijaya'; the sad nobility of waning love in 'Ephemera'; the inspired, almost Poe-like, Druidical insanity of 'The Madness of King Goll'; the authentic note of the Irish love-song in 'Down by the Sally Gardens'; and the 'come-all-ye' flavour of the three ballads. When one considers also the epigraph it seems reasonable to suppose that Yeats thought he had found appropriately manifold expression for that Celtic quality which, considered in its essence, bore affinity with the immeasurable. In other words, appropriately expressive 'vessels'. Not surprisingly, the poems make the nature of Druidical–Brahminical philosophy part of their subject-matter, as we have already observed in the case of the shepherd poems and 'The Indian upon God'. But 'Ephemera' and 'The Madness of King Goll' provide examples of this tendency which are especially noteworthy, both in the way they treat the subject and in the way they anticipate some of Yeats's later styles and manners.

'Ephemera' (*P* 15), like another poem from this group, 'The Falling of the Leaves' (*P* 14–15), is about the waning of love. So much is clear from the very first lines, spoken by the male lover:

> 'Your eyes that once were never weary of mine
> Are bowed in sorrow under pendulous lids,
> Because our love is waning.'

But the reference to sorrow alerts us to the fact that this is another poem about that prime pair of contraries, Joy and Sorrow. The lovers have moved from the one to the other. This, as we know, is the way the world goes. And they possess, as it were, the right attitude: they have taken this fact to heart. That in itself offers promise for future joy: they will not attempt to hold on to the husk of happiness once the substance has departed:

> . . . 'Ah, do not mourn,' he said
> 'That we are tired, for other loves await us;
> Hate on and love through unrepining hours.
> Before us lies eternity; our souls
> Are love, and a continual farewell.'

This can be read in two, closely related ways. It can be seen as referring to this life, and the attitude and behaviour appropriate to it. These render the experience of life similar to that of eternity, with which that attitude and that behaviour possess an affinity. On the other hand, the lines can be seen as referring to the transmigration of souls and to the many future lives of the lovers. Each reading supports the other. Metempsychosis is the destiny of the soul in eternity. The soul that realises this will treat this life as many lives in miniature, with all the loves and contrariety ('Hate on and love') that this implies. And in living this life according to their kinship with the immeasurable the lovers are also living on the lively boundary between Eternity and Time. Their condition thus corresponds to that of the good poem: a tissue of meanings determined by the shape of that boundary when properly constituted; which is to say, when not imposed and fixed as an external husk, but derived from the idea of a place of mediation between Time and Eternity. Appropriately enough, the poem is full of images of borders and boundaries. The lovers stand 'By the lone border of the lake'. The time is twilight: temporal as well as physical boundaries were traditionally magical in Celtic mythology and might mark a point where the supernatural would intervene. It is autumn, at the time when the leaves are beginning to fall: appropriately melancholy, but also another boundary of the same kind.

The king in 'The Madness of King Goll' (*P* 16–18) progresses further than these lovers in his understanding of ultimate things; so far, indeed, that he becomes subject to a form of inspired and estranging insanity, akin to that of the 'crucified' poet. This poem offers, in fact, an early version of the unsettling Druid wisdom to be found in 'Fergus and the Druid', although Goll does not progress to the same disabling conclusion as Fergus. There are also similarities with 'The Song of the Wandering Aengus'. The warlike king is valorous and successful in repelling the Viking marauders, but on one occasion things become a trifle wild and strange: in his berserk frenzy he intuits a connection between his own energy and the fire in the stars which is our best image of the eternity for which we yearn. He is then able to generalise his intuition: he becomes aware that the same fire is at work in others, and can be discerned in their 'keen eyes'. His spiritual fire, like that of Aengus, is 'wandering', which guarantees the reality of the connection Goll has made. If Time is a moving image of Eternity, the wandering spirit is that which best corresponds to the eternal spirit. This is also the reason why 'Ephemera' contains the memorable words: 'our souls/Are love, and a continual farewell.' By the same token, 'The Madness of King Goll', like 'Ephemera', makes covert reference to the doctrine of transmigration, the ultimate form of wandering.

In *The Rose*, which we shall consider next, Yeats seeks to provide a syncretic account of the connections between Ireland and the philosophy of wandering through eternity in such a way that it is meaningful to use an expressive flowering, as far removed as possible from the idea of the husk, as the dominant symbol of the series.

5

ROSE, MIRROR AND HEM

I

Yeats's Rose is the chief symbol in his early work of a boundary between Time and Eternity, and the one that in the whole of his *oeuvre* most suggests that this boundary can be inflated to an expressive fullness. At the same time, the symbol bears on his Irish identity: it is as if the hyphen in the word 'Anglo-Irish' were thus inflated, overpowering the antinomal adjectives that flank it, instead of stretching tenuously between them as a sign of division: for the Rose is also a symbol for the poet's unity with Celtic sensibility and of his ability to express this in suitable measure for the instruction and nurture of modern Irish sensibility. In sum, and very much in accordance with the account we have been giving of other Yeatsian images of form, the Rose conforms with measure but conveys a sense of the immeasurable; and it symbolises the satisfaction of desire, but also, as it must in the living world of contraries, alludes to the thwarting of satisfaction.

Thus this group of poems has 'The Rose of Peace' and next to it, like some Blakean contrary, 'The Rose of Battle' (*P* 37–8). And thus it is true, of course, that Yeats saw in the Rose 'Eternal beauty wandering on her way', but equally true that he found it doing so 'In all poor foolish things that live a day' ('To the Rose upon the Rood of Time'; *P* 31). Hence that important notion of wandering again: in so far as Eternal Beauty participates in the foolish things of this world, it must, for the reasons already given, wander as it

60

does so. For to be fixed would be a complete denial of the creative energy of Eternity. John Unterecker's formulation cannot be bettered: the Rose 'represents that intersection of mortality and immortality which seemed to Yeats man's richest experience.'[1] Yeats's prayer, in the second stanza of 'To the Rose' – that the rose breath come near but not engulf him – is a prayer to be allowed to function at the intersecting point, that point at which – mortal but in touch with immortal things – he is able to hold fixed in mind on Time's destructive cross, the Rose, symbol of imperishable order. A full understanding of the Rose depends, then, on an understanding of this Cross, upon which it blooms, according to Rosicrucianism and the Golden Dawn. It also requires some insight into the Kabbalistic ideas to which both symbols are related.

Yeats's notions about these things would perforce have been influenced by his reading of A. E. Waite's *Real History of the Rosicrucians* (1887). Waite notes that 'According to the Kabbala Denudata of the Baron Knorr de Rosenroth, the Rose signifies the Shecinah',[2] the Schechinah being the indwelling or immanence of God in the world.[3] Before the fall the unity between God and this, His final manifestation, was complete. But now that unity is broken and the Schechinah is in exile, only to be perceived in particular places and times.[4] One can see how easily this notion could be conflated in Yeats's mind with the evanescent glimpses of the Eternal Beauty evoked in Shelley's 'Hymn to Intellectual Beauty', and also how, in a rather obvious way, it could provide Yeats with one way of theorising the nature of those transitory heightened moods that went to the making of a poem.

The Cross can be understood in the light of the title of the *Crossways* group. It represents the spheres and paths into which the divine light had been disseminated in the world of time, now fallen. Upwards through those spheres and paths the adept must progress towards union with God, though in doing so he encounters variety and contrariety, and most of all the two essential contraries of Sternness and Mercy, around which the Tree of Life is organised: crossed ways. This is why Yeats says that eternal beauty is wandering 'under the boughs of love and hate'. For she is to be found amid the contraries of the Kabbalistic Tree, which may be imaged as a cross. But she is not herself marked by contrariety. To ascend towards God on the Tree is to approach more nearly the principle of the Rose's beauty. But it is not, in fact, to approach more closely to the Rose. For the Rose really is a liminal concept: its very definition includes not merely 'eternal beauty', but also 'wandering'; not merely the Infinite, but the Infinite in the Finite. Deduct from the Rose its concreteness and you may still encounter the eternal, but you will not encounter the Rose Yeats had in mind. Yet it would be equally misguided to err in the other direction and forget the sacred over-tones with which it was invested.

The double or compromise nature of the symbol explains the hesitation of 'To the Rose'. At the beginning of the poem Yeats invokes the symbol in support of his effort to sing 'the ancient ways' of Eire – Cuchulain and the saga material. This ambition is not at first seen as conflicting with the desire to find beauty in 'poor foolish things that live a day'. The ideal seems appropriately pre-Raphaelite in a general sense: it comprises the beauty of passionate legend and that of transient 'common things'. But too long spent in esoteric eavesdropping and one might learn 'to chaunt a tongue men do not know'. No chance, in that case, even of singing of 'old Eire and the ancient ways' to good effect. The dangers of courting the infinite thus redound on methods of handling the saga material. Although he does not say so, Yeats is in fact recording an anxiety not only about the correct approach to esoteric studies, but also about the correct way of handling an ancient story: do not treat it as dry archive or wooden archetype, which is to say as dead letter, husk or mechanical measure.

The Rose, like *Crossways*, is also an attempt to capture some of the essence of ancient Ireland. The difference in symbol goes with a more conscious and single-minded attitude to that attempt, as befits a group of poems most of which were selected from *The Countess Kathleen and Various Legends and Lyrics* (1892), Kathleen being, as we have seen, a personification of Ireland deliberately modelled on similar figures in the traditional *aisling* poems. The symbol of the Rose, as is well known, is made to bear the sense of uniting disparate areas of experience and tradition, not merely occult ones, in a not-able grafting of roses. It is not only the Schechinah but (to stay for the moment with Irish associations) it is also the dark-haired girl (Róisín Dubh), who may symbolise Ireland notably in the poem sometimes attributed to Red Hugh O'Donnell, and best known in Mangan's English version, 'My Dark Rosaleen'. The Rose may also allude to the Red Branch dynasty of Ulster, which gave its name to the Cuchulain cycle. And of course, as well as referring to love in general, it may refer to Maud Gonne in particular, who herself might represent Ireland. That this group is intended to illustrate Celtic sensibility is also suggested by the original title of 'The Rose of Battle', 'They went forth to the Battle, but they always fell', which is an allusion to Macpherson's *Ossian: 'The sad, the lonely, the insatiable'* (*P* 38) must be seen as characteristically Celtic.

The homogeneity of this group is only a relative condition. But unlike *Crossways* it has no oriental poems, only one ballad, and it tends to cultivate a high, noble style throughout. This homogeneity was required by the connotations of unity invested in the group's symbolism. Yet for the reasons given, the volume had also to embody contraries, and Yeats's self-distrusting methods were not so easily shuffled off: some of the juxtapositions, as one might expect, are carefully contrived to heighten the sense of contrariety. It could hardly be otherwise, given his belief that fixities and definites could offer only a false infinite to wandering humanity. The essence of ancient Eire has to be proved on the pulses. And these were the pulses of a man in love with Maud Gonne, and whose love has conditioned his sense of what ancient Eire is and what eternal beauty is.

Speaking of love and the pulses, it should not be assumed that a generation familiar with Rossetti and Swinburne would think of the Rose as deficient in carnality, nor that Yeats thought of it thus. Just as in general it signifies the infinite in the finite, in the case of love it signifies love's essence embodied in the sensuous appreciation of a particular woman. Yeats was well aware, and would have learnt from Waite, that the Cross was a masculine principle, the Rose a feminine one. He would also have known that in its earliest form (that of the sign of Venus) the Rosy Cross was regarded as 'typical of the male and female generative organs in the act of union'.[5] Such hints were enthusiastically worked up by the notorious occultist Joséphin ('Sar') Péladan, in many ways a typical 1890s figure. He was the author of *Constitution de la Rose Croix* (1893) and other Rosicrucian tracts. But his interests extended to the Roman decadence, the supposed pagan *cultus* shared by the Albigensians and the troubadours, and the similar *cultus* supposedly embodied in the Mysteries of Eleusis. The books in which his views on these subjects were expounded – *L'Origine et esthétique de la tragédie* (1905) and *Le Secret des troubadours* (1906) – were enthusiastically reviewed by Ezra Pound, and appear to be the only source for his belief in a sexual mystery cult descending from Eleusis to Provence.[6] The ultimate source of these ideas is to be found in Masonic speculation about the origins of Freemasonry: according to some they were to be found in 'Eleusinia'.[7] Thinking of the

Golden Dawn in some such light may have commended itself to Aleister Crowley, who was to join the Order in 1898 and would later become a practitioner of 'Sex Magic'. In this role he was to be found in the early 1920s in his Abbey of Thelema, modelled on Rabelais's Thélème.[8] These facts put Yeats's dreams of an Irish Eleusis in Lough Key in a revealing light:

> I believed that the castle could be hired for little money, and had long been dreaming of making it an Irish Eleusis or Samothrace. An obsession more constant than anything but my love itself was the need of mystical rites – a ritual system of evocation and meditation – to reunite the perception of the spirit of the divine, with natural beauty. (*Mem* 123)

Mystical rites are an obsession second only to 'my love', and their character would be such as to invite comparison with Eleusis and to join natural with spiritual beauty. Now it is scarcely likely that Yeats had in mind an orgiastic cult. But it seems surpassingly likely that he pondered using occult symbolism in such a way that its sexual connotations could not be ignored or easily separated from those which could be regarded as spiritual. On the next page he speaks of initiating 'young men and women'. Such practices might prepare the initiate for the ideal marriage. And such initiates might include Yeats and Maud Gonne.

The light from Eleusis shines directly into ancient Ireland. And Ireland reflects it back into the world. In the 1890s Crowley had joined an eccentric group called 'the Celtic Church'.[9] And one of the rites of Freemasonry, it was claimed, had originated in a place in Scotland called 'I-Colm-Kill'.[10] The reference is to St Columba (Columcille), who brought Celtic Christianity from Ireland to her colonies in Dalriada.

But Yeats found more immediate guides than these in pre-Raphaelite poetic practice. While it could be said that this offers a version of the broad Romantic concern with the relations between the finite and the infinite, it did so, following Keats, unencumbered by metaphysics. And while Yeats is clearly a thinking poet, his thoughts tend, at this stage in his career, towards the critique of abstraction. Dante Gabriel Rossetti's 'The Blessed Damozel' is as close as one gets to a theory of the untheoretical character of pre-Raphaelite poetry. It is notably self-reflexive and conducts its reflections through the symbol of an ideal woman who is at the boundary between time and eternity: 'the golden bar of heaven'. Everything in the poem works towards reinforcing and clarifying the liminal character of that bar. She seems only to have been a day in heaven, and thus partakes of this world as well as the next (st. 3). Her bosom, it seems, is able to 'warm' the bar (st. 8), and we are thus invited to erotic thoughts about a spirit who is still partly physical. And she makes herself felt to the speaker through the phenomena of nature ('Even now, in that bird's song,/Strove not her accents there . . . ?' (st. 11). There is even a curious graphic representation of this permeable bar. For the speaker's imagining of the Damozel's heavenly existence is divorced from his fancies about her communicating with him through natural phenomena by a device of punctuation: by pairs of brackets. These curved lines are the textual signs of a boundary that does not divide, but permits commerce between, time and eternity.

It is the combination of these facts with the parallel symbolism of the Blessed Damozel herself (spiritual and physical, sacred and erotic) that makes this poem a precursor of such fertile suggestiveness. And this is especially so when all the implications of blessedness have themselves been drawn out. For while in broad terms Rossetti is indebted to a tradition of mingling the sacred and erotic which harks back to Keats's *Eve of St Agnes*, there is a specific allusion to the Blessed Virgin (not least in the title itself) which is typical of Rossetti: it is to be found also, for instance, in his painting 'Rosa Triplex'.[11] This conflates the sacred and profane by alluding not only to the triple goddess, but also to the litany's description of the Blessed Virgin as 'Rosa Mystica'.

'Rosa Mystica' is also the title of a sequence of poems by Oscar Wilde composed partly in response to the Italian stages of the trip to Greece in 1877.[12] On the return journey he kissed the hand of Pope Pius IX – though on the same evening he prostrated himself on Keats's grave in the Protestant cemetery.[13] One might divine a preference here. Yet the poems are surprisingly explicit in their admiration of Rome and of Mary, two subjects which come together in the third stanza of 'Rome Unvisited':

> O Blessed Lady, who dost hold
> Upon the seven hills thy reign!
> O Mother without blot or stain,
> Crowned with bright crowns of triple gold![14]

Yet as we have seen, Wilde could combine papal and Masonic emblems, and did so on the title-page of the very volume containing these poems. And he was well aware that the Rose had Masonic connections. Nor are these the only apparent contraries mingled in the poems, for Wilde can mix the carnal and the spiritual as well as Rossetti. A poem such as 'Madonna Mia' leaves it deliberately unclear whether he is speaking of his lady or of Our Lady. It begins with a lingering description of virginal delights:

> Pale cheeks whereon no love hath left its stain,
> Red underlip drawn in for fear of love,
> And white throat, whiter than the silvered dove,
> Through whose wan marble creeps one purple vein.[15]

Yet he avows that his love will remain spiritual, since he feels 'Like Dante, when he stood with Beatrice' in Paradise. But perhaps the most unexpected feature of Wilde's 'Rosa Mystica', and the one most reminiscent of Yeats, is the way that it culminates with a long poem on Helen of Troy which is very explicit about her sensuality, and about her status as object of desire and *casus belli*:

> Where hast thou been since round the walls of Troy
> The sons of God fought in that great emprise?
> . . .
> For surely it was thou, who, like a star
> Hung in the silver silence of the night,
> Didst lure the Old World's chivalry and might
> Into the clamorous crimson waves of war![16]

In 'The Rose' Yeats evokes Helen of Troy both in 'The Rose of the World' (*P* 36) and in 'The Sorrow of Love' (*P* 40), but in the former he also asks the archangels to bow down. Similarly, the final stanza of Wilde's poem identifies Helen with Our Lady by making explicit reference to the litany's *Turris eburnea*:

> Lily of love, pure and inviolate!
> Tower of ivory! red rose of fire!
> Thou hast come down our darkness to illume:
> For we, close-caught in the wide nets of Fate,
> Wearied with waiting for the World's Desire,
> Aimlessly wandered in the House of gloom . . .[17]

Thus Wilde contrives to combine the contraries of warfare and peace, of purity and sensuality, in one group of poems dominated by the emblem of the Rose.

Are we to infer that Yeats's Rose stands for the Blessed Virgin? Not really. But that it makes allusion to her seems to me indubitable. Yet the allusion is, of course, by no means straightforward. A painter such as Edgard Maxence, in his 'Rosa Mystica' (watercolour, 1903), might offer a fairly unambiguous celebration of the Virgin as a figure of pure yearning, or yearning purity.[18] But such a course is hardly open to Yeats. On the other hand, there was a tradition in Protestant occultist circles, or those who made use of occult imagery, of seeing the Virgin as a malign misrepresentation of the Eternal Feminine. This could be illustrated from Disraeli's *Lothair*, or, more to the point, from Blavatsky's attitudes to Her.[19] Yeats's *The Rose* uses the shadowy but recognisable presence of the Virgin as a foil for its own Rosicrucian presentation of the feminine, Celtic sensibility, the more successfully to mesmerise the Irish nation by practising upon their mental associations. These associations take us into proximity with an eternal feminine object of yearning which never loses its contact with life. The dim allusion to the Blessed Virgin, on the other hand, constitutes a ghostly measure or outline, permitting access to Yeats's Rose, but in danger of becoming a dead husk if taken too substantially. The traditional role of Mary as intercessor and intermediary with God (the response in the litany is *ora pro nobis*) also proffers analogies with Yeats's liminal concept and with the position of the poet. But the former is again a straightforward relay process by contrast with Yeats's deliberately vagrant and unpredictable principle.

Finally, there is a further clarification to be made: just as in 'The Song of the Happy Shepherd' there was 'no truth/Saving in thine own heart', so the expressive fullness of the Rose is not some vague realm of emotion opposed to husk and limit, but to be found in the spontaneous longings and promptings of the individual heart. As the old man conveys the words of the 'knight of Palestine' in the story 'Out of the Rose':

> He had seen a great Rose of Fire, and a Voice out of the Rose had told him how men would turn from the light of their own hearts, and bow down before outer order and outer fixity, and that then the light would cease, and none escape the curse except the foolish good man who could

not think, and the passionate wicked man who would not.
(*VSR* 22–3)

II

Yeats dramatises the dangers of heading in a purely spiritual dir-
ection in a poem which is deliberately placed after 'To the Rose',
'Fergus and the Druid' (*P* 32–3). Fergus, one of the Red Branch
kings, abdicated when Queen Ness agreed that he could have her
hand on condition that her son Conchobar took the throne. Fergus
was happy to comply, feeling the crown a burden; the very thought
of it torments him even when he has laid it down, as the poem
makes clear. He contemplates the Druid's shape-shifting antics,
antics which are available to those whose wisdom includes know-
ledge of transmigration. After being successively a raven and a
weasel, the Druid ends up as 'A thin grey man half lost in gathering
night'. This is unexpectedly ominous. And the Druid warns Fergus
that his own lot is unenviable, that his 'thin grey hair and hollow
cheeks' are the emblem of a life of renunciation. For Yeats those
hollow cheeks connote the starved inanition of life, and the hunger
for it, as they come to do in the case of Maud Gonne. But Fergus,
undeterred, opens the Druid's 'bag of dreams' and himself gains
insight into the mysteries of life and transmigration, as we are
shown in the famous passage already quoted about having been
'many things' (*P* 33), including 'A green drop in the surge', a slave
and a king. This looks like the familiar tale of Truth opposed to
Life. In a way it is. But note that the Druid's version of grey Truth
is here associated with 'dreaming' (Fergus wishes to 'learn the
dreaming wisdom' that is his). This is a notable twist in the hand-
ling of that opposition. For it puts the Truth that is the principle of
all dreams on a par with the pursuit of abstract truth: both are
movements away from the directness of the heart and towards
'externality'. Better for Fergus, perhaps, had he stayed a king, or
been happy as an ex-king. By contrast, in 'Who Goes with Fergus?'
(*P* 43), he becomes a kind of happy version of King Goll; signifi-
cantly he there 'rules . . . all dishevelled wandering stars', thus
having moved away from kingship as external compulsion and
entered into the wandering principle of the cosmos. But in 'Fergus
and the Druid', he is tired of life, and feels the burden of his former
office even when he has abdicated. This is perhaps to be too

sensitive and wanting in vigour: like the sad shepherd, Fergus possesses a heart undeniably but inexplicably weak.

The same opposition of heart and externality is treated in 'The Two Trees' (P 48–9). The first stanza asks the beloved to be confident in subjectivity, and gaze into her own heart, where she will find 'the holy tree' growing, its branches beginning in 'joy'. We recognise this as the Kabbalistic Tree of Life subjected to a Druidical interpretation. The emphasis is on the peaceful love that can be realised by trusting to the sources of joy within us: the root of the tree has 'planted quiet in the night'. Within its leaves 'the Loves' are 'borne on in gentle strife' in all versions of the poem until 1929 (when Yeats changed several lines in order to introduce the notion of 'Gyring'): another version of the benign view of contrariety. What the beloved must not do, we learn in the second stanza, is to gaze any longer into 'the bitter glass'. Above all it is important to realise that this 'glass of outer weariness' is just that: externality, a dead reflector of life, and not a looking-glass of 'vanity or self-absorption'.[20] If one looks into the glass, one courts not so much the pleasures of vanity (though no doubt a kind of brittle vanity may be involved) as the dangers of becoming, as Yeats put it in a letter to Katharine Tynan of 1888, a 'dead mirror' (CL, I, 94). 'When the tide of life sinks low', Yeats was to write in Samhain in 1904, it is 'life in the mirror', although a pictorial kind of art (he cites Keats's 'Ode on a Grecian Urn' and Aeneid VI) may be made out of it; but to this condition he opposes, quoting Blake, 'the energy that is eternal delight', which finds its expression in 'drama and gesture' (Ex 163). The sleep of God mentioned in 'The Two Trees' refers to the Lurianic Kabbalah's description of His withdrawal from the universe, and thus also to Urizen with his dead 'circumference' of Reason. This Blake opposed to 'Energy' in The Marriage of Heaven and Hell. The mirror is itself a husk in the sense of a hard reflecting wall around life, which has no contact with that life except the very function of reflecting. It corresponds, then, to the description already offered of the type of art symbolised in the Other World of The Wanderings of Oisin, which, it will be recalled, was seen as an edge to this world containing empty pictures of life, and was compared to the Cold Pastoral wrought around the void at the heart of the Grecian Urn.

If 'The Two Trees' reveals the lifeless circumference of the mirror, 'To Ireland in the Coming Times' (P 50–1) offers us instead an opposed kind of boundary, a version of the lively edge between time and eternity: the 'red-rose-bordered hem'. This hem belongs to Eternal Beauty, and since it 'Trails all about the written page', it is clear that her principle really gets into the writing. Indeed, the hem itself is the writing: the lines of poetry are the red-rose-bordered hem. The image is mentioned in Yeats's essay 'Symbolism in Painting' (1898), where he speaks (E&I 151-2) of seeing in a vision a company of people sweeping by with 'little roses embroidered on the hems of their robes'. One of the company communicates with Yeats 'by showing me flowers and precious stones, of whose meaning I had no knowledge', and he seemed 'too perfected a soul for any knowledge that cannot be spoken in symbol or metaphor'. It is by means of magical symbols flickering among the words on the page that poems may imperfectly approach the perfection of such direct communication: flowers and stones, images of compact, essential, self-present and radiant meaning. The 'hem' idea is a means of representing the deferred, flickering and wandering expression which is a deflection of such immediacy, but is the nearest we can come to encompassing the eternal. Pondering the blue-robed company, Yeats wonders if they are 'the eternal realities' of which we are the reflection 'in the vegetable glass of nature'. This is the language of Blake's revised neo-Platonism. And it is Blake himself who said in *Milton* 26, concerning visions of Eternity, that 'we see only as it were the hem of their garments/When with our vegetable eyes we view these wondrous Visions.' This makes the notion of deferral very clear.

But especially in a poem with a title such as this, it would be wrong to let this matter of deferral rest in isolation from the question of the poet's relationship to Ireland. One is not, of course, surprised to find that the faeries accompany man in pursuit of the hem, especially in 'A Druid land'. More arresting, and more problematic, are those famous lines in which he seems to concede that the occult character of his writing may lead to the accusation that he is not accessible enough to help in the revival of Irish culture:

> *Nor may I less be counted one*
> *With Davis, Mangan, Ferguson,*
> *Because, to him who ponders well,*
> *My rhymes more than their rhyming tell . . .*

This is ambiguous. Does the poet ask to be deemed patriotic in spite or because of his occult depth? If the latter, then problems soon cease, for the occult things are also Druid things. If the former, then he is asserting that he possesses an evidently patriotic surface and that the deeper matter is a bonus for 'him who ponders well'. There is no way of resolving this ambiguity, which corresponds to a substantial doubt as to the patriotic role of such poetry. The doubt is enabled by a distinction between 'My rhymes' and 'their rhyming', in which the former is understood as the fullness of the well-pondered poem and the latter as an external part of that fullness: both form and symbolic integument; 'measure' in the widest sense, but externality nevertheless. The fullness corresponds to the hem, but it would cease to be confined even to this beautiful border were it not for its time-bound dependence on 'rhyming'. These lines are profoundly revealing, for they show Yeats, for all his fervour, divided by that hem, and uncertain which side of it should truly be called Irish.

The well-known lines that include the word 'measure' were only added to this poem in 1927, and are an index of Yeats's increasing self-consciousness about the concepts it might cover. Of course, much that for him is implied in the word is already present in the 1890s. But that increasing self-consciousness, which, as here, is entangled with questions of identity, will be the subject of the second part of this book. It was, however, a self-consciousness which had to await the waning of Yeats's confidence in his syncretic Irish Rose.

6

FIN-DE-SIÈCLE FENIANISM: THE WIND AMONG THE REEDS

I

There is a change of attitude in *The Wind Among the Reeds*. It would be too much to say that this was complete, and indeed, a number of the poems in the earlier pages date from the time when those in *The Rose* section were being composed. Nevertheless, there is a relative change of emphasis. There is much about the happiness of unrequited love.[1] And in so far as love is attached to the theme of wandering desires and moods, there is occasionally a new note of weariness about the restless journeys of life and its energies. Since the beloved woman is in touch with Faery and is thus of 'the wind' (*sidhe*), and since Faery is a name both for the substance and the temper of the Celtic apprehension of the sacred, the volume also conveys a less than happy relationship with the matter of Ireland, for 'Irish' and 'Celtic' were still near-synonyms in Yeats's thinking – something they were to cease to be for him in the early years of the twentieth century.[2] These facts become both more obvious and more ironic when one considers the extent to which *The Wind Among the Reeds*, at least in the version to be found in the first edition, is an occult tribute to Fenianism by one who had been in the I.R.B., deliberately devised to fulfil the prospectus suggested in 'To Ireland in the Coming Times': that of making rhymes that tell more than their rhyming. The acute ambivalence of the volume towards both Faery and Fenianism may be gauged best of all from the poem which originally concluded the series, 'Mongan Thinks of his Past Greatness' (now 'He Thinks of his Past Greatness when a Part of the Constellations of Heaven': *P* 73).[3] The most obvious sign of that ambivalence is present in the line in which Mongan says: 'I became a man, a hater of the wind', since this puts him at odds with the wind of desire, which is also referred to in the title of the whole book. He also becomes 'a rush that horses tread', which is to say, a reed.

This poem is as good a place as any to start unravelling Yeats's meanings. Its subject-matter is linked to the themes of Druidic lore and transmigration. And since Mongan is one of a number of *personae* who were, according to the titles in the original volume, the putative speakers of many of the poems, it offers a convenient way into an understanding of this aspect of the first edition as well.

Mongan's father, we learn from the French Celticist de Jubainville, was the god of the sea, Manannán mac Lir, and this has some significance, as we shall see.[4] But the most important thing to know about him is that he is a reincarnation of Finn mac Cumhail:

> Now, according to the Irish legend, he was not only the son of a god, but by another miraculous occurrence, consequent upon the first, he was a rebirth of Find mac Cumaill, the hero of the Ossianic cycle, the Fingal of Macpherson; and Find died three hundred years before the birth of Mongan.[5]

Yeats need not have read this passage in de Jubainville's original French of 1884, although even allowing for his indifferent proficiency he may well have known of it. But he might have come across the very full discussion of the Mongan story in the first volume (1895) of Meyer and Nutt's *Voyage of Bran*. This includes the succinct remark that 'Mongán, however, was Find, though he would not allow it to be told.'[6] It is, nevertheless, a fact known to modern Gaelic scholars.[7] Yeats, however, would not allow it to be told, either, and it is possible to suspect that that very phrase may have possessed a charm for him, chiming with his predilection for the arcane, and specifically for the arcane treatment of Irish mythology, a process for which Mongan must have seemed like an extraordinarily apt symbol.

Mongan also embodied in a most unusual degree the shamanistic, shape-shifting qualities which would have seemed like a survival of Druid magic: for he 'was wont to enter at his leisure into divers shapes'.[8] But the lesson is also about the persistence of the heroic Fenian spirit in Ireland, symbolised by the rebirth of Finn. In a consoling poem composed much earlier, 'Into the Twilight' (*P* 59), we learn that 'Your mother Eire is always young'. Of this fact Yeats was minded to provide secret corroboration to those who ponder well. Or even not so secret: for 'O'Sullivan Rua' appears in the titles originally assigned to four of the poems. This is Yeats's version of the name of an admirable eighteenth-century survivor of the bardic tradition: Eoghan Ruadh O Suilleabháin (Owen Rua – or Roe – O'Sullivan) who, as we have seen, wrote Jacobite poems. 'O'Sullivan Rua', then, is clearly intended to represent a late rebirth of the Irish spirit. Nevertheless, we are suggesting that by the end of the 1890s that rebirth begins to seem to Yeats about as youthful as Little Father Time in *Jude the Obscure*.

One factor contributing to the sense of weariness is internal division. For the secret matter also comprised the fact that Finn's formidable companion and rival, Goll mac Morna, was originally called Aedh (fire) until his eye was put out by a lance. Now ten of the poems in the first version of *The Wind* are given to a character called 'Aedh'. And while we may well feel that Yeats is concentrating on the symbolism of fire, as indicated by his note (pp. 73–4/*VP* 803), rather than on the Fenian provenance of the name, it seems likely that he was pleased to be able to press the legend of Finn into service as part of his little drama of the elements, the occult ramifications of which have been exhaustively studied by Allen Grossman.[9] Clearly, the first version of *The Wind Among the Reeds* dramatises variety of mood by the use of speakers (including also Hanrahan and Robartes). But variety may be internal conflict or division. For while Aedh mac Morna was for many years Finn's closest companion, he was also originally Finn's rival for the leadership of the Fianna, and, it was discovered in the end, the murderer of Finn's father, Cumal. The conflict, then, is located at the heart of the Fenian material. Of course, at the level of love-lyric it symbolises a conflict between the ardent temperament (Aedh) and a reflective, watery, melancholy one (Mongán, son of the sea-god) in pursuit of the 'white woman' mentioned several times. But she also reveals a hidden reference to Finn mac Cumhail. For she bears the same name as the women of the *sidhe* in several of Finn's adventures as translated by Standish Hayes O'Grady in *Silva Gadelica* (1892). In particular, when Finn took 'Sabia daughter of the Daghda's son Bodhb Derg' in marriage, he was marrying the fairy granddaughter of the highest of the old gods, and daughter of the king of the Munster *sidhe*, who resided at *sidh na mban fionn*, the fairy-hill of the white women.[10] Seen in an allegorical light, then, we have what might be called a divided and belated Finn mac Cumhail, or at least a Fenian principle, in pursuit of an Irish muse, with the accent increasingly on melancholy and failure, an accent significantly stressed in the poem which originally, and significantly, concluded the volume, 'Mongan thinks of his Past Greatness'.

II

To return, then, to that poem: Mongan knows 'all things' because he has 'drunk ale from the Country of the Young', or Tír na nÓg. But as with Fergus, the knowledge has brought him no happiness. On the contrary, it causes him to weep. As far as the poem is concerned, his knowledge consists of information about his former lives:

> I have been a hazel tree and they hung
> The Pilot Star and the Crooked Plough
> Among my leaves in times out of mind:
> I became a rush that horses tread:
> I became a man, a hater of the wind . . .

> (p. 61/*P* 73)

Originally Mongan has been the Cosmic Man, the Kabbalists' Adam Kadmon, and has contained the starry heavens in his limbs, as Blake put it when referring to his Albion in the proem to Chapter Two of *Jerusalem*. The Kabbalistic Tree of Life has become, in Yeats's poem, appropriately Druidical, as a magical hazel tree. What follows is like the Fall of Albion, and is so swift and demeaning that it seems to show Druid pantheism in a very bleak light. Instead of some glorious progress through the elements of nature, Mongan goes from Tree of Life to trodden rush in the space of one line. But the fall of the Tree is also a descent into husk and devitalised outline. For as we have seen, the separation of the stars from man is, in Yeats's mind as in Blake's, associated with the Kabbalistic conception of the removal of divine light from the forms or vessels of the universe, which become lifeless shells. So

Mongan's is a descent into what Yeats elsewhere calls 'externality'. He has been blown by a malign wind away from the expressive heart of things onto a lifeless margin.

So when he becomes a man, he becomes 'a hater of the wind': that is to say, of the wandering principle of life Yeats has praised so often, but which seems here to ensure misery and humiliation. This principle has made itself felt most effectively in Celtic mythology and magic, and that fact is also referred to in the word 'wind', for as well as meaning 'fairy', the word *sidhe* 'is also Gaelic for wind', as Yeats reminds us (p.65/*VP* 800). Therefore, Mongan is also a hater of Faery and of the Celtic lore and insight which it may symbolise. As a man, Mongan has been humiliated and depressed by one tragic fact: that he will never possess the woman he loves 'until he dies'. There is an ambiguity here, however: possibly he may, in some sense, possess her after death, since, we may surmise, she has an affinity with the Infinite. This sort of ambiguity is important in a number of poems in *The Wind*, as is the related one about wishing for the end of Time. But it consorts, as here, with another ambiguity: is not annihilation the speaker's true desire, born of exhaustion? At any rate, bitterness and weariness there is, for nature retains its affinity with the wandering spirit, so that, even though he cannot have his desire, everything keeps reminding him of it: 'Although the rushes and the fowl of the air/Cry of his love with their pitiful cries.' From a philosophical point of view the content of this is no different from that of some earlier poems of Druidical import. But the fact that Mongan will never in his whole life possess his beloved renders painful and ironic the ubiquity of desire, and painful the whole lengthy business of transmigration.

This disillusion with Druid lore colours the whole volume of poems. For being alienated from the cry of the rushes; thinking of a rush as a passive weed, trodden by horses; and hating the wind: these ideas do not suggest an entirely happy meaning for the title of the book, *The Wind Among the Reeds*. By the same token, even the task of writing poetry is affected by weariness and disillusion. Allen Grossman has shown how the image of the Aeolian harp lies behind this title.[11] It was always capable of being transferred to purely organic instruments, as in Shelley's 'Ode to the West Wind': 'Make me thy lyre, even as the forest is.' Grossman shows how the Aeolian harp idea had very close links with the figure of Macpherson's Ossian in the mind of the nineteenth century.[12] But Yeats would have known that it had more genuine Ossianic ancestry than that. For in the May-time song with which Finn mac Cumhail celebrates the start of his career, the 'harp of the woods' is said to play music. Here is a translation by Yeats's friend T. W. Rolleston, which provided the title for Katharine Tynan's Irish anthology, *The Wild Harp*:

> Through the wild harp of the wood
> Making music roars the gale –
> Now it settles without motion,
> On the ocean sleeps the sail.[13]

This provides us with another gauge of the decline from tree to rush: it is also a decline from the robust music of setting out on life – and on the Fenian principle – to the thin, weary, bitter-sweet music that is half in love with death, and feels no optimism about the vigour of that principle.

Mention of Shelley and Aeolian harps might lead one to wonder how far Yeats is commenting on the degree of confidence he can feel, at the time of writing, in his ability to impart strength to the Irish poetic tradition. It seems probable that, in placing this poem at the end of a volume published in 1899, he was, at least for a moment, inviting the reader to think in terms of a *fin-de-siècle* weariness which was also, among other things, the weariness of the Romantic tradition in general and of his own efforts in Ireland in particular. It is instructive to compare this poem with another one about the century's end, Hardy's 'The Darkling Thrush'. This also alludes to the image of the Aeolian harp:

> The tangled bine-stems scored the sky
> Like strings of broken lyres,
> And all mankind that haunted nigh
> Had sought their household fires.

We go on to learn that the features of the land look like the Century's corpse and, interestingly, that the wind sounds like his 'death-lament'. Weariness affects everything, including the speaker:

> The ancient pulse of germ and birth
> Was shrunken hard and dry,
> And every spirit upon earth
> Seemed fervourless as I.

But Yeats, in evoking the decline of the Ossianic wind-harp, is also suggesting that the Irish poetic tradition is tainted with weariness. This is not an incongruous idea in the context of this poem, since Mongan is a sort of Finn mac Cumhail as well as a sort of Albion. Yet it represents a somewhat unexpected turn of thought, like so much about this poem.

In 'Into the Twilight', Yeats had offered the spirit of Eire as an antidote to the kind of malady offered in 'Mongan Thinks'. If one ignores the difference in date of composition it is hard to square the circle that runs between these two poems. We may observe that in this one the twilight, apart from being restful, is once again the boundary time, the moment of the intervention of the super-natural. It therefore represents the desirable middle term in the Yeatsian triad: the creation of meaning at the intersection of the infinite and the finite. For this reason, to a degree paradoxically, the twilight is a youthful time: but only to a degree, because the poem leaves it uncertain whether or not the twilight is essentially that of dawn or also that of the evening. And this uncertainty is part of its meaning: the Druid spirit of ancient Ireland is a *philosophia perennis*, where the opposites of age and youth meet and dissolve. Nor is hopefulness the only mood of the poem, for the final conces-sive clause bleakly undermines the prescription on offer: 'Though hope fall from you and love decay,/Burning in fires of a slanderous tongue.' But if this poem maintains the attitude of hope in the face of hopelessness, 'Mongan Thinks' asserts that humanity is fallen from Eternity, and that, in virtue of this fallenness, a life may be, or at least feel, irremediably and tragically damaged. What price mother Eire in that case? Such are the contradictions consequent on a system where one must believe in the restless and unfixed principle of life and its many moods, even when one of those moods is disgust and weariness at life. The word 'moods', Yeats's chosen term for the variety of states of mind, is itself suggestive of unanalysable diversity, even of potential perversity. This fact be-comes clearer if one compares the term with possible alternatives: Blake's 'states', for instance. Certainly Yeats's poem, 'The Moods' (p.4/*P* 56), which takes third place in *The Wind*, suggests tu-multuous multiplicity: 'What one in the rout/Of the fire-born moods/Has fallen away?'

On the side of relative hopefulness again, in a poem such as 'The Song of the Wandering Aengus', Yeats is able, as in *The Rose* group, to suggest the bitter-sweet beauty of wandering hopefully towards the beloved through all the 'hollow lands and hilly lands' – the contraries – of Time. In practice, though, the difference of mood that is most interesting to Yeats, perhaps because most problematic, is the large, essential one embodied in the difference between 'Mongan Thinks' and 'Into the Twilight': the difference between participation in the spirit of Joy and complete alienation from it. It is also the difference that most interests the reader because of the amount of energy invested in describing the negative contrary. The difference, as we have seen, is the same as that between the two aspects of the Tree of Life in 'The Two Trees': the flourishing one, and the dead one that is subdued to 'outer weariness'. But it is also the same as the contrast between the *sidhe* as beautiful representatives of Joy, or as delusive and dangerous enchanters. For in their latter aspect they bring their victims to realise that the appearance of beauty and joy was hollow, and this realisation is the same in content as that which leads one to grow weary with the lively process of existence. The *sidhe* figure ambiguously in a number of poems in *The Wind*. It is they who are 'The Everlasting Voices' in the poem of that title (*P* 55), for Yeats recounts in *The Celtic Twilight* that he had been told by a voice 'out of the Golden Age' that:

> [the] perfect world still existed, but buried like a mass of roses under many spadefuls of earth. The faeries and the more innocent of the spirits dwelt within it, and lamented over our fallen world in the lamentation of the wind-tossed reeds, in the song of the birds, in the moan of the waves. . . . It said that if only they who live in the Golden Age could die we might be happy, for the sad voices would be still; but they must sing and we must weep until the eternal gates swing open. (*M* 104–5)

The poem, written in 1895, adds to this notion the familiar note of weariness, and the familiar immanence of the fairy spirit in the world of nature, imparting a sense, which is to become equally familiar, that it is the world, as much as the fairies, that has made us tired. But significantly the fairies greet us in their most sinister aspect in the first poem in *The Wind*, 'The Hosting of the Sidhe' (pp.1–2/*P* 55), where Niamh, the fairy enchantress who spirited Oisin away, reveals more clearly than elsewhere the perverse delight of her kind in tormenting mere mortals. Enticing us with the time-honoured cry of 'Away, come away' she goes on to inform us that:

> . . . *if any gaze on our rushing band,*
> *We come between him and the deed of his hand,*
> *We come between him and the hope of his heart.*

But how, precisely, do they do this, since they bear an essential affinity to the winds of life and desire? *The Wanderings of Oisin* provides an instructive, if not entirely exact, analogy. Bringing us too close to Immortal Beauty, they render us unfit for mundane existence. But lest we should be too happy in their happiness, they add insult to injury by reminding us that we can never be more than mere mortals. Thus are we left with hollow existence and hollow aspirations: hollow, and deferred with respect to the directness of the desires of the 'heart'. For like the daughters of Herodias, to whom Yeats compares them in his note (p.65/*VP* 800), the *sidhe* go on a frenzied dance of deferral away from the heart of things, just as the former dance away from and around the severed head of prophecy. In this respect the *sidhe* provide imagery which works in parallel with that of the tree of externality, not only in their uncanny proffer and withdrawal of satisfaction, but in their dancing around a void.

This is an emphasis that gathers strength towards 1899. And as in 'Nineteen Hundred and Nineteen', so in *The Wind Among the Reeds*, where there is a persistent strain of speculation about the end of the world, the *sidhe* might be associated with dangerous apocalyptic violence. A political meaning for this violence is part of the background to 'The Valley of the Black Pig' (pp.35–6/*P* 65–6), and that meaning, as in the case of 'Mongan Thinks', points in the direction of political ambivalence, though rather less indirectly. The poem describes a twilight dream of some ferocious, unidentifiable battle, and goes on to depict those who live and labour bowing down to God at that hour, as if waiting upon his will. Yeats's notes make the vague symbolism clearer: at one level the battle is that which will liberate Ireland from her enemies, an idea also alluded to in 'The Secret Rose', the original title of which, 'O'Sullivan Rua to the Secret Rose', makes the political intent much clearer: 'Surely thine hour has come, thy great wind blows,/ Far-off, most secret, and inviolate Rose?' In his notes Yeats observes that,

> All over Ireland there are prophecies of the coming rout of
> the enemies of Ireland, in a certain Valley of the Black Pig,
> and these prophecies are, no doubt, now, as they were in
> the Fenian days, a political force. (pp.95–6/*P* 591)

Yet Yeats's original note, in the lengthy form in which it appeared
in the first and some subsequent editions, puts this point into such
a long and erudite perspective of anthropology and folklore that the
political import is rendered transitory and ineffective, and the com-
mentator seems distanced from the naive folk whose beliefs he
somewhat obscurely lauds in the poem. Much of the meaning of
the note revolves around the distinction between two species of the
sidhe: the tribes of Danu, who are supposedly beneficent (though
we know that they are not always so) and the Fomorians, who are
undoubtedly evil:

> I suggest that the battle between the Tribes of the goddess
> Danu, the powers of light, and warmth, and fruitfulness,
> and goodness and the Fomor, the powers of darkness, and
> cold, and barrenness, and badness upon the Towery Plain,
> was the establishment of the habitable world, the rout of
> the ancestral darkness; that the battle among the Sidhe for
> the harvest is the annual battle of summer and winter; that
> the battle among the Sidhe at a man's death is the battle of
> life and death; and that the battle of the Black Pig is the
> battle between the manifest world and the ancestral dark-
> ness at the end of all things; and that all these battles are
> one, the battle of all things with shadowy decay. (p.101/*VP*
> 810)

Yet the distinction between good and bad fairies is notoriously
hard, in practice, for mortals to grasp. And the uncertainties Yeats
himself creates about the *sidhe* in his poetry are in this respect
merely true to the tradition. The result is that the battle to liberate
Ireland begins to wear a somewhat ambiguous aspect, as well as
being effectively patronised by references to Frazer and Rhys
(p.97/*VP* 809). The battle takes place at 'the end of all things', and
it seems that 'all things' lose the fight in true Celtic fashion. Thus
the political references are not really at odds with those poems,
most signally 'Mongan Thinks of his Past Greatness', which sug-
gest that the results of the Fall have begun irreparably to damage

the spirit of old Eire. Other references to the battle in the Valley of the Black Pig, or to the end of the world, suggest a violent cataclysm, the only value of which will be to liberate the speaker from the agony of separation from his beloved. Thus in 'Mongan Laments the Change that has Come Upon him and his Beloved' (later 'He Mourns for the Change . . .') Mongan is driven to a despairing hope about a Boar which is the same as the Black Pig, as Yeats's notes make clear:

> I would that the Boar without bristles had come from the
>   West
> And had rooted the sun and moon and stars out of the sky
> And lay in the darkness, grunting, and turning to his rest.
>
> (p.23/*P* 61–2)

These lines are merely, perhaps, the bluntest embodiment of the familiar note of weariness, and of a figuring of the coming battle as mindless and destructive, rather than liberating. This conditions the reader's response to such political content as the volume, rather indirectly, proffers. For if readers have found it hard to infer a confident political message from *The Wind Among the Reeds*, this is not only for the obvious reason that it submerges political reference in a more general Matter of Ireland which seems to have much to do with love and occult lore; it is also because, when we encounter specific passages which refer to Ireland's struggle, they are so ambivalent, with an ambivalence which, I would submit, is measured partly by a certain congenital distance from Irish Republican ideals. This distance is the more striking when one realises the true extent of the role played by Fenian references in the covert symbolism of the volume, an extent which this chapter has attempted to indicate. It is a distance also from that unity with Irish mythology and the cause of Irish liberation which Yeats had at first proposed to himself as something he could forge simultaneously with his own unity. Now instead of the unity found in the heart of the Rose, he was somehow expelled to the lifeless boundaries of his own circle. The voluminous notes to the original volume (Eliot's notes to *The Waste Land* are in part a satire upon them) offer a textual correlative of Yeats's exile from unity, taking up not far from half the book and presenting a scholar of Celtic folklore who comments drily on the melancholy matter of his own poems. Indeed, the book is a concrete textual embodiment of that division.

The fervent melancholy of the poems makes a piquant juxtaposition with the notes. The sense of rosy unity with Ireland seems to fall, as it were, through the gap in the middle.

To look forward: the years after 1899 must be recognised as years of transition by whatever standards one might test such a notion. One way of gauging the character of that transition is to trace Yeats's increasing self-consciousness and subtlety about the idea of the husk or shell which is everywhere just below the surface of *The Wind Among the Reeds*.

Part Two

The Measure

7

THE MASKS OF DIFFERENCE

I

Irish harps have metal strings, a fact alluded to when Con-
chubar touches 'the brazen strings' in 'Cuchulain's Fight with
the Sea' (*P* 34). There is much about harps in the poetry of
the years from 1899 to 1908. And gentle though the image may
seem, there is reason to believe that this is not only a by-product of
Yeats's experiments with chanting and 'Speaking to the Psaltery'
(*E&I* 13–27). It also seems to fit into a general, though by no
means smooth, transition towards the cultivation of increased
hardness, both in manner and in metaphors of artistic activity: it is
thus intended to supply a deliberately hard and artificial contrast
with the melancholy and organicist connotations of the reedy
wind-harp. In *Baile and Ailinn* (1901) the two lovers set out to meet
one another in the land of the dead, each accompanied by harpers.
The narrator, who occasionally is moved to general discourse in
italicised passages, which themselves serve to distance the poem
and offer it as artifice, remarks on the disappointing nature of
'common love' when compared with that which 'Awoke the harp-
strings long ago' (*P* 398). We are, however, moved to this dream-
ing 'folly' by 'wandering birds and rushy beds', and by 'grey reeds':
the persistence of the Aeolian harp image, and of the philosophy of
wandering desire which accompanied it, however disappointing
this world may be when compared with that of legend and story.
We are somehow incited both by the failure and by the spirit of the

mundane world. Once out of nature, however, Baile and Ailinn, turned to a pair of swans linked by a golden chain, encounter Aengus, the god of love, playing his harp (*P* 401). In this land of 'undying things', they themselves are like the essence of love in all things. The processes of nature tend to seek and find fulfilment in eternal images which are at a remove from the natural.

In *The Shadowy Waters* (completed by 1900) the voyager, poet and hero, Forgael, actually manages to wield the Harp of Aengus for himself, and with it spread enchantment around. And he also is pursuing an undying ideal: his true love, who will, he thinks, be 'the world's core' (*P* 419), and thus should not be 'one that casts a shadow' (*P* 419). The general point is made at the end of *Baile and Ailinn*:

> . . . *for never yet*
> *Has lover lived, but longed to wive*
> *Like them that are no more alive.*

Or as Forgael puts it, with more emphasis on the fabulous aspects of such longings,

> . . . but it must be love
> As they have known it. Now the secret's out;
> For it is love that I am seeking for,
> But of a beautiful, unheard-of kind
> That is not in the world.
>
> (*P* 414)

The Platonic overtones that Yeats attaches to this quest gradually become more obvious. Forgael expresses his desire thus, speaking to his helmsman, Aibric:

> . . . Fellow-wanderer,
> Could we but mix ourselves into a dream,
> Not in its image on the mirror!
>
> (*P* 416)

To which Aibric replies, 'While/We're in the body that's impossible.'

But the dream's the thing. Though Dectora's husband has been killed by Forgael's sailors, she cannot help but succumb to his magic harp, entering a trance-like state; and when she does, she loves Forgael 'like them that are no more alive', at first equating him with a hero called 'golden-armed Iollan' who died a thousand years ago (*P* 424). The spirit of some long-dead woman has entered her dream. But this is Yeats's allegory of the nature of passionate love. And when Forgael tries to explain that he is not this Iollan, she responds that she does not care, since it is him she now loves. The metonymy of desire is more important than the identity either of Iollan or Forgael. When Forgael explains that he is not Iollan, she says,

> What do I care
> Now that my body has begun to dream,
> And you have grown to be a burning sod
> In the imagination and intellect?
>
> (*P* 427)

Desire and its satisfaction may bring us to 'the world's core' in the sense of the meaning of meaning. Yet *The Shadowy Waters* is a sustained ironic critique of the idea that 'core' is really an appropriate phrase for this: it is deferral that drives desire and creates meaning. Identity is constituted in relation to an other.

So the play's the thing, too. As Forgael explains:

> There is not one among you that made love
> By any other means. You call it passion,
> Consideration, generosity,
> But it was all deceit, and flattery
> To win a woman in her own despite . . .
>
> (*P* 426)

But what does 'in her own despite' mean in the context already established? At the very least it must mean 'in ignoring her essence, core or heart and deliberately manipulating her propensity to pursue images'. Both partners are party, then, to a game of deferrals, and understanding this is the precondition for understanding the next line: 'For love is war, and there is hatred in it.' For whatever compromises the game may involve, its mainspring is the selfish desire which will seek to find the images that move it, come what may. Love's way is precisely like the Way of the Serpent through the different aspects of the Tree of Life.

'Never Give All the Heart', one of the poems added to *In the Seven Woods*, puts the same message into the mouth of a speaker,

embittered by the unavailingness of his devotion, who explains the
ways of women in these terms:

> O never give the heart outright,
> For they, for all smooth lips can say,
> Have given their hearts up to the play.
> And who could play it well enough
> If deaf and dumb and blind with love?

(P 79)

The failure of the lover lies in having offered 'heart' or core: a
fellowship with essence that leaves one incapable of responding to
the deferrals imposed by time and nature: 'deaf and dumb and
blind'. In this dance all women are Salome, and in offering one's
heart one might as well offer one's head on a platter. The only
answer lies in becoming more like 'woman', in a game where, admit-
tedly, the terms are set by her: note that Forgael does not impose his
own image-kitty on Dectora: he has to put up with sneaking into
hers. Nevertheless, he does not intend to lose. From this period on,
Yeats's poetic imagination operates in the circles of the changing
moon, but seeks to do so with masculine assertiveness.

The doctrine of the mask was developed in part out of the cre-
ative metonymies of desire. Love employs the lies of art. Or rather
it is bound up with them. The lies of art allude to eternal images.
Eternal images are already deferred aspects of the truth. Glimpsed
in the world of time they entice desire but seduce our immortal
longings into deferral too. The music of the brass-stringed harp
provides Yeats with a metaphor he now finds truer than the wind-
harp, for he wishes to suggest not only a vehicle for the expression
of longing, but the eternal and non-natural character of the images
we pursue: 'the world's core', even in the ironic sense intended,
may be 'the world's bane' ('The Happy Townland': *P* 85–6). De-
spite the fact that all this shows the poet once again inhabiting a
line between this world and eternity, the emphasis is a new one in
so far as it gives a more effective role in art to the formed and
artificial: to hard qualities that partake of husk or shell.

II

'Never Give all the Heart' is one of those poems in which Yeats pioneers a direct and passionate plain style, compounded of pure diction and strong, but not ostentatious, rhetorical sinews. Certainly, the effect of a strong speaking voice is one that Yeats prizes. But this style may sometimes look simpler than it really is. For Yeats comes to value the forceful mask over consecutive reasoning. This point can be illustrated from a poem in *The Green Helmet and Other Poems*, 'The Fascination of What's Difficult' (*P* 93), a magnificent, manifold, and not entirely focused grouse against the difficulties of working as a poet, which begins thus:

> The fascination of what's difficult
> Has dried the sap out of my veins, and rent
> Spontaneous joy and natural content
> Out of my heart.

But the poem proceeds with a complaint about the nature of the speaker's personal Pegasus: it has to sweat and labour:

> . . . There's something ails our colt
> That must, as if it had not holy blood
> Nor on Olympus leaped from cloud to cloud
> Shiver under the lash, strain, sweat and jolt
> As though it dragged road metal.

But where at first it had seemed that the poet was complaining about a congenial, if self-maiming, fascination with the laborious, here, it seems, he is complaining about something in his gifts that is slow, plodding and lacking in facility – unless it be that we should now read the first sentence as meaning that 'what's difficult' for him is simply poetry itself, rather than a particular type of poetry or endeavour set apart by its difficulty.

The next complaint concerns time-consuming theatre business, and 'every knave and dolt' he has to fight with: there are a lot of knaves and dolts in this volume. But this seems yet another kind of grumble, more on the lines of 'All things can tempt me from this craft of verse' (*P* 97–8), the penultimate poem in the group. Finally, Yeats cries resoundingly: 'I swear before the dawn comes round again/I'll find the stable and pull out the bolt.' This goes with escape from theatre business: let's get on with the important work of poetry – a solitary endeavour ('before the dawn'), and an exciting one (a midnight gallop on Pegasus, who bolts along like a thunderbolt, for those words hover in the background). But wait: can it really be like that if, when Yeats reaches the stable, he only discovers the same sweating and difficult colt as before? Perhaps this is the point. But it is not a point which is achieved with any precision. Different possibilities are allowed to coexist within a framework which pretends that they are the same possibility. This fact clarifies something about the mask as it operates in Yeats's lyric poetry: it is an effect of sameness which is achieved out of palpable difference, and this fact in itself reinforces a sense of artificiality.[1]

This is quite a telling example. For while it is clear (especially from the context) that Yeats regards himself as taking great pains with his work, these are not always consistently expended in imparting either clarity or consecutiveness to an argument. Clarity of diction, indeed; purity of diction, as Donald Davie says.[2] Also the impassioned, but not usually inflated, rhetoric which employs all the devices to articulate the movement of the poem: *exclamatio, quaestio*.[3] In this respect, and not only in this, Yeats is offering an implied rebuke to his former guide, Verlaine, who had enjoined poets to wring the neck of rhetoric: 'Prends l'′eloquence et tords-lui son cou!' Such a rebuke is all of a piece with a self-conscious rejection of 'decadence'. This is the new Yeats, in fact, the Yeats who has changed his manner: *The Green Helmet and Other Poems* is a real watershed in his development, as Ezra Pound recognised, and an impressive one at that.[4] Most of the poems in fact postdate the establishment of acquaintance with Pound, and his influence on some of them cannot be entirely ruled out. Yeats was later to worry that he had taken a wrong turning, but it is instructive to note that these worries revolve around the question of rhetoric: 'I have spent the whole of my life trying to get rid of rhetoric. I have got rid of one kind of rhetoric and have merely set up another.'[5]

But how certain is it that the new Yeats is not concerned about clear and consecutive argumentation, however passionate? Consider also the slightly different case of 'King and No King' (*P* 91–2). This is the poem in full:

> 'Would it were anything but merely voice!'
> The No King cried who after that was King,
> Because he had not heard of anything
> That balanced with a word is more than noise;

> Yet Old Romance being kind, let him prevail
> Somewhere or somehow that I have forgot,
> Though he'd but cannon – Whereas we that had thought
> To have lit upon as clean and sweet a tale
> Have been defeated by that pledge you gave
> In momentary anger long ago;
> And I that have not your faith, how shall I know
> That in the blinding light beyond the grave
> We'll find so good a thing as that we have lost?
> The hourly kindness, the day's common speech,
> The habitual content of each with each
> When neither soul nor body has been crossed.

Here the problem is not the absence of a shaped argument, but the difficulty of laying bare its articulation by making sense of both public and private allusion. It is quite hard to make anything beyond a hazy sense of the first few lines unless one knows that the reference is to the Beaumont and Fletcher play *A King and No King*, in which King Arbaces falls in love with his supposed sister, Panthea, and wishes that he could destroy the words 'brother and sister', as if fancifully supposing the incest taboo to be merely a matter of language. It transpires, however, that Arbaces is really adopted, and therefore is 'No King'. But by the same token he is now able to marry Panthea: thus 'King' again. Only with this knowledge can we bring a sense of impossible love to bear on our interpretation, although Yeats also plays on the idea of 'King' being merely a word, and 'cannon' being merely matter and 'noise'. Now we can ask what is the 'pledge' that she gave long ago. Probably a vow never to marry Yeats: although one cannot have a positive certainty about this, it, or something of the same kind, is the only possibility that makes sense of the latter half of the poem, since the pledge has to be some 'word' or 'voice' that prevents their marriage or union. The reference to 'your faith' – that is, to Maud Gonne's Catholicism, adopted in 1903 – though not entirely impervious to conjecture, is still a private allusion.

Once these matters are clarified one perceives a rather fine conceit about the power and powerlessness of words in different, and sometimes urgent, contexts, embodied in an example where paradoxically an old Romance lets physical power win, whereas real life allows a word to destroy the possibility of happiness. The style of the poem is direct and nobly rhetorical, its movement finely modulated, from the address of the opening, through the straightforward casualness of 'Somewhere or somehow that I have forgot', to the almost Wordsworthian exalted plainness of the last three lines. What is at issue, then, is not necessarily the presence of a clear argument, so much as that of Yeats's concern to present one. In 'The Fascination of What's Difficult' he had cast a number of different but overlapping grumbles into a fluent rhetorical form which suggested that there was only one grumble. In 'King and No King' he presents an economical and shapely idea, again in fluent rhetorical dress, through casually evoked public allusion and unclarified private allusion. All this implies a very particular balancing act: Yeats's concern that art should conceal art is so thorough-going that he will purchase the effect of spontaneity at the expense of clarity. But his equally pressing concern that art should be no less than art means that he will also sell clarity in return for a finely judged rhetorical period. There is a sort of artful expressionism in this, which dimly prefigures certain phases of 'Confessional Poetry' – the poems in Robert Lowell's *History*, for instance. Yeats would find his descendant too dishevelled, however, and the best guide to his own practice is in the developing concept of the mask. The rhetorical force this encourages, and the effect of sameness wrung from difference, are congruent with the new thematic stress on artifice and are witness to a serious attempt to work out the role and relative importance of music and rhetoric. In *Discoveries* (1906) there is a section on 'The Musician and the Orator' which suggests a preference for rhetoric that consorts very well with the kind of poetry one finds in 'The Fascination of What's Difficult':

> I in my present mood am all for the man who, with an average audience before him, uses all means of persuasion – stories, laughter, tears, and but so much music as he can discover on the wings of words . . . . Music is the most impersonal of things, and words the most personal, and that is why musicians do not like words. (*E&I* 268)

There is a gradual change of emphasis, then, from brazen strings as suitable trope for music's evocation of a realm of images we pursue, to the mask that arrests, by main force of personality, the drift of images, and gives it a unity that is not the unity of reason. Both are conceptions that can be seen in terms of measure, but the latter, in seeing this in relation to the mask, constitutes perhaps the most important and characteristic moment in Yeats's aesthetic thought, and we should now turn to a more extended consideration of that thought and its practical effects.

III

It will be worth considering in what way some of these relatively early ideas about form and measure influenced Yeats's poetic practice, and how far they might help one to characterise that practice: might they, for instance, enable one to specify the characteristics of 'early Yeats', characteristics many feel may be contrasted in general terms with those of later Yeats? We have already noted a tension between the desire for measure and the need to express the immeasurable. The same tension is expressed at greater length in Yeats's essay on 'The Celtic Element in Literature'. The early Celts like other early peoples had once believed 'that trees were divine' (E&I 174). Those who lived 'among great gods whose passions were in the flaming sunset, and in the thunder-shower, had not our thoughts of weight and measure' (E&I 178). Blake, thinking about the 'Ancient Poets' in The Marriage of Heaven and Hell, Plate 11, noted that they 'animated all sensible objects with Gods or Geniuses, calling them by the names and adorning them with the properties of woods, rivers, mountains, lakes, cities.' On Plate 7 of the same work one of the Proverbs of Hell proclaims, 'Bring out number, weight & measure in a year of dearth.' But like Blake, Yeats felt it as a problem that perceptions touched by the wing of the Eternals had to be embodied in measure. His solution was to attempt in his versification a fusion of measure with intimations of the immeasurable such as he believed had been achieved especially in Celtic nations, and was still to be found in the folk poetry of Ireland. This desired fusion at the level of technique corresponds to the concepts and symbols of wandering Beauty with which we are regaled at the thematic level: both attempt to inhabit the line between inexpressible infinity and the living death of too strictly bounded forms.

This last fate Yeats felt he could avoid by the use of his famous 'faint and nervous' rhythms (E&I 5). His readers are familiar with what he says about these, as they are with his belief that poetry moves us because of its symbolism. This idea being accepted:

we would cast out of serious poetry those energetic rhythms, as of a man running, which are the invention of the will with its eyes always on something to be done or undone; and we would seek out those wavering, meditative, organic rhythms, which are the embodiment of the imagination, that neither desires nor hates, because it has done with time, and only wishes to gaze upon some reality, some beauty. (*E&I* 163)

Indeed, possibly Yeats's readers are too familiar with these notions, since they appear to have given rise to the unexamined conviction that his early poetry is almost entirely composed in tremulously irregular rhythms. Such is by no means the case. In her useful *Study of Rhythmic Structure in the Verse of William Butler Yeats*, Adelyn Dougherty refers to 'the high percentage of 8-syllable tetrameter lines' in the poems up to and including *The Wind Among the Reeds*.[6] She goes on to point out that, along with this, 'the correspondingly high incidence of co-lineal speech-units [this means that phrases end at line-endings] underscores the lineal identity and contributes to a certain monotony in the rhythmic flow of the verses.'[7] She offers 'The Song of the Wandering Aengus' as an example, and it is a good one. The contribution of such a rhythm to this poem and others is, I think, in the light of the subject-matter, to enhance an atmosphere of simple, naked intensity. But it is not a wavering or uncertain rhythm. Indeed, it is the rhythm of one who is following a metrical norm, and partly on the basis of this aspect of his early work, Dougherty asserts that Yeats is 'in the mainstream of the English tradition as a metrist'.[8] This, as I hope to indicate, is only a slight overstatement of the case.

Yeats owed much to the example of William Morris, and this is true for the particular case of his early tetrameters. Consider these lines from Morris's 'The Hill of Venus' (*Earthly Paradise*, xi):

> Before our lady came on earth
> Little there was of joy or mirth;
> About the borders of the sea
> The sea-folk wandered heavily;
> About the wintry river side
> The weary fishers would abide . . .
> . . .

Unkissed the merchant bore his care,
Unkissed the knights went out to war,
Unkissed the mariner came home,
Unkissed the minstrel men did roam. [9]

Compare with these the lines on Joy from *The Wanderings of Oisin*,
Book I, quoted above:

[Joy] for the peewit paints his cap,
And rolls along the unwieldy sun,
And makes the little planets run:
And if joy were not on the earth,
There were an end of change and birth . . .

(*P* 362)

In fact, these lines are fairly unusual in context, for they contain the
slightly irregular line 'And if joy were not on the earth' (/x/x/xx/, or
possibly even xx/x/xx/). But this may serve to introduce us to another
feature of Yeats's versification, a tendency to what Dougherty calls
'loosening' of the 'basic iambic meter', either by 'trochaic substitu-
tion' (/x) or by 'anapaestic substitution' (/xx).[10] Despite some con-
temporary attempts to dispense with them, I assume, at the very
least, pragmatic utility for these 'classical' terms for English stress
patterns, and also for the idea of 'feet'.[11] Trochaic substitution at the
beginning of an iambic line is a normal feature of English iambic
verse, and is deemed regular. Replacement of other iambs by
trochees may not (depending on position) always look so orthodox,
and certainly the line in question would look fairly adventurous to an
Augustan author. But its most typically Yeatsian feature is the ana-
paest at the end ('on the earth': xx/). Typical, that is, because fre-
quent use of anapaests, which may occur anywhere in the line, is a
marked feature of many well-known poems by Yeats. And some of
these poems are sometimes offered as examples of Yeats's 'faint and
nervous rhythms'. But not all volumes make great play of the ana-
paest. Dougherty's table showing the incidence of 'trisyllabic units'
records that in 'The Rose' group there are 22 anapaestic units, in the
'Crossways' group 39, but in *The Wind Among the Reeds* 92: the
percentages are 3.20, 5.98 and 16.22 respectively.[12] There is no
book, apart from *The Wanderings of Oisin*, Book III (for the obvious
reason that it is composed in loose anapaestic hexameters) which
contains such a high percentage of these patterns. The style enters

Yeats's work in *The Wanderings*, and it is learnt from William Morris. Thus, compare Yeats's line 'Fled foam underneath us, and round us, a wandering sky' with the first line of Morris's *Sigurd the Volsung*: 'There was a dwelling of kings ere the world was waxen old.' The very first poem in *The Wind Among the Reeds* gives a good example of the kind of verse which supports Dougherty's findings:

> The host is riding from Knocknarea
> And over the grave of Clooth-na-Bare;
> Caoilte tossing his burning hair,
> And Niamh calling *Away, come away.*

(*P* 55)

The effect here accords well with Allen Grossman's description of 'the diction and metric of manic dream'.[13] He contrasts this with what he calls the 'trance style', in which he asserts that 'Every word of the poem bears the same weight of emotion' under the influence of French syllabic metric, and offers the second poem in the volume as an example:[14]

> O sweet everlasting Voices, be still;
> Go to the guards of the heavenly fold
> And bid them wander obeying your will,
> Flame under flame, till Time be no more.

(*P* 55)

Yet there is, in fact, no difference in use of metre or handling of anapaests between the former poem and the latter. One knows, however, what Grossman means: he was wise to mention diction as well as metric as a factor in his estimation. He might also have mentioned that hoary category of 'tone'. With regard to diction, in the widest sense, the choice of collocations such as 'everlasting Voices' or 'wander obeying' often renders the stress less emphatic than in the other poem. And the tone of weariness enforces an appropriately unemphatic reading in any case. One is brought back to the unexciting realisation that quantification of metrical features only makes sense when it is combined with an assessment of other characteristics of the poem. When it is generalised, this perception may indeed offer a way of distinguishing early from late Yeats.

One unexpected discovery in Dougherty's investigation was that the anapaestic pattern was relatively salient in Yeats's work throughout his career, though nowhere so striking as in *The Wind*. Thus, alongside any anapaestic example from the early poems one may put, as equally typical of the later period, this line from 'Lapis Lazuli': 'If worthy their prominent part in the play' (x/xx/xx/xx/). Yet diction and tone render the effect completely different from 'trance' or 'manic dream'. So although readers are right to discern a degree of freedom in Yeats's poetic practice throughout his career, some of the more subtle effects they note are caused by the interaction of metre with other elements of the poem. Among these, one might also mention yet again the tendency for the phrase to end with the line in the earlier work. The effect of this is to increase the sense of lyric artifice, aligning the poems with the aesthetic or with the immemorial songs of the folk; or both, in pre-Raphaelite fashion. By contrast, 'the pull of the sense units across the line boundary is stronger in the later verse'.[15] And this is of a piece with the movement towards 'impassioned speech', which is facilitated also by Yeats's increased readiness to use an urbane diction, sometimes spiced by well-placed colloquialisms.[16] But the early verse is rather more conservative metrically than has sometimes been assumed. Its 'loosening' is effected, where it occurs, almost entirely by the use of the anapaest, a use that is only salient in two volumes. But if Yeats thought of this as his 'faint and nervous' rhythm, it was only because of its consorting with his equally faint and nervous subject-matter and tone.

But are we, in fact, right to identify anapaestic 'loosening' with the kind of rhythm Yeats desiderates in his criticism? The remarks quoted at the beginning of this chapter date from 1901 and 1900. Apart from the fact that some of the poems one might mention, such as 'The Everlasting Voices', seem to accord with their bearing, there is also the evidence of *Baile and Ailinn*, finished in August 1901, which, according to Dougherty's quantification, yields a relatively high incidence of 'loosening'.[17] Further, the phrases about seeking wavering rhythms come from 'The Symbolism of Poetry', the leading ideas of which are consonant with those expressed in an essay of 1898, 'Symbolism in Painting'. Yeats's rather limited rhythmic experiment is at its height, then, in the latter half of the 1890s, and in the earliest years of the new century, in a period when he was seeing possible connections between the doctrines of symbolism and his occult and Druid beliefs. It is scarcely original to note the probable influence, in a general sense, of Verlaine's recommendations in 'Art Po'etique'. But it may be stressing that 'l'Impair' (uneven or odd) in the music of poetry, while it suggests Yeats's 'wavering' rhythm, also consorts with the general conception of 'la chanson grise/Où l'Indécis au Précis se joint' (the grey song where the Indistinct joins with the Exact). This conception, though it does not carry the same metaphysical burden, is at least congruent with Yeats's tendency to imply that the lovely line of significant song is at the borders between this world and the other. It is also reminiscent of the twilight hours he sometimes uses as a metaphor for those borders. Verlaine's very phrase is recalled in Yeats's essay on 'The Symbolism of Poetry', in a passage which provides a striking instance of his tendency to reinvest the symbol with a literal sense of the supernatural:

> All sounds, all colours, all forms, either because of their preordained energies or because of long association, evoke indefinable and yet precise emotions, or, as I prefer to think, call down among us certain powers, whose footsteps over our hearts we call emotions. (*E&I* 156–7)

It is interesting to see that when Yeats is thinking of 'decadence' primarily in the visual arts, as at certain points in 'The Autumn of the Body' (1898), he finds in 'faint lights and faint colours and faint outlines and faint energies' (*E&I* 191) an analogy for 'wavering rhythms'. 'Outlines' and 'energies' recall Blake, who becomes, by virtue of his insistence on energy and strong outline, the term in relation to which decadence is measured. But it is voice that concerns us, and it is instructive in this connection to consider Yeats's proposals, in his essay 'Speaking to the Psaltery' (1902), for the speaking of poetry, in particular his own poetry. This looks a bit like singing, or at least chanting, and Yeats prints a notation provided by Arnold Dolmetsch for 'Impetuous heart be still', which is a musical score in the important sense that it employs orthodox musical notation (*E&I* 17). It is, however, eccentric in the way that it employs this: as in a Catholic missal there are no time-signatures or bar-lines; and it uses the old C clef. But 'speaking to the psaltery' was certainly not to be singing, nor chanting 'as they chant in churches' (*E&I* 13): these are 'gross effects' which one has to learn to surrender (*E&I* 18). Yet clearly the method has a musical aspect. For Yeats took the idea from George Russell ('A. E.'), whose efforts are like 'very simple Arabic music' (the oriental imprint), and may even have been like Blake's tunes for *Songs of Innocence* (the imprint of the master) (*E&I* 15). It is clear that Yeats conceives of himself as resuscitating an ancient Bardic delivery of poetry, common alike to ancient Greece and ancient Ireland, for Homer is mentioned, as well as 'the Irish *File*' (*E&I* 19), which could open the door to confusion, for the *file* was the composer of poems, while the bard recited them to the accompaniment of a harp. In the background is Catholic chanting, as a fallen, priestly corruption of the true mode: when Yeats tries to sing his poems 'in the ordinary way', they 'turn into something like a Gregorian hymn' (*E&I* 15). And Florence Farr, in a note added in 1907, speaks of trying to improve on the 'speaking by priests at High Mass' (*E&I* 21). As so often, Yeats's thoughts turn to a quasi-Masonic alternative to Catholicism: 'I am not certain that I shall not see some Order naming itself from the Golden Violet of the Troubadours or the like, and having among its members none but well-taught and well-mannered speakers who will keep the new art from disrepute' (*E&I* 19).

Celtic verse technique may also have suggested Yeats's way with rhyme. In her book on *Rhyme and Meaning in the Poetry of Yeats*, Marjorie Perloff quotes from the introduction of George Sigerson's *Bards of the Gael and Gall*.[18] Sigerson, an acquaintance of Yeats, speaks of the Gaels' avoidance of monotony and cultivation of 'echoes and half-echoes', and Perloff suggests that Yeats's knowledge of such descriptions may have influenced his own cultivation of approximate rhyme. In general terms this is a fertile suggestion. But the precise ways in which it cannot be of use are also worthy of note. Gaelic poetry employed complex patterns of rhyme, assonance and internal assonance or rhyme, frequently involving stress-displacement. Yeats never attempted anything like a true imitation of Gaelic rhyming, something which is perfectly feasible in English, and has been attempted by a number of poets, most notably Austin Clarke. His free translation of a middle Irish poem on the life of the scholar provides, in its third stanza, a very good example:

> The showery airs grow s*o*fter,
> He pr*o*fits from his pl*ó*ughl*and*
> For the share of the schoolm*en*
> Is a p*en* in h*á*nd.[19] (emphases and accents added)

Frequently, Gaelic poetry will employ straightforward assonance in patterns such as the above, without consonantal rhyme. Yeats's approximate rhymes, by contrast, overwhelmingly tend to use consonantal identity without assonance.[20] This form is not common in Gaelic poetry. Yeats's approximate rhymes, in line with the pervasive tendency to compromises, represents a deformation of conventional English rhyme, guided by a notion of Gaelic subtlety, rather than a submission to Gaelic norms. It is also significant that the number of approximate rhymes increases markedly in the early years of this century, at the very time when Yeats was devoting so much thought to the speaking of poetry, which suggests a deliberate attenuation of the musical quality of rhyme.

The way in which Yeats describes this special speaking, distinguishing it alike from music and ordinary speech, makes it the middle term of another triad, with a meaning closely related to that of those we have already seen. Singing is not 'delicate' enough for poetry (*E&I* 13); it belongs, no doubt, with the 'gross effects'. But so does naturalistic speaking, as in modern theatre, for it has made us concentrate on 'the intonation that copies the accidental surface of life' at the expense of 'rhythm': it is rhythm that 'separates good writing from bad, that is the glimmer, the fragrance, the spirit of all intense literature' (*E&I* 18). Yet the term 'rhythm' is not sufficient on its own to describe what Yeats has in mind, for he also speaks of the method as 'lyrical verse spoken to notes' (*E&I* 19). So, while it is not singing, it half-aspires to the condition of singing, being both rhythmical and spoken to notes. In this condition it captures spirit, but remains identifiable as passionate speech, rather than alienating itself completely in the unnatural realm of song. But it is a passionate speech that goes deeper than the surface of life, precisely because it is seeking there the giant forms of the eternal passions or moods. So as in 'To the Rose upon the Rood of Time' one has to find eternal beauty, but not in entire forgetfulness of 'common things': it would be fruitless to 'chaunt a tongue men do not know', and it would also be deadening. The poet finds the Infinite where it intersects with Time, and his method of 'speaking' must negotiate a path between submission to the superficial and immersion in the eternal. But not only the poet, apparently. The essay on 'Speaking to the Psaltery' shows Yeats thinking simultaneously about speech in drama and in lyric poetry. Such thoughts grow increasingly important to him as he becomes ever more involved in the writing, performance and management of drama. One thing must be clearly borne in mind: the separation in Yeats's mind between a type of speaking suitable for lyric poetry and another for drama is a distinction within one kind, rather than of two different kinds. Indeed, a memorable passage from his essay 'First Principles', in *Samhain* (1904), is in part so arresting precisely because it shows him attempting to summarise the change that is coming about in his own verse-practice, and doing so in terms of a movement from 'pictures' to an art that is both dramatic and singing:

> There are two kinds of poetry, and they are commingled in all the greatest works. When the tide of life sinks low there are pictures, as in the *Ode on a Grecian Urn* and in Virgil at the plucking of the Golden Bough. The pictures make us sorrowful. We share the poet's separation from what he describes. It is life in the mirror, and our desire for it is as the desire of the lost souls for God; but when Lucifer stands among his friends . . . when Timon makes his epitaph, we feel no sorrow, for life has made one of her eternal gestures, has called up into our hearts her energy that is eternal delight. In Ireland, where the tide of life is rising, we turn, not to picture-making, but to the imagination of personality – to drama, gesture. (*Ex* 163)

At the same time, thinking perhaps of the *file* and the bard, Yeats recognises a difference, within a similarity, as between 'the player' and 'the reciter': the art of the latter is 'nearer to pattern than that of the player', for 'what he tells of' is 'distant' (*Ex* 215). In sum, both reciter and player should assume personality in large and gestural shape, and give expression to this in a kind of musical utterance that is neither song nor naturalistic speech. Both inhabit the line between measure and eternal qualities, though the reciter, being the 'messenger' of the poet, is closer to the 'far-off things' which are the eternal principles of life, and that is why he is permitted more musicality (*Ex* 215).

Yeats's conceptions here, then, show a concern both for energetic expression of personality and for measure (musical pattern and the shape of personality). While the reference to Blake helps to reveal the organicist basis of these ideas (artistic form is the shape taken by a strong personality), as with Blake the notion teeters on the edge of something coercive and potentially 'external'. In *The Marriage of Heaven and Hell* (Plate 20) the opponents of energy may feel 'imposed' upon, and Blake accepts that 'imposition' is a condition of energetic discourse. Similarly, Yeats is very concerned in the early years of this century with 'strength' (*E&I* 265) and with a type of forcefulness he terms 'masculine', finding it in Chaucer and other 'old writers', but not in 'effeminate' modern literature (*Ex* 221, 220).[21]

IV

Yeats was also theorising in a more general way about art in this period. Writing to George Russell ('A. E.') in March 1903, Yeats declared his loss of sympathy with the vagueness, the flight from definite form, which had characterised those years, and which are praised in his own essay, 'The Autumn of the Body'; now, he says, 'I feel about me and in me an impulse to create form, to carry the realisation of beauty as far as possible' (*L* 402). He sees this change in his thinking in terms of Nietzsche's contrast between the Apollonian and the Dionysian: 'The Greeks said that the Dionysiac enthusiasm preceded the Apollonic and that the Dionysiac was sad and desirous, but that the Apollonic was joyful and self sufficient' (*L* 402). Written a month after Maud Gonne's marriage, this might seem tinged with wishful thinking, but its timing certainly indicates a depth of need. In any case, Yeats felt that the change was significant of a fundamental bipolarity, for the next day he wrote to John Quinn: 'I have always felt that the soul has two movements primarily: one to transcend forms, and the other to create forms' (*L* 402–3). It was a bipolarity the rudiments of which he would have found in Blake, and his sense of it would have been sharpened by the reading of Plotinus, in Thomas Taylor's translation, which he seems to have undertaken in the late 1890s.[22] This, of course, is the translator through whom Blake would have encountered the neo-Platonists. For these, the world of 'Spirit', or 'Intellect' – the 'Intelligible World' – consisted of distinct bounded Forms or 'Ideas'. Thomas Taylor refers to 'those regions of mind, where all things are bounded in intellectual measure; where every thing is permanent and beautiful, eternal and divine'.[23] These Eternal Forms, paradoxically, exist in a mode of infinity, and are not limited by Time and Space. Furthermore, their ultimate source – and the ultimate Reality – the unknowable *One* or *Good*, is entirely immeasurable, and nothing can be predicated of it with respect to its form, or anything else about it. The One, 'though immense, is not measured by any magnitude, nor limited by any circumscribing figure, but is every where immeasurable, as being greater than every measure, and more excellent than every quantity.'[24] R. T. Wallis speaks of the problem for the neo-Platonists 'of reconciling the mystical desire to transcend form and limit with the Classical Greek view of them as the essence of perfection.'[25] On Nietzsche's account, of course, this tension is endemic to Greek culture. Blake, attempting to create 'original' forms, while believing they were also eternal, and believing in 'definite' vision as well as in 'the Infinite', found that neo-Platonic terminology served to describe a similar tension. Thus on the one hand, he can say, in *There is No Natural Religion*, that 'The bounded is loathed by its possessor'; while on the other, he can assert in *The Book of Los* that 'Truth has bounds. Error none.' The former notion fits with Blake's celebrated resentment of limitation; the latter with his engraver's insistence on the 'distinct, sharp, and wirey . . . bounding line' (*A Descriptive Catalogue*), an insistence to which he imparted a consciously neo-Platonic significance under the influence of Winckelmann, Flaxman, George Cumberland, and, of course, Thomas Taylor's translations and commentaries.[26]

Yeats would have been very familiar with this aspect of Blake's thought. The point is this: at this stage in his career he seems to have associated the imposition of form and measure with clarity, spareness, distinctness, the creation of a clear poetic *persona*, and an effect, so to speak, of exalted spontaneity within formal constraint – at least, if one is to judge by such poems as 'Adam's Curse' or 'Never Give all the Heart'. Probably under the influence of his reading of Nietzsche, he associates the resultant style with masculinity, finding his own earlier verse, as he tells George Russell in 1904:

> an exaggeration of sentiment and sentimental beauty which I have come to think unmanly . . . . I have been fighting the prevailing decadence for years . . . it is sentiment and sentimental sadness, a womanish introspection . . . . Let us have no emotions . . . in which there is not an athletic joy.(*L* 434–5)

But women clearly do not need to be introspective:

> For they, for all smooth lips can say,
> Have given their hearts up to the play.

> And who could play it well enough
> If deaf and dumb and blind with love?

Women will submit (give their hearts up) to those who, like themselves, are prepared to put delighted and energetic labour into the creation of the mask: for women the mask of beauty, for men the mask of assertion. To Nietzsche, of course, 'Truth is a woman', by which he means something comparable to what Yeats is implying: Truth is veiled and adorned with an alluring mask, but there is nothing worth knowing under the veil or the mask, no essential objective Truth. The veil, on the other hand, is beautiful, multi-faceted and elicits pursuit. If a man (and for Nietzsche and Yeats it has to be a man) will realise this and live energetically in the masks his individual mode of existence proposes as increasing his power, the woman Truth will come to him. According to this formula, then, Truth is at most the way in which 'philosophy' should come and go at the beck and call of the Will to Power. For Nietzsche there really is nothing behind the veil. Yeats is clearly less certain about this, as about most things: as we have seen, there may be nothing, or Death, behind the veil; or there may be 'the world's core'. In either case, at this stage Yeats is inclined, much of the time, to think one must plunge into the creation of new images and masks without any capacity to know their ultimate source. But being Yeats he remains curious.

V

The move towards an insistence on definite form, however, is accompanied (at least in its first phase) by a striking new image of the hollowness of form: the hollow moon. In 'Under the Moon' (*P* 82–3) Yeats recounts his weariness with old legends of the happy Otherworld or of unhappy love 'Because of something told under the famished horn/Of the hunter's moon', a phrase which connects his own unhappiness and thwarted desire with a metaphor for art that is empty and shell-like because too hungry, too giving of 'heart': a generosity that evacuates the core. In 'Adam's Curse' (*P* 80–1), a poem that itself breaks new ground in the development of a conversational 'middle' style, art is the overt subject. The poet compares his labours to a woman's stitching, the woman notes that 'we must labour to be beautiful'. In the world, 'Since Adam's fall' we are in Eve's element, where the condition of deferral and the necessity of the mask go together. As we have seen, it is necessary to enter into Eve's game, though by no means with the expectation that she should win. Yet, in a characteristic gesture, the poem proceeds to subvert some of the implications of its own premises. As daylight fades the companions watch the moon:

> A moon, worn as if it had been a shell
> Washed by time's waters as they rose and fell
> About the stars and broke in days and years.

> I had a thought for no one's but your ears:
> That you were beautiful, and that I strove
> To love you in the old high way of love;
> That it had all seemed happy, and yet we'd grown
> As weary-hearted as that hollow moon.

Both love and literature (to which 'the old high way' alludes, for it is the way of Romance) may become mere externality and dead form unless replenished by the energy that is eternal delight. And in any case, the image of the moon encompasses temporality: Yeats is already using progress through the lunar phases as an emblem of the progress of a mode of life or a mood. He often does so, as here, in conjunction with the related idea of the ebb and flow of the tides. As he had already announced at the beginning of 'The Autumn of the Body' (1898), 'Our thoughts and emotions are often but spray flung up from hidden tides that follow a moon no eye can see' (E&I 189). By the time he has written the last version of *The Shadowy Waters*, the barest outline of a system is in place. It is not the system of *A Vision*, though it certainly bears some relation to this. The greatest success for the piracy of Forgael and his crew is associated with the full moon, when they sink a galley, while Forgael plays his magic harp much of the night. The great dead lovers with whom Forgael is obsessed are, however, 'those that can outlive the moon' (P 416). The moon, then, is associated with the cycles of this life, and, at least at the full, may represent these cycles as imbued with imagination. But to 'outlive the moon' and enter into the eternal reality of great lovers, is to enter a world for which the most appropriate emblem is the sun:

> . . . It's not a dream,
> But the reality that makes our passion

As a lamp shadow – no – no lamp, the sun.
What the world's million lips are thirsting for
Must be substantial somewhere.

(*P* 415)

The difference is that in *A Vision*, the principle of Beauty for which great lovers strive is represented by the full moon rather than the sun, which is reserved for the opposing principle of objective Truth. Yet when one considers the irony to which the play submits Forgael's conception, perhaps the difference is not that great, for when it comes to capturing a woman one must do so through the reflected images of the sublunary world.

Yeats's thinking about the moon symbol is therefore already more complicated by 1906 than might be suggested by his marginal annotation of Thomas Common's selections from Nietzsche (1901), in which we find these words next to a passage from *On the Genealogy of Morals*:

HUMAN PRINCIPLES.   PLANETARY DIVISION.

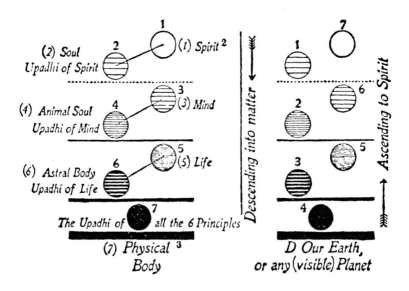

Figure 7.1 From H. P. Blavatsky, *The Secret Doctrine*, 2 vols (London, 1888), vol. I, p.153.

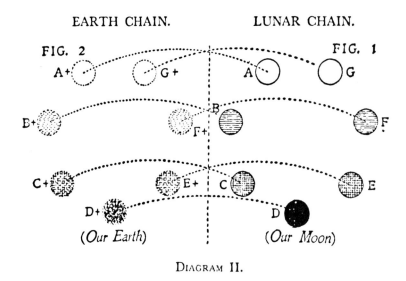

Figure 7.2 From H. P. Blavatsky, *The Secret Doctrine*, 2 vols (London, 1888), vol. I, p.172.

| Night | {Socrates}
{Christ} | one god | night | – denial of self in the soul turned towards spirit, seeking knowledge. |
| Day | {Homer}
{   } | many gods | day | – affirmation of self, the soul turned from spirit to be its mask and instrument when it seeks life.[27] |

Yeats ends up, in *A Vision*, by almost completely inverting the values here accorded to sun and moon. But his thinking in the early years of the century already recognises the possibility of using the moon symbol to represent development or decay in mode of life or mood, so that the character of the waning moon is different from that of the full.

Yeats had, however, received a long preparation for this kind of thinking in his reading of the Rosicrucians and in the works of Madame Blavatsky. In *The Secret Doctrine* she describes a seven-fold universe, on the analogy of the Ptolemaic system of planets.

There simplicity ends. Each planet has seven forms, and the spirits on each go through these seven forms in a cyclical process, first moving down from spirit to matter, and then ascending again to spirit (see Figure 7.1). Blavatsky refers, as does Yeats in *A Vision*, to the ancient tradition of thinking in terms of vortices. The development of spirit in the cosmos has passed from the moon to earth in a complex but orderly fashion (see Figure 7.2). When she is speaking of this fact it is often with respect for our lunar fathers or 'Pitris' as she calls them. Furthermore, perhaps confusingly, in that it seems to contradict the septenary model, Blavatsky sometimes speaks of two paths, the solar and the lunar. When she does this, however, the moon is the path of error. Blavatsky is an important source and model for *A Vision*, but her influence, of course, is an early one.

VI

We have already on occasion referred to Yeats's habit, like Blake, of finding contraries within contraries. Thus within the large contrary of Objectivity versus Subjectivity, if one simply looks at the latter one finds a lesser contrary of passionate spontaneous dreamer versus escapist or learned dreamer. Fergus, it will be recalled, seeks the principle of all dreams, but ends up 'nothing, knowing all' every bit as successfully as if he had taken the path of objective truth in the first place. There are thus at least two major ways of courting the danger of declining into the hollowness of externality: one is that of the philosopher, scientist or (in Yeats's estimation) priest; the other that of the escapist dreamer or the learned dreamer who, for instance, may read too deeply in occult and magical science. This, though closer to a genuine truth than the theology of the priest, may still lead its initiates away from life.

In order to fill out the picture of Yeats's attitude to form and externality at this stage, to show how these are still bound up with his relationship to Ireland, and also as a preparation for appreciating the complexities of his attitude to the matter of *A Vision*, it will be worth glancing at a group of poems which, at least in their original versions, showed the occult researcher as frustrated and defeated by love's reality. These are the poems at the beginning of *The Green Helmet* group, one of them being 'King and No King', each of which was originally given the extra title of 'Raymond Lully and his wife Pernella' (*VP* 253–60). Lully, or Ramón Llul (*c.* 1232–1315) was a Catalan mystic, philosopher and theologian influenced by neo-Platonism and by alchemy. He was born in Majorca and learnt Arabic through contact with the considerable Moorish population of that island. Through this medium he also came under the influence of Arabic philosophy and Sufi mysticism. He undertook missions to convert the population of North Africa to Christianity, and it is thought that he was stoned to death near Tunis in the course of one of these attempts. These associations would have rendered him irresistible to the Rosicrucian author, who was captivated by the idea of Moorish society. Yeats himself avers, in an erratum slip in the 1910 edition, that 'by a slip of the pen' he had put Lully instead of the alchemist Nicholas Flamel (1330–1418). Yeats's Golden Dawn colleague, the Reverend William Wynn Westcott, had in 1890 brought out a reprint of Flamel's most celebrated work, a book of 'hieroglyphs', or allegorical emblems, in the Introduction to which is a discussion of Flamel and 'his wife Pernelle or Perrenella'.[28]

The implication of this title is ironic. Not that Yeats's identifying himself with an alchemical philosopher is entirely surprising. But the poems are mostly about his relationship with Maud Gonne. John Harwood, writing of an earlier period, has put well the two thoughts which lie behind this title: Yeats felt 'fear of estrangement from the everyday as the price of occult entanglement', and 'Even in 1891, [he] was aware that [Maud Gonne] would not be content merely to disseminate "secret mystic propaganda"'.[29] She was also less than satisfactorily enthusiastic about 'Willy', and there is therefore something painfully unlikely about her ever adopting the attitude of Perrenelle, who, according to Westcott, 'became by [Flamel's] teaching and her own intuitions as learned and successful a mystic and occult operator as himself'.[30] Yeats's title is, in fact, like one of those desirable images which draw us, yearning after them, through our lives; and he has built into it a bitter ironic awareness of the true distance of the image from anything that is likely to happen to him in reality. In other words, like Forgael or Dectora, Yeats had been infatuated because he was able to link Maud Gonne to prior images. But she was unable to link her own imagery to his, and his role as occult researcher had come to seem hollow and external. There is ambivalence, though, for in one of these poems, 'Words' (*P* 90), Yeats suggests that unsatisfied desire has fuelled his writing: otherwise, 'I might have thrown poor words away/And been content to live.' But the bitter irony here suggests a doubt: may not even his poetic words, like Kabbalistic names, partake of the quality of husk and externality, or be in constant danger of assuming it? A suggestion of the Faustian bargain hangs over both the large occultist framework and the urgent matter of poetic composition.

Why Lully? It may have been a slip of the pen, but such things are not to be ignored, though there is no intentional Freudianism here. Lully had had a profane youth, but had become ardent in his Catholicism and in his desire to convert Islam. His study of Arabic was only one part of an immense, wide-ranging, intellectual labour devoted to this end. The substitution thus unwittingly reveals Yeats's suspicion that his own growing immersion in philosophy, as an adjunct to his occult speculations, is distancing him from the type of life in which his desires are likely to find satisfaction. Perhaps even the ghost of Ebremar, from *Mosada*, hangs over the *persona* of these poems. Ebremar, after all, had also left behind a profane youth, and was also in contact with the Moors. Might not Yeats, in seeking his own Rosicrucian surrogate for Catholicism, be becoming a species of philosopher-theologian, increasingly at odds with that very Celtic spirit (allegorised by Moorish spirit) which he had been attempting to formulate, and certainly at odds with modern Ireland? But as so often there is a reversion to the contrary thought. One of these poems is 'No Second Troy' (*P* 91). We are not sure at first how seriously to take the suggestion of bitterness:

> Why should I blame her that she filled my days
> With misery, or that she would of late
> Have taught to ignorant men most violent ways,
> Or hurled the little streets upon the great,
> Had they but courage equal to desire?

If bitterness it be, it concerns not mystical but political propaganda. Yet the ensuing lines, with their tributes to Maud Gonne's 'nobleness' and 'beauty', seem to settle our doubt in favour of sweetness, until the final rhetorical question raises ambivalence to the highest pitch: 'Was there another Troy for her to burn?' Helen's beauty and Helen's infidelity and destructiveness. Of course, the question is only rhetorical to the degree that Troy is not Ireland. And the lines about 'little streets' suggest an unexpected mock-heroic intent in the question. Yet Ireland, like Troy, is a polity, and it can be ruined: 'Pernella' might have been better employed in mystic propaganda after all. Bitterness towards modern Ireland, as well as towards political propaganda, becomes a frequent theme of Yeats's middle years, and, as here, is closely bound up with his attitudes towards artistic form.

8

FRAMING IRELAND

I

Noh plays and Zen Buddhism might seem to have little to do with Yeats's attitude to Ireland. Masks, ghosts, ancestor-worship and desirable images that drift around the void: these are the topics on which Yeats found Eastern instruction for his thoughts on Irish society. One of two epigraphs to the volume *Responsibilities* (1914), 'In dreams begins responsibility' (*P* 100), touches on the topic of desirable images and links these to the ethical. One way of looking at the remark, then, is to see it as a clear derivative of the whole nineteenth-century critique of abstract morality, from Wordsworth and Coleridge down to Carlyle and Newman. But dreams for Yeats are repositories of archetypes. So we may add the refinement that his and our sense of responsibility is ultimately nourished by the symbols and images encountered in dreams and imaginings: nourished, that is, at that point where the archetypes of human life bear on ethical and social questions in the widest sense. Further light is shed on the aspect of dreams Yeats had in mind by pondering on the second epigraph, from 'Khoung-Fou-Tseu' (Confucius, *c.* 551–479(?) BC), which he probably discovered through Pound's guidance: while the two of them were sharing Stone Cottage in Sussex in the winter of 1913–14, the latter was working on the manuscripts of Ernest Fenollosa, the American scholar of Chinese and Japanese literature, as well as acting as Yeats's secretary. The epigraph runs like this: 'How am I

114

fallen from myself, for a long time now/I have not seen the Prince of Chang in my dreams.' What is it to fall from oneself? It is to be bereft of the apparition (the ghost) of another – in this case, of the image of a virtuous scholar and prince, long dead (Châu-kung, d. 1105 BC). We have learnt that desire seeks to attach images from the past to present existence. For Yeats our desire for order, beauty and virtue is only a species of the same desire. We seek their images, usually human images, in a dream of the past. Where a civilisation has to be built, we seek them in a dream of the future, also, in a sense. But this too will perforce be defined in terms of images from the past.

Pound's work on the Fenollosa papers allowed Yeats to link the themes of tradition, family, the spirit-world, desire and the possible void at the heart of existence in what seemed to him a coherent way: it was by no means merely an instigation to technical experimentation (beginning with *At the Hawk's Well*, composed in 1916) under the influence of Japanese Noh drama. Indeed, that very notion is a Western misapprehension: the Noh, like most manifestations of Japanese art, is imbued with Zen Buddhism. It is also profoundly influenced by Shinto ancestor-worship, and by the dance and music of the Samurai warrior-aristocrats.[1] From Zen Buddhism Yeats derived an interest in the concept of 'non-attachment', which, by an apparent paradox, affirms life and action, but only to the extent that they are entered into in a spirit devoid of grasping, being aware of the transitoriness and unsatisfactoriness of all phenomena. He was already temperamentally prepared for this attitude, though perhaps not for all that it implies, as is revealed in a letter of *c.* 1906, to Florence Farr:

> I have myself by the by begun eastern meditations – of your sort, but with the object of trying to lay hands upon some dynamic and substantialising force as distinguished from the eastern quiescent and supersensualizing state of the soul – a movement downwards upon life, not upwards out of life. (*L* 469)

Here again is the affirmative way among the leaves of the Tree of Life familiar from the Golden Dawn. The Zen attitude (not necessarily the same as that implied in Yeats's letter) is enabled, in those who are enlightened, by the state of 'No-Mind', which may be attained in meditation; for nothing can be predicated of the ultimate reality, even the negation of attributes. This is what Yeats later terms 'Buddha's emptiness'. His familiarity with Plotinus might have led him to perceive a similarity with the neo-Platonic One. That a class of warrior-aristocrats should have embraced a religion of this kind must have seemed irresistibly attractive to Yeats. His attitude to Buddhism remains ambivalent: positive when he can associate it (the association remains, admittedly, problematic) with heroic Nietzschean affirmation in the face of the void; negative when, like Nietzsche himself, he tends to regard it as life-denying.

There are other obvious reasons why he should have been drawn to the Noh. A very common feature of the Noh play was the 'Noh of spirits', in which ghosts, dissatisfied in death as in life, wander lamenting, or are, as in *Nishikigi*, set free by a Buddhist priest.[2] It is not always realised that Yeats's interest in spiritualism as such did not begin in earnest until 1909, and that he only pursued it seriously from 1911: although as a young man he had attended a seance with Katharine Tynan, the Blavatsky Lodge and the Golden Dawn were both opposed to passive mediumship.[3] The visualisations of the Golden Dawn, for instance, should be conceived as an active pursuit of supernatural knowledge by the *magus*. In spiritualism, an interest in automatic writing was very much in vogue in the early years of the century, and this aspect of it engaged Yeats's attention from 1912 onwards: the automatic writing out of which *A Vision* emerged has to be seen in this light.[4]

Then, of course, there is the use of masks in the Noh. There were fifteen varieties of these, for different roles: hero, villain, demon, madwoman, and so on.[5] From one angle they would have seemed to Yeats reminiscent of the Tarot (The Fool, The Emperor, The Hanged Man, The Lovers), and of course, they are just as much a source for the twenty-eight phases of *A Vision*: more so, perhaps, in that each phase there has its mask. But he would also have felt that the Noh could provide striking analogies with the point at which his thinking had arrived as he was writing the poems in *Responsibilities*, for this postulates more or less willed attitudes (masks) revolving around one of two possible versions of Death: either Nothingness; or a state of Eternity so unlike life that Death seemed a reasonable description of it.

Finally there is ancestor-worship: in the context of the Noh, specifically aristocratic ancestor-worship. The idea of encountering, memorialising and entering into dialogue with the ghosts of his ancestors suggested a way of recording Yeats's valuing of his own Anglo-Irish tradition and background at a point in his career when his estimation of the potential for culture of Catholic Ireland was at its lowest.

Fittingly, for a poet seeking to define the dreams (or ghosts) in terms of which his own responsibilities begin, he opens this volume with some introductory rhymes ('Pardon, old fathers' (*P* 101)), by which he seeks to place himself in the tradition of his own family. In the same gesture, as he himself well realises, he is offering his own image of that tradition. He begins by invoking the shade of the first Yeats in Ireland, a Dublin linen-merchant who was exempt from customs duty (*'free of the ten and four'*). Next he refers to his great-grandfather, John Yeats (1774–1846), Rector of Drumcliffe: *'Old country scholar, Robert Emmet's friend'*. Yeats is evidently proud of the lineage represented by these two: *'Merchant and scholar who have left me blood/That has not passed through any huckster's loin.'* The reasons for the pride are not as evident as he appears to think. To be proud of not being a huckster is an aristocratic sort of pride, as he is aware, for the aristocratic life is free of all taint of use: by implication, therefore, his blood has remained pure. Yet a huckster, a dealer in small wares, is only a petty kind of merchant. And 'merchant', you might say, is a grand name for a grand kind of huckster. At any rate, a merchant deals in material wares, and is the prototype of the bourgeois existence Yeats is so often quick to condemn, not least in this volume. A scholar, of course, is a fine thing; but a country parson is unlikely to be very much of an aristocrat. There is a touch, then, of the creative in Yeats's handling of his ancestry. And the true source of this creative energy becomes clearer in the following lines:

> *Soldiers that gave, whatever die was cast:*
> *A Butler or an Armstrong that withstood*
> *Beside the brackish waters of the Boyne*
> *James and his Irish when the Dutchman crossed.*

Yeats is proud of his roots in the Ascendancy, for while he himself is better described as a mere member of the Protestant middle class, the descent from Mary Butler (1751–1834), a member of the Ormonde family, means those roots are indisputable. He is proud also of those who stood braving death with King Billy against Catholic James 'and his Irish' at the Battle of the Boyne: this line represents an extraordinary *volte-face*, at least in terms of overt attitudes, and imparts to the very word 'responsibility' a sense of the prodigal son's return. Mention of Robert Emmet hardly conflicts with such pride, for he, like most (though not all) of Yeats's nationalist heroes is also drawn from the Ascendancy. By contrast, the Catholic Daniel O'Connell is dismissed in 'Parnell's Funeral' as 'the Great Comedian'. And how does Yeats sum up the values of courage, enterprise and intelligence he discerns in his tradition? In a phrase that, as a boy, he was inspired to think of when contemplating his 'silent and fierce' maternal grandfather, William Pollexfen (1811–92), a sea captain and merchant. The phrase is: 'Only the wasteful virtues earn the sun.' This sounds aristocratic, and it encapsulates one of the main themes of the volume. Indeed, the poem serves its introductory purpose fairly well, since tradition and its nurture, aristocratic virtue, contempt for hucksters and nationalist, Ascendancy heroes all crop up again. That appears to leave out a specific reference to art; but Yeats ends his introductory lines by asking pardon from his fathers that he has no child, *'nothing but a book . . . to prove your blood and mine'*. We have been advised: the poems in this volume will be worthy of these virtues and these fathers. Yeats, like a good son of tradition, sees his new 'masculine' style as a patrilineal inheritance.

Art and its role in civilised society are the themes of a group of poems written as part of the controversy surrounding Sir Hugh Lane's offer of his collection of French Impressionist paintings to the Dublin Municipal Gallery of Modern Art, which he himself had founded. The offer was made on condition that they be properly housed, and this required funds. But the response from members of the Dublin Corporation and important members of the Catholic bourgeoisie, especially the newspaper-owner William Martin Murphy, was one of ungrateful and vicious philistinism. Lord Ardilaun, it is thought, offered to put up some of the money if it could be proved that there was a general desire to have the pictures in Dublin (*L* 573). This is the situation referred to in the lengthy title of the first poem on this subject: 'To a Wealthy Man who promised a second Subscription to the Dublin Municipal Gallery if it were proved the People wanted Pictures' (*P* 107–8). Yeats has no time for this deference to the opinions of 'Paudeen' and 'Biddy' (such are the revealing sobriquets he bestows on the people of Dublin). Duke Ercole d'Este did not deign to seek the opinions on drama of the onion-sellers when he encouraged the imitation of Plautus in Italian comedy. Nor did the other great aristocratic patrons of the arts, about whom Yeats had read in Castiglione's *Courtier*, consult the people. If they had done so, then, it is implied, there would have been no Renaissance. And if wealthy, cultured members of the Irish Ascendancy do so, there will be no Irish Renaissance. The noble thing would be to give for the pride of giving, 'What the exultant heart calls good' (a Nietzschean touch). Thus, by the generous nurturing of the highest values of a cultured class, and by their embodiment, protection and endowment in institutions and traditions which outlast the individual life of the giver, is civilisation created and continued: 'Because you gave, not what they would,/But the right twigs for an eagle's nest!' This degree of cultural theorising (it is scarcely original to describe it as implying a High Tory ideal of an organic community) is new to Yeats's poetry. But it would be wrong to see it as, in its outline, radically at odds with what has gone before. Yeats thinks of civilisation in general, like art, as something built out of the desire for the beauty and achievement of the past (the imitation of Plautus, or else 'sucking at the dugs of Greece', in this poem). What is thus built is handed down, both as tradition and image, through the generations. Civilisation, like art, can thus be regarded as partaking of something not essentially of flesh and blood. This is shown to be true even within the life of the individual artist, and in 'The Grey Rock' (*P* 103–6) Yeats shows the poets of the Cheshire Cheese as ghosts of naturally aristocratic disposition (*P* 104): he is able to guide his actions in the light of the ghostly image of their probity. The new and surprising thing, then, is not so much the cultural theory of the ghost and image (though the emphasis on spirits is novel) as the extent to which ghost and image are of the Ascendancy.

Yeats's poems about beggars and hermits (*P* 111–19) link the Buddhist theme of non-grasping with aristocratic contempt for the mean monetary measure. Some of these beggars are not unlike 'our old Paudeen in his shop' with his 'fumbling wits' and, more significantly, his 'obscure spite' (*P* 109). Humourless, timid and resentful of those who possess energy, his calculating spirit is the opposite of that proud, bountiful, self-delighting generosity Yeats lauds. He or his like would be among those who hated *The Playboy of the Western World*, and whom Yeats compares to eunuchs running through Hell to stare at Don Juan, 'Even like these to rail and sweat/Staring upon his sinewy thigh' (*P* 111). And Ireland is coming under the domination of the Paudeens, as we are memorably informed in 'September 1913':

> What need you, being come to sense,
> But fumble in a greasy till
> And add the halfpence to the pence
> And prayer to shivering prayer, until
> You have dried the marrow from the bone;
> For men were born to pray and save:
> Romantic Ireland's dead and gone,
> It's with O'Leary in the grave.

(*P* 108)

John O'Leary was something of a despiser of the bourgeois, informing Yeats that the average member of this class would never make a good rebel, 'for here the risk is immediate and certain, and the material advantage distant.'[6] It is easy to see precisely why Yeats would regard him as 'Romantic'. But of course, he also possessed the advantage, in terms of Yeats's strategy for this volume, of being both a spiritual ancestor and dead. What is not quite so obvious is how he consorts with those who fought James 'and his Irish', but light is shed on this when O'Leary's own spiritual ancestry is enumerated. It is an instructive list: not so much because it includes the expected Anglo-Irish patriots – Edward Fitzgerald, Robert Emmet and Wolfe Tone – but because it also mentions 'the wild geese': that is to say, those remnants of the ancient Gaelic aristocracy and their followers who fled Ireland following the submission of Hugh O'Neill (1603) after the Battle of Kinsale, and were very often employed in the armies of Austria, Spain and particularly France. They were, thus, the last remnants of an aristocratic, Gaelic, Catholic order, which Yeats could easily bring himself to admire, not least because, as he well knew, the sagas and poetry of ancient Ireland, and even some of its extraordinary bardic institutions, had been kept alive until that period, and even slightly later.[7] This is the first example in Yeats's work of the creation of a tradition for his idea of Ireland in terms of specific modern historical groups, and it provides a striking instance of his urge to forge factitious unity out of his divided inheritance. The example of Yeats's later occupancy of the Norman-Gaelic tower at Ballylee confirms that he saw a kind of continuity between the Gaelic aristocracy and the Anglo-Irish, where others could only perceive, in the earliest stages, usurpation accompanied by a destruction and savagery without parallel in the annals of Europe until the twentieth century. Fitzgerald, Emmet and Wolfe Tone might be said to have made some recompense for that destruction. And there they 'troop' in Yeats's ghostly band of heroes, while on either side of them Hugh O'Neill joins hands with Lady Gregory across the centuries. All possess the aristocratic virtues: they 'weighed so lightly what they gave' and would never stoop to counting pennies, like Paudeen. But Yeats's tradition remains notable – has become more notable at this stage – for its wary ambivalence towards that great, ungainsayable fact about Ireland: a Catholic peasantry, with aspirations of its own.

This might seem a slightly surprising conclusion: had not Yeats thought that Ireland's advantage over England was that it had the potential for an organic culture, in that it was still possible to believe that there could be a direct transaction between a true peasantry and a cultured national elite, leaving out the middleman of commercial culture? That was only a few years back: in 'The Galway Plains' (1903) he had written of England's disadvantage:

> England or any other country which takes its tunes from the great cities and gets its taste from schools and not from old custom may have a mob, but it cannot have a people. In England there are a few groups of men and women who have good taste, whether in cookery or in books; and the great multitudes but copy them or their copiers. (*E&I* 213–14)

Back in 1899 Yeats had seen it as a problem, surpassable no doubt, that 'the Irish educated classes' felt an 'antagonism to the life about them', occasioning their 'imaginative sterility' and encouraging the English disease in Ireland: a 'small minority', however, have been 'fruitful in imagination' (*UP*, II, 141). It is with this cultured and patriotic minority that many of Yeats's hopes had resided. They were, I have been suggesting, the middle term in a triad, mediating Celtic sensibility to the nation in terms of an idea of measure which (however it might be described) had many English or cosmopolitan associations, in a form which, nevertheless, was conceived as organic, and derived its energy from the people: ' to belong to any aristocracy, is to be a little pool that will soon dry up. A people alone are a great river . . .' (*E&I* 214).

But by 1907 there is a great change in the estimation of the worth of aristocracy, one which gives it a leading, rather than an expressive, role. And there is a new awareness of the political efficacy of the Catholic lower-middle and shopkeeper class. The problem is that this class will become the conduit for the culture and aspirations of the Catholic peasantry. A better conduit, one feels, would have been a reformed Ascendancy. In both opinions one senses, even discounting Yeats's own value-judgements, a new realism about the character and consitution of real and potential political power in modern Ireland. It is a realism which is profoundly at odds with the organicism of the people. The essay on 'Poetry and Tradition', published in *The Cutting of an Agate*, ends with a kind of valedictory to Yeats's earlier political hopes, a survey of lost opportunity, which itself is an instructive text to put alongside 'September 1913':

> Power passed to small shopkeepers, to clerks, to that very class who had seemed to John O'Leary so ready to bend to the power of others, to men who had risen above the traditions of the countryman, without learning those of cultivated life or even educating themselves, and who because of their poverty, their ignorance, their superstitious piety, are much subject to all kinds of fear. (*E&I* 260)

The most obvious thing about this is that, whatever Yeats may have intended, he has let slip some of his true opinions about the condition of these people before they rose in life. For much of their ignorance comes with them to their new station; and though 'traditions of the countryman' is a nod in the direction of the old conception of a living peasantry, the damage has been done. Less obviously, it seems that in practice the only route out of the peasantry is by way of this destructive status. In general, it can be said that a surprising revaluation occurs in Yeats's political thinking over this period, so that even England may now appear as the site of a superior civility: in the *Memoirs* Yeats records how Thomas MacDonagh had complained that the Gaelic League was 'killing Celtic civilisation'. Yeats reflects:

> In England this man would have become remarkable in some way, here he is being crushed by the mechanical logic and commonplace eloquence which gives the most

power to the most empty mind because, being 'something other than human life' [a reference to Blake's opinion of parliamentary politics] it has no use for distinguished feeling or individual thought. I mean that within his own mind this mechanical thought is crushing as with an iron roller all that is organic. (6 March 1909) (*Mem* 178)

Not only superior civility, then, but access to the organic. This thought can be linked to the conception of aristocracy adumbrated in *Responsibilities*. For though his thoughts on how to attain it have changed, Yeats definitely retains the ideal of the organic nation: his next thought in the *Memoirs* was: 'The soul of Ireland has become a vapour and her body a stone.' The right union produces earth. But Yeats now feels that this union is brought about not simply by the mediations of a bardic caste, but rather by an alliance between aristocracy and artist in which both partners possess aristocratic qualities: 'A great lady is as simple as a good poet. Both possess nothing that is not ancient and their own . . . ' (22 January 1909) (*Mem* 140). It is from this caste, so defined, that cultivation works mostly downwards in an asymmetrical relationship with the culture of the people. In *Discoveries*, in 1906, still castigating the failings of the English, Yeats had asserted, 'you cannot have health among a people if you have not prophet, priest and king' (*E&I* 264). This, an adherence to the most vaunting pretensions of the Romantic poet to become once again the legislator of mankind, here purged of all democratic taint, is combined with the organic idea of the growth and propagation of such a caste, and the retention of an organic notion of the connection to the people. Such was increasingly to be the emphasis in his work. And this brings us to two related contradictions in Yeats's political ideology in its bearing on aristocracy and tradition.

That part of his thinking which stresses the organic growth and nurture of a civilised society – the endowment and rooting of the arts, learning, and leisured aristocratic families – is to a significant degree at odds with, on the one hand, the part that sees the ordering process involved as ultimately invoking eternal images; and on the other, with the part that stresses self-delighting individualism.

Taking the first problem: the organic ideal for social order and growth seems to imply modes of perception and even imagination which are far more tentative, unpredictable and this-worldly than the stiff, visionary and sometimes deathly aspect of eternal forms.

Cairns Craig, in a highly original study of the politics of poetry in Yeats, Eliot and Pound, stresses the essential part that association and memory play in Yeats's conservative ideology, and insists that their role had been prepared even in the early poetry, in, for instance, his formulations of symbolist doctrine.[8] Not that many would ever maintain that associationism in itself was inimical to symbolism. And there had always been, as we remarked above, a tentative, Shelleyan, feel to Yeats's 'moods' when one compared them to Blake's symbols and 'states'. Craig maintains that Yeats's work (like Shelley's) is deeply imbued with associationism, at least of the kind represented by an aesthetician such as Archibald Alison, in his *Essays on the Nature and Principles of Taste* (1790), which is 'Platonist rather than materialist in bias', maintaining that 'mind is the primary reality and association is an account of those principles by which the mind orders itself – not an account of how the mind is ordered by mechanical forces.'[9] Craig discusses a passage from 'The Philosophy of Shelley's Poetry' (it is at *E&I* 89–90), where Yeats describes how 'ancient symbols' occur to us in fantasy and dreams, adducing 'a vision that a friend of mine saw when gazing at a dark blue curtain': for Craig this is an example of 'casual contingency' and 'pure associational recall'.[10] Whatever it be, the passage does not present the purely associational in any obvious sense; nor can it be concerned entirely with contingency, casual or otherwise, if it shows that our associations end in ancient symbols from the Great Mind. Yeats does not, of course, maintain a consistent philosophical position, and he is quite capable, without reference to eternal symbols, of writing poems about aristocracy and order which seem to be mainly concerned with maintaining certain traditions and modes of feelings so that their associations may be preserved to help build and mould future minds, which is the kind of thing Craig has in mind when he refers to political poetry. We shall recur to this in the next chapter. Craig insists, alluding to poems such as 'The Madness of King Goll' or 'Fergus and the Druid', that the minds even of Yeats's visionaries are trapped, against their wishes, in a world of time, following only an endless movement of association.[11] But in context, even this rather loaded evidence is equivocal, since these are typical examples of Yeats examining the negative possibilities of an idea: in 'Fergus and the Druid', for instance, the danger that even visionary pantheism could degenerate into a static truth: a Blakean point.

With respect to the other ideological contradiction we mentioned, that between individualism and order, Terry Eagleton has these perceptive words to say, in a lecture delivered to the Yeats Summer School in Sligo in 1985:

> The conflict I have in mind is simply this. Adherents of aristocratic ideology like Yeats are committed on the one hand to the values of order, ceremony, peace, stability and tradition – that's to say, to an impersonal organic hierarchy to which the individual subject is – precisely – subjected. All the values, in short, of the artistically admirable, politically revolting *Prayer for my Daughter*. But this 'organicist' vein of aristocratism co-exists with its opposite: with a swaggering, anarchic, Byronic affirmation of the individual subject as autonomous and absolute, utterly self-grounded and self-generative, stooping (as Yeats writes) to no man's beck and call.[12]

We have been connecting the latter aspect to Yeats's well-authenticated admiration for Nietzsche, but Eagleton is quite right to identify Byron as the English-language figure with whom Yeats could most easily identify these attributes: one who also offered certain practical hints about 'masculine' poetic style. It is not often realised how important a figure Byron becomes for Yeats, as we shall have to observe in other contexts. Eagleton's overall thesis, which is about 'Politics and Sexuality in W. B. Yeats', is a perceptive interweaving of Marxism and psychoanalysis. It first rehearses the Freudian hypothesis about castration, in its bearing on the male view of women, with the implication of its relevance to Yeats's view of Maud Gonne:

> By fetishising woman, converting her to an untouchable totemic object, man can hope to use this object to plug the nameless void in being which the woman incarnates, turning her against herself, perceiving her as at once poison and cure. For Freud, all fetishism is essentially a defence against castration, the construction of a substitute phallus for the one you might always lose. Woman as madonna is thus, paradoxically, woman as phallus, even if it is equally true (for the unconscious knows absolutely no contradiction) that she is idealised beyond sexuality altogether.[13]

It is possible to fill out this suggestion by observing that the metonymic drift we have already noted, of desire around the void at 'the world's core', is also the pursuit of fetishised images of Maud Gonne (her image is attached to those of 'dead lovers', or the Rose) around the 'void in being' of castration.

Eagleton's thesis states that Maud Gonne represented a profound psychic threat to Yeats:

> As both rose of Ireland and rancorous demagogue, Maud dramatised for Yeats with virulent intensity a contradiction always latent in the patriarchal unconscious; she is at once unity of being and what destabilises all such unity, the strictly unthinkable, the deadlock or aporia beyond which not even the most grandiosely synthesising thought can push.[14]

Yeats's defensive response to this aporia is the Byronic 'masculine' style. Further, his social theory sees 'the violent, demonic, libidinal male' as 'the architect of order'; but that organic order 'itself is somehow feminine'.[15] I do not, myself, see that 'somehow' as entirely obscure. Yeats had been distancing himself, not from the abstract idea of devotion to Maud Gonne, but from any hint of acquiescence in her ideology, attitudes or companions. This new assertiveness and independence was part of the new 'masculinity'. G. Kline has suggested, in *The Last Courtly Lover*, that Lady Gregory became a 'mother-substitute' for Yeats;[16] and certainly she inducted him into many of the mysteries of the aristocratic ideology. The suggestion is a fruitful one, at the very least in so far as it points to the idealised, desexualised 'feminine' mode which Yeats associates with the kind of social order he describes in 'A Prayer for my Daughter'. The problem is that this idealisation threatens the potency of the masculine impulse which is supposed to enact it. This threat can be conceived from two related Freudian angles. One, suggested by *Beyond the Pleasure Principle* (1920), posits the death-instinct on the basis that self-destructiveness, which according to Freud is often found to be inexplicable on the hypothesis of the universal application of the pleasure principle, can however be explained if one postulates a universal tendency of all organisms to regress to the state of rest enjoyed by inorganic matter. Such a state may best be achieved in death. The other, related, angle is that supplied by *Civilisation and its Discontents* (1930), in which Freud attempts to generalise this hypothesis – worked out originally in relation to certain types of anxiety dreams and neurotic compulsions – to the broad field of society. Here the emphasis is far more on the destructive course which may be taken by Thanatos in pursuit of that final quietus: the more a society seeks, by sublimation, ideal order, the more likely it is that the instinctual will rise up in rebellion and tear the body politic apart in Dionysiac frenzy.

In this perspective, as Eagleton indicates, it is scarcely surprising that Yeats should entertain the fears expressed in 'The Second Coming', especially if one considers that he felt that the social order he valued really was threatened by anarchy and violence. And on the same explanation, I think it is quite intelligible that his aristocratic order should be a slow, organic growth, conceived in terms of an idealised feminine, and that above this, so to speak, should be a world of relatively static eternal forms which have an affinity with death, but which draw organic, social aspiration after them, just as they do the desire of lovers. At the heart of these two layers is the void, the absence of 'core'.

II

We expend our lives, what we think of as our hearts, our 'core', in pursuit of those images and the patterns they make. In 'The Wild Swans at Coole' (*P* 131–2) the swans belong to the apparent eternity of Keats's Nightingale, and – since it is Yeats of whom we are speaking – a real eternity too. The regularity of their appearance, of the sound they make ('bell-beat of their wings'), and the order they assume ('lover by lover') suggests an eternal pattern. Organic life has seemed to be of the same order, but it is expending itself in counting, in making image and pattern, and the last stanza shows the poet divided between his mortal self and the pattern that will outlast him. Yet since the only hearts we do have are to be found in pursuit of image and pattern, division and deferral are an indispensable part of making, even as they also derive from a world of transience and death: in this case there are two reasons why one's 'heart' should be 'sore' and 'grow old', and why the final note of the poem is one of emptiness.

Such are the thoughts that become involved with Yeats's political contradictions in 'In Memory of Major Robert Gregory' (*P* 132–5) for this poem quietly pits Yeats's two versions of the aristocratic against each other: on the one hand, the traditional and rooted; on the other, the daring free spirit, with its echoes of Nietzsche and Byron. It does not, however, resolve this contradiction, nor even confront it.[17] This, like other such dubieties, was to remain richly unresolved. The poem takes its stanza form, and something of its plain, dignified manner, from Abraham Cowley's elegy, 'In Memory of William Hervey'. Yeats regarded his reading in the seventeenth century as a way of giving strong but noble sinew to his diction, and probably also of seeming withdrawn from modern baseness. In the case of Cowley there were congenial sentiments about a life of retired scholarship and contemplation, away from the tawdriness of urban existence, to be found in his *Essays*, for which he had in Yeats's youth been chiefly remembered, if at all. Cowley expresses a knowing nostalgia for the pastoral which hovers in the background of Yeats's thoughts both in this poem and in his other elegy for Robert Gregory, 'Shepherd and Goatherd' (*P* 141–5). In 'The dangers of an Honest man in much company', Cowley wishes 'that we might have our Woods and our Innocence again instead of our Castles and our Policies', but notes ruefully that he has been disappointed in some of his hopes of rural life:

> I thought when I went first to dwell in the Country, that without doubt I should have met there with the simplicity of the old Poetical Golden Age: I thought to have found no Inhabitants there, but such as the Shepherds of Sir *Phil. Sydney* in *Arcadia*.[18]

Yeats and his wife have retired to the old Norman keep in Galway ('Now that we've almost settled in our house' is the first line of the poem) but 'Our Sidney and our perfect man', Major Robert Gregory, has died in the Great War, and is not there to welcome them.

The anarchy of the modern world is already threatening 'the ceremony of innocence'. But so is the aristocratic contradiction we observed. For much of the poem celebrates Gregory's skills in such a way as to suggest their affinity with the nurture and continuance of order: he loved the landscape down to the last detail, even to the stir of the cattle who startle a water-hen (st. VII), as only they can who have an intimate relationship with the setting of their birth and upbringing. He would perhaps have been a great painter, and his potential was expressed in an ability to capture the essence of his own locality, 'cold Clare rock and Galway rock and thorn' (st. IX). He could have offered the Yeatses advice on how to restore their house, helping them to put down and nurture roots (st. X). All this imparts a kind of absurdity to the description of Gregory's death (st. XI), quite apart from the vagueness and equivocation of it, which are perhaps intended to be delicate in the handling of a subject painful to Lady Gregory:

> Some burn damp faggots, others may consume
> The entire combustible world in one small room
> As though dried straw, and if we turn about
> The bare chimney is gone black out
> Because the work had finished in that flare.
> Soldier, scholar, horseman, he
> As 'twere all life's epitome.
> What made us dream that he could comb grey hair?

This makes Gregory sound like an artist ('the work') of swift genius, whereas he had in fact died in action on the Italian front in January 1918, shot down in error by an Italian plane. Nothing in the rest of the poem leads us to conclude that 'the work' has been 'finished': quite the contrary, the impression is of wasted potential. Yeats is uneasy here in dealing with the fine daring, careless of one's own life, which the aristocrat should properly possess, and of which the harmless form was being a brave horseman (st. VIII). For in following his bold inclination, Gregory has nullified his other aristocratic duty, which is to nurture order and tradition in his own demesne. And he has done so at the time when Yeats has made a strengthened commitment to order, within that very demesne, and through the painful sacrifice of both Maud and Iseult Gonne: a bargain, in fact, which had deep resonances for Yeats, and which he was at times inclined to regard as involving the sacrifice of passion. Gregory had shown the ultimate contempt for such a bargain, a contempt which could never be answered, and moreover one for which Yeats himself felt an emotional sympathy: in 'The Collar-Bone of a Hare' (P 136–7) the speaker imagines himself staring coldly at 'the old bitter world' and laughing at 'all who marry in churches'.

The critical train of thought is more obvious in 'Shepherd and Goatherd', in which Gregory is described as 'a cuckoo,/No settled man' (*P* 143). But as for 'In Memory', for everything nuance can show about Yeats's ambivalence with respect to Gregory, he did include in the poem his sense that Gregory was potentially a 'great painter'.[18] The death of the potential artist is proleptic of the death of all artists, including the one who is writing the poem. Indeed, potential is a quality that evokes deferral, and the labour of art which, though in principle endless, must always be terminated by the casualty of death. Gregory alive is a figure of imaginative fullness: in stanza VII we are told that 'all things the delighted eye now sees/Were loved by him', and we are given an inventory: trees, tower, ford, water-hen. Gregory is an Adam, but a lost Adam, who leaves the poet and his wife contemplating a landscape – cold and rocky, in any case – which echoes the void at the heart of existence: like the final stanza of 'The Wild Swans at Coole', this is the desolation of a Nature always barren where man is not. Gregory dead is Adam fallen, and is therefore a fit type of the artist, who has to wring form from this haunted world. That Gregory should join Johnson, Synge and George Pollexfen and start to troop with them as a ghostly gauge of value is something that Yeats says he is not 'accustomed' to: but that is the point: he has been shocked into an authentic response. Of course, that Gregory should join those others is in principle something Yeats would accept as possible. But the sudden death of one who should have acted as an imaginative aid to Yeats's own fashioning of the landscape has the cold force of a fact and has reawakened a knowledge, always subject to evasion, that art is wrung out of conflict and in the face of death; that all artists labour after Adam's fall.

This makes the poem self-reflexive in a more profound sense than is entailed by the mere fact of Gregory's being a painter, and nowhere is that self-reflexivity more evident than in the final stanza, which notes how, 'seeing how bitter is that wind/That shakes the shutter', Yeats had meant to compose a more conventional elegy, recalling exemplars of virtue or heroism, with 'some appropriate commentary on each', but instead, 'a thought/Of that late death took all my heart for speech'. For while this frames the poem, in post-Romantic fashion, as a sincere subversion of stiff convention, and thus as full and expressive utterance, it also says that the truest art is improvisational.[19] For the heart may need conventional images to motivate it, but it only finds itself in the deferrals and exfoliations imposed on this motivation by time: that is, in 'speech'. Expressive utterance is not really 'full'. Furthermore, since this exemplary poem has shown Yeats shocked into authentic speech by the death of one who would alive have left him in a state of complacency about the task of imagination, it suggests both that the truest art always remembers death, and that 'the imagination may live most vigorously in the absence or death of its object'.[20]

In an analogous way, Gregory ends up being more exemplary than Johnson, Synge or Pollexfen. He is torn by the same conflict that rends his elegist: that between the *sprezzatura* of the aristocratic artist and the 'responsibilities' of the essentially aristocratic temperament. That he gets it wrong, and makes a bargain in which he relinquishes the latter in favour of the former, is shown by 'An Irish Airman Foresees his Death' (*P* 135). Even Yeats liked to see more sense in heroism than is offered in this, for neither heart nor head seems to offer a convincing reason for the adoption of the attitude described: explanations are explicitly ruled out. The poem is an enigma: 'lonely impulse of delight' in what? Flying? Air combat? The following lines seem to cast doubt on these adolescent images of heroism:

> I balanced all, brought all to mind,
> The years to come seemed waste of breath,
> A waste of breath the years behind
> In balance with this life, this death.

This sounds far finer than adolescent heroics, for it suggests a moment of profound existential insight. But the content of this insight (punctuation properly construed) is that past and future life seem a waste compared with a present which is defined as 'this life, this death': that is to say, the perceived moment of heroism. 'Waste of breath', on the other hand, is the same as the expenditure of the heart required by a settled life of compromise between deferral and measurement. It takes some hard arguing to see much in this choice that would consistently commend itself to Yeats's reason; indeed, an important strand of underlying negative feelings is revealed by 'Reprisals' (*VP* 791), a poem not published in his own lifetime, which essentially convicts Gregory of gross irresponsibility in deserting his tenants.[21] Yet we are all subject to the tormenting, contrary pulls of immediate significance and deferred significance, and we all – Yeats included – make bargains with life. Given that the components of Gregory's character are the approved aristocratic and artistic ones, he is the more truly a hero because of the tragic imperfection of his choice, and the more truly exemplary because that choice, like so many choices, is irrational, and because it reminds us that every life is one of wasted potential.

As for Yeats's political aesthetic, whether one considers the virtues he lauds, or the type of settled life in which they are deemed to flourish, or the images of those virtues and that life, or even the careless aristocratic freedom that may subvert all this: all are explicitly seen, here and elsewhere, in terms of the Ascendancy. Yeats's assertive style, and his critical and appraising attitude to modern Ireland, take the value-judgements that lend them confidence from a conscious sense of Anglo-Irish tradition. And the body of images that surround his world, measuring desire and the conflictual life of Ireland, also has a strong Anglo-Irish content. The hardness, the sense that there is value in stern measure, in Urizenic 'personality', as Yeats had once put it, even for the creation of lively and flexible form, shows him positioned as external limit with respect to Ireland, rather than at her rosy heart. Indeed, this is later what he was to think of as his 'bitterness' towards her. The events of 1916 were to tax his ability to frame modern Ireland, but in the event he was equal to the challenge, according to his Anglo-Irish lights.

III

Nations, too, need their images to build a tradition and sustain their enterprise. In 'Easter 1916' (*P* 180–2) Yeats sets about making a national image out of the chief insurgents, most of whom had been shot. He responds with apparent magnanimity to the unexpected refutation of the despair he had expressed over the fate of the national ideal in 'September 1913' – a refutation offered largely by members of that very Catholic middle class of which he had despaired. The poem begins by contrasting the sometimes tawdry, sometimes ridiculous, reality of the insurgents' imperfect lives with hints of the vague and powerful image into which the poet will work them. Much space is given to the reality.

Justice dictates that the role of Paudeen be recognised, and Yeats gives a nod in this direction by recalling that in everyday life he used to meet some of the insurgents coming 'From counter or desk'. At such occasions he had sometimes spoken 'polite meaningless words'. But this poem is not the place for meaninglessness, and he is absolved of the need for politeness by the gravity of his task. The ensuing cameos of some of the leaders are fairly unsparing. And furthermore it is fair to say that they show the insurgents as profoundly damaged in their essential humanity by the very cause which prompted their heroism. The picture of Constance Markievicz (whose life was spared) is a summary of a course that should not be taken by a woman, especially a beautiful one. Considered carefully, this portrait, offered in Yeats's most precise and urbane manner, reveals itself as a studied insult:

> That woman's days were spent
> In ignorant good-will,
> Her nights in argument
> Until her voice grew shrill.
> What voice more sweet than hers
> When, young and beautiful,
> She rode to harriers?

'Ignorant good-will' is a splendidly judged phrase. She can hardly have been mollified by the amplification Yeats supplies three poems later in 'On a Political Prisoner' (*P* 183–4): 'Blind and leader of the blind/Drinking the foul ditch where they lie.' This dreadful transformation has been wrought (she has been 'changed utterly' in an unpromising sense) admittedly through her own stupidity, by a woman whose youth at Lissadell as a child of the Ascendancy had started so finely: riding to harriers carries inescapable social connotations. Next comes Patrick Pearse, a teacher, who 'rode our wing`ed horse,' unlike Con Markievicz, who was born to ride a real one. Pearse is here condescendingly accorded the role of chief nationalist poet by Yeats, a condescension made easier by the fact that he is secure in his estimation of their relative merits, as the calculatedly facile phrase reveals. But since it is 'our' wing`ed horse, the implication is that every nationalist movement has to retain a bard, who is likely to be given to sentimental or vatic inflation, and thus ruined as a poet. Thomas MacDonagh fares better, but the chief drift of Yeats's remarks is that his promise has been wasted. John MacBride, Maud Gonne's former husband, requires careful handling, and Yeats confesses that he had 'dreamed' him a 'drunken, vainglorious lout'. He does not, however, expressly assert that he has awoken from his dream, but explains that MacBride had done bitter wrong to 'some who are near my heart', and then, in a generous concessive clause,

Yet I number him in the song;
He, too,has resigned his part
In the casual comedy . . .

There follows a verse-paragraph in which Yeats implies that the
hearts of the insurgents had seemed to be 'Enchanted to a stone/To
trouble the living stream.' This is, in part, another form of the
imputation that they had been damaged by the cause. Again, the
woman's crime is to be seen as greater: 'Women . . . give all to an
opinion as if it were some terrible stone doll,' Yeats remarks in
'The Death of Synge' (*Au* 504). In contrast to this petrified en-
durance, which comprises the idea of damaged or diminished
humanity, Yeats evokes the detail of common mutability, in su-
perbly modulated phrasing which enacts the quiet passage of time
through repetition, parallelism, balance and antithesis:

The horse that comes from the road,
The rider, the birds that range
From cloud to tumbling cloud,
Minute by minute they change;
A shadow of cloud on the stream
Changes minute by minute;
horse-hoof slides on the brim,
And a horse plashes within it;
The long-legged moor-hens call;
Minute by minute they live:
The stone's in the midst of all.

There have been two changes to the insurgents, then: in the first,
before the insurrection, their hearts had seemed enchanted to
stones, and this transformation had entailed diminished humanity, a
damage compounded by the fact that they seemed to be merely a
part of the casual comedy without realising what kind of play they
were in. They had thus succeeded in appearing simultaneously irk-
some, cold and ridiculous. The second change had, through their
martyrdom, taken this stony condition and transformed it into a
'terrible beauty'. It is a fair inference, then, that the word 'terrible' is
not merely a deliberately indefinable gesture to the sublime, with its
traditional association of 'Terror' and 'Obscurity', in Burke's par-
lance. In this context it also means simply 'painful' or 'bad' (to quote
the dictionary) in a manner conditioned by Yeats's ambivalence.

Yet this double process can, of course, be seen in another aspect, which shows that petrifying themselves in life had only been part of a process of changing into a heroic image, a process completed in martyrdom. In this aspect, the insurgents bear a tragic similarity to the artist, forced to choose 'perfection of the life or of the work'. They have, at least, succeeded in transforming themselves into an image for their nation. This image is, as images often are in Yeats, hard, cold and inhuman. But wrested from the self-maiming of lives of promise, baptised in blood and coloured by the associations bestowed by previous martyrs to the cause, it is indeed beautiful and sublime in a way that is awe-inspiring and obscure. One specific echo in the line, that of Blake's 'fearful symmetry', is instructive in this connection. Blake is also responding to notions of the sublime as terrible. The emblem of 'The Tyger' alludes in part to a merely fashionable aspect of these notions, as exemplified in Stubbs's pictures of lions devouring horses. But it also alludes to the terrible aspect of God revealed in the Old Testament, for in asking who made the Tyger, Blake is implying that the deity must be to a degree tigerish. Further, the poem is in that sense about creation. This creation is conceived in terms of a harsh manufacturing process ('What the hammer? what the chain . . . ?') albeit probably an artisanal one. In the context of Blake's other poems of the period, including his other *Songs*, it is not hard to see a very oblique reference to the revolutionary potential of the working class, which tended to be symbolised by related images of fire, energy and wrath, as in the figure of Orc. None of this would have been strange to Yeats. The point of similarity is that what has been 'born' in 'Easter 1916' is not merely an icon, but the aura surrounding it and the effects that aura will bring to pass. It is a poem, as 'The Tyger' is in part, about the genesis of a new revolutionary movement.

The sublime terror of this movement, however, unlike in Blake, is feminine: it is Dark Rosaleen a shade or two darker than before. Indeed, the most likely immediate source for the phrase 'terrible beauty', as Carmel Jordan has shown, is in Sheridan Le Fanu's long poem, *Duan na Glave*, which is about a Munster goddess called Fionuala: 'Like Cathleen Ni Houlihan, she demands the ultimate sacrifice of her devotees, and Cathair, a young hero like Cuchulain, gladly accepts death for her sake. . .'[22] The lines in question are these: 'Fionuala the Cruel, the brightest, the worst,/ With a terrible beauty the vision accurst. . .'[23] But these are not the only traces of Gothic femininity in the poem. Nina Auerbach, in *Woman and the Demon*, notes how in *Dracula* 'The word "change", sometimes modified by "strange" and "terrible", almost always accompanies Lucy in the text. . . .'[24] In so far as the insurgents have until now had any commerce with the feminine, it has been in a form too contemptibly susceptible of definition: the small, stony, living death of opinion and propaganda. But now, in one leap, they have transcended the definitions proposed by Yeats, and identified themselves with the very life and future of Ireland, which, always personified as female, is now both fearful and hard to define for one who is both sympathetic to the national cause and alienated from those currents in national life which are now its chief bearers.

But this does not mean that Yeats will not make an attempt at defining them. It is interesting to compare his grappling with the question of definition with Blake's. In 'The Tyger', the question, 'What immortal hand or eye,/Dare frame thy fearful symmetry?' is partly self-reflexive, for in invoking the Divine Craftsman, it also invokes the idea of the poet. Yeats disclaims divine foreknowledge of the future course of the national movement ('That is Heaven's part'), but allows himself the task of creating the new national icon by the act of poetic naming: 'our part/To murmur name upon name'. This act of definition is so important that it has to be signified to the reader twice – the second time with direct reference to the creation of the poem itself: 'I write it out in a verse'. The analogy Yeats finds for his role, though, is not to that of the Godhead, but to that of the mother: 'As a mother names her child'. When Yeats acceded to what he thought was Lady Gregory's sense of his place in the social order, he acceded to the apparent paradox of a mother founding a patriarchal system. He offers her rooted perspective as a competitor to that of the terrible goddess of insurrectionist Ireland, who has stolen each poor 'child' away, like a kidnapping woman of the *sidhe*.[25] The act of naming and framing from this position will allow for the precision of qualification, such as that offered in this very poem and in poems such as 'On a Political Prisoner', and for unillusioned political realism, including the feeling that 'England may keep faith' and, as promised, reintroduce the Home Rule Bill at the end of the war. If so, perhaps it was 'needless death after all', an irrationally heroic one, not unlike the one Robert Gregory was to suffer.

But if there was admiration bestowed there, for Yeats did admire heroism even of that kind, there is yet more admiration here, for even if the insurgents misunderstood politics, they were fighting in a cause still near his heart. And cannily percipient as usual, he already suspected that the die was cast (see 'The Rose Tree' (*P* 183)), and that, by the folly of executing the insurgents, the government had ensured a confidence and determination in the national cause which meant that Ireland would have her freedom whatever England did. This would happen despite any ambivalence he or Lady Gregory might feel about some of the chief actors and some of the likely consequences of their actions. In the end, then, the act of naming, a difficult enterprise which has had to struggle with so much that might detract from a sense of the heroic, is undertaken in the knowledge that when the insurgents were 'changed utterly', everything else was changed utterly too. Yeats had the greatest respect for historical change won by blood and heroism; and if readers have imagined that the chief note of the poem is positive, that is surely because, however grudging the expression of respect might be, it ends up not merely by juxtaposing a grudge with a portentous nod of respect, but by finding the grudge outweighed by the heroic act. Concessive praise and concessive blame are corollaries, in Yeats's work, of the philosophy of contraries which allows one to consider both truth and 'counter-truth'. The weighing and judging involved are sometimes offered with an air of grave wisdom. Nevertheless, the force, even the sincerity, if one may say so, of the positive side of Yeats's response to the insurgents can be gauged by the fact that he is, in effect, praising them in the highest terms he knows: like true heroes they have endured a tragic sacrifice akin to that which the poet has to make, while it required immeasurably greater courage. It will nevertheless be obvious that this powerful concession has been wrung in part from a cold-eyed attitude of weighing and judging in which the Anglo-Irish postulates, so to speak, of Yeats's thinking remain fully operative. These postulates are, however unlikely it might seem, just as much at work in Yeats's occult writings as they are in the poems we have been studying here. They, and in particular *A Vision*, are every bit as much about 'framing Ireland' as are the more obviously political poems studied here. It will be the task of the next chapter to suggest how this is so, not in yet another explication of the workings of gyres, but in an examination of the associations Yeats held with some of central images involved in his system.

9

REFLECTIONS ON YEATSIAN OCCULTISM

I

The nature of woman, whose emblem is the moon, and who, through the mediumship of George Yeats, relayed the knowledge imparted by the instructors, can help in providing some insight into *A Vision*, at least when it is considered in relationship to ideas about the Orient, about the Celtic and about occult science. When, in the poem 'Michael Robartes and the Dancer' (*P* 175–6), '*He*' announces to '*She*' that 'Opinion is not worth a rush', he argues that women should put the cultivation of beauty, the 'looking- glass', in its stead. One of the things implied, as elsewhere, is that women have an instinctive propinquity with the mask, and with the rituals and games of passion that can be played through its agency. The use of the 'looking-glass' image already recognises self-consciousness and division, but also recognises one of the instinctive rights of women: to be unselfconscious precisely about self-consciousness of this kind, to play the game of measured deferral with ease, 'as those move easiest who have learned to dance'. By contrast, the pursuit of opinion, of abstraction and of being 'Learned like a man' can, as we saw in the last chapter, make a 'stone' out of woman's 'heart': that is to say, instead of the heart's being expended in the game of life, it shrivels to a petrified parody of the 'core', something that does not even exist except as a parody.

On the other hand, the role of women as mediums suggests that they may get in touch not only with spirits but also with truths about the spiritual world. Notwithstanding woman's essential antipathy to abstraction, what his wife's mediumship brought him was geometrical patterns – diagrams of the phases of the moon and their relationship to human character; gyres and vortices coloured black and white, by means of which he could plot mathematically the whole of history – and these objectifications, while they might appeal to his bent for occult theorising, could also be seen precisely as another form of 'inverted' and possibly sinister escape from life, and in particular from the passion of a living woman. On the other hand, these very patterns, precisely by virtue of their discipline, their provision of 'measure', could be seen as an attractive and necessary part of the codification of experience. Hints of these ideas are to be found in 'The Gift of Harun Al-Rashid' (*P* 445–50), originally published in the first version of *A Vision* (1925) as 'Desert Geometry or the Gift of Harun Al-Raschid' (*AVA* 121–7). The poem has to be seen in the light of the fiction he maintained at that juncture to the effect that the system derived from the wisdom and writings of one Kusta ben Luka (820–[?]92), a Christian doctor and philosopher in Harun's court, according to Yeats. The doctor is real, though the writings are not, and he could not possibly have been at the court of Harun Al-Rashid.

The poem describes how the Caliph presented Kusta (clearly symbolising Yeats) with a new bride. A few days after the wedding she begins to talk in her sleep – an obvious reference to the automatic writing: 'A live-long hour/She seemed the learned man and I the child . . .' (*P* 449/*AVA* 125). Note that in becoming learned she also becomes like a man. The poem assures us that despite the complicated and forbidding appearance of the occult philosophy, with its diagrams and abstract terms, it is merely a codification, an abstract ordering, of life:

> All those abstractions that you fancied were
> From the great Treatise of Parmenides;
> All, all those gyres and cubes and midnight things
> Are but a new expression of her body
> Drunk with the bitter sweetness of her youth.
> And now my utmost mystery is out.
>
> (*P* 450/*AVA* 126–7)

Yet it would hardly be churlish to say that this was protesting too much if one recalled that it was the abstractions which, at least in those very first days of Yeats's marriage, had apparently seduced him away from the dream of a young girl (Iseult Gonne) and the memory of her mother. But this is his own problem, so to speak: it is for the male sage or mage that abstractions such as this possess a seductive character, and possibly a dangerous one, as tending to lead away from life. The lines continue, 'A woman's beauty is a storm- tossed banner;/Under it wisdom stands.' A woman's beauty may be best nurtured in the cultivation of the mask and its deferrals. But for that very reason it will not be a focus for peace. The wisdom that lies beneath it will express the principles of conflict, contrariety, *différance*. Despite the dangers of abstraction, then, these are the best abstractions on offer, being as it were a theory of anti-abstraction. Partly for this reason, one ingredient of the magical haze with which Yeats seeks to surround *A Vision* is the idea of feminine wisdom. The first version is also dedicated to 'Vestigia', that is, to Moina Mathers (under her Golden Dawn name), wife of MacGregor Mathers, the translator of the diagrammatical *Kabbalah Unveiled*. It bids fair in its inclusiveness – and, as we have seen, in its own diagrams (Figures 7.1 and 7.2) – to compete with works such as Madame Blavatsky's *Secret Doctrine* and *Isis Unveiled*, this last being another tribute to the moon, symbol of the goddess. And, as Jon Stallworthy has noted, 'The Gift of Harun-Al Rashid' finds some of its source material in *The Thousand and One Nights*.[1] It thus makes allusion to Shahrazade, and as Warwick Gould has pointed out, 'Yeats shares with Shahrazád a simple need – time-gaining'.[2] The gaining of time, that is, for the definition and re-definition of experience where it is understood, as we saw in the last chapter, that such definition is best offered in the recognition of death. Gould shows how such a perspective can be illuminating about the different versions and subdivisions of *A Vision*: they are, in a sense, different tales, each of which works 'to place a finite shape upon an infinity of potential experience': *A Vision* is 'a "moving image" of its author's developing thought'.[3] And then there is the fact that 'Many stories of the *Nights* use wise girls as geomancers.'[4] Geomancy, a topic to which we shall have occasion to return, was begun in a state of trance, in which diagrams were produced, and these were later subject to conscious ordering and interpretation. It is not entirely surprising to find that in Yeats woman expresses life's wisdom in a trance or somnambulistically. The danger for the interpreter and codifier is that he will seek the abstraction instead of the life.

II

But before considering that danger, it will be worth looking at the topic of Orientalism, which is raised by the *Arabian Nights* and which offers some parallels, in Yeats's handling, with the subject of woman. It will be recalled that in Chapter 1 we suggested that the Oriental could be seen as a matter of passionate temperament, or in terms of a propensity for alchemy, astrology, occult science in general – to which we might now add geomancy. We also referred there to the 'Leo Africanus' episode, in which Yeats undertook automatic writing, as a result of a seance in 1912, in an attempt to make contact with this Moorish traveller. This episode fed into the fictions that surrounded the first version of *A Vision*, for the fictional tribe who were supposed to have preserved the wisdom of Kusta ben Luka were at first called 'Bacleones', 'an Arab sect well known at Fez in the time of Leo Africanus' (*AVA* 31).

What, if anything, can one infer from Yeats's references to Moorish culture, or at least, from the associations suggested by *Mosada*, by the Lully poems, by the figure of Leo Africanus, and by the fact that Yeats kept his 'barbarous words' (magical invocations) in a 'gilded Moorish wedding-chest' (*M* 366)? Ebremar, in *Mosada*, had loved a Moorish girl, but then become a fanatical Catholic Inquisitor. Lully, from a profane youth, had become a devout Catholic, but had steeped himself in Arabic learning, including alchemy, by long contact with the Moors of Majorca, with a view to converting the Muslims of North Africa. Leo Africanus, born a Moor, was apparently versed in alchemy (Yeats writes to him about 'the Alchemists of Fez'), and possibly in 'barbarous words' (words of Barbary?).[5] His travels were recorded in his geographical texts. He had converted to Catholicism out of expediency, but on his return to Fez had renounced it.

Catholicism does not come well out of this: not only codifier, it is also cruel denier, of life and passion. On the other hand, it offers a system which Lully felt had a worthy if misguided antagonist in Islam. Leo Africanus, however, on the basis of roughly similar knowledge to that possessed by Lully, made the opposite choice as soon as he was free to do so. Moorish sensibility (and by extension Arabic sensibility) is not, then, at odds with system: it inherits Arabic skill and learning in geometry, alchemy and astrology. But it does not make abstract knowledge the enemy of passion. Moorish and Arabic civilisation are, rather, given the general characteristic of expressing passion in pure oriental (which for Yeats is allied to Celtic) manner, while being able to codify in abstract form the universal intuitions to which this passion gives rise, without doing Catholic violence to the body. Now the ancient Celts had, in the Druids, also possessed a caste which was able to 'geometricise' the roots of passion. So Yeats is again, and more firmly, setting himself on the side of the Oriental, Celtic and occult against Catholic denial of energy and corruption of the perennial truth. The status of *A Vision* as both imitation and correction of Dante also supports such an interpretation: Cary's translation, which Yeats used, was called *The Vision*, and the change from definite to indefinite article, as Gayatri Spivak has pointed out, is significant.[6] Dante offers the apodictic truth of Catholicism; Yeats the subjective and provisional – in line with the perspective suggested by his allusions to the *Arabian Nights*.

The Epilogue to *Per Amica Silentia Lunae* prompts further thoughts on Catholicism. It is addressed to 'Maurice' (Iseult Gonne) and, recalling time they had spent together in Normandy, it naturally alludes to Yeats's earlier experiences of France in the 1890s. He especially recalls the fascination which magic and the occult held for French writers of that generation, as well as for him. But Iseult had been reading the younger French poets to him: Claudel, Jammes, Péguy, all Catholic:

> It was no longer the soul, self-moving and self-teaching – the magical soul – but Mother France and Mother Church.
> Have not my thoughts run through a like round, though I have not found my tradition in the Catholic Church, which was not the Church of my childhood, but where the tradition is, as I believe, more universal and more ancient? (*M* 368–9)

He had never meant that his magical practices lacked tradition, but in his youth that he was not so much concerned with this as with the relatively spontaneous experiments of the Golden Dawn. Now, however, he is becoming learned in his tradition, reading Henry More, uncovering the roots of Rosicrucianism. Although he does not say so, he is happy enough that his tradition is not Catholic, not only because he regards it as more universal and ancient, but also because his associations with Catholicism are strongly negative, as his reflections on the Moors make plain.

III

It will be helpful at this stage to consider in slightly more detail the associations one may glean from the broad outlines of the system of *A Vision*, before adverting, at last, to the question how far Yeats felt himself tempted by a dangerous or Urizenic abstraction. For the system of *A Vision* is Oriental, Celtic, Rosicrucian and Masonic; and these adjectives, as I hope to show, can be glossed in illuminating ways.

The fictional tribe who were supposed to have preserved the wisdom of Kusta ben Luka were at first called the 'Bacleones', 'an Arab sect well known at Fez in the time of Leo Africanus'. But they soon changed their name, moved from Morocco to Mesopotamia, and became Bedouin: their new title was the 'Judwalis'. This, according to Yeats, in a formulation which recalls his interest in the concept of measure, 'means makers of measures, or as we would say, of diagrams' (*VP* 825). The word, as S. B. Bushrui points out in a detailed discussion of 'Yeats's Arabic Interests', derives from the Arabic word '*jadwal*', meaning 'a stream or canal or mathematical table or diagram', though the tribe itself never existed.[7] The Judwalis were incorporated into the first version of *A Vision* where, it will be recalled, they danced in such a way that their footprints left in the sand the pattern of the phases of the moon which is one of the cornerstones of Yeats's system (*AVA* 9–11). Bushrui points out that this is also a reference to the Bedouin art of geomancy, or 'sand divination' ('Khatt al-Raml', literally 'line [or lines] drawn on sand'.[8] But Mrs Yeats made a revealing remark to Dr Bushrui, which indicates that Bedouin geomancy is a disguise – though a plausible one, since it does exist – for Golden Dawn practices: she remarked that the 'sand diagrams' were 'part of the Order to which Yeats belonged'.[9] If so, there is an obvious Rosicrucian source for them – and it is the only Rosicrucian source – in the works of Robert Fludd, who was a strong believer in geomancy, and who incorporated a theory of it into the vast Kabbalistic and neo-Platonic synthesis he created.[10] Fludd is given a chapter in an important book, *The Real History of the Rosicrucians* (1887) by Yeats's Golden Dawn acquaintance, A. E. Waite.[11] He had also been the subject of a more recent study by J. B. Craven, in 1902, and of a 'homage' by the Reverend Wynn Westcott, the very man into whose hands the documents which founded the Golden Dawn were supposed at first to have come.[12] More important, he was

simply the most significant figure in the history of English Rosicru-
cianism, and was generally thought of as such.[13] And since there is
no other occult writer who pays so much and such learned atten-
tion to the subject of geomancy, his are probably the 'sand dia-
grams' to which Mrs Yeats refers. In fact, these diagrams consisted
of patterns of dots made at random in the sand or earth, and
further patterns consciously derived from them.

A number of details of Fludd's theory and practice are suggestive
of *A Vision*: the fifteen compartments into which the dots resolved
themselves could be seen as roughly corresponding to half the
lunar cycle; more convincingly, the random series of dots with
which the geomancer begins have to be laid out in lines of four, and
this is reminiscent of Yeats's description of the sand dance as per-
formed by 'Four Royal Persons' – the Four Faculties, as they be-
come, corresponding to the Four Elements and Blake's Four Zoas.
But perhaps more illuminating than any such detail is the initial
state of the geomancer. The task is described by Keith Thomas as
'interpreting the meaning of the pattern of dots produced by the
wizard in a state of semi- trance'.[14] Everything that is known about
geomancy, including from the works of Fludd, supports this de-
scription. The automatic writing, then, has more than a perfunc-
tory similarity with the magical practice which provides the chief
metaphor for it. This points up another conformity: in both ac-
tivities there are two stages: first there is semi-conscious expres-
sion, and then conscious, exact, 'diagrammatical' interpretation. In
the case of Mrs Yeats's automatic script, she was supposed to be
the relatively unconscious oracle; Yeats was the chief interpreter
and magus, codifying feminine wisdom.

The system he arrived at was Rosicrucian in other, more funda-
mental ways than those already hinted at. In Robert Fludd's *Utrius-
que Cosmi* we are regaled with many beautiful diagrams expressing
emanation from the Godhead. While the result arrived at by Yeats
and his Instructors is palpably indebted in a general sense to the
whole occult tradition, there is no more significant specific debt
than that which they owe to Fludd's diagrams of intersecting light
and dark triangles, showing the progress away from divinity and
then back towards it again; or the related ones in which that pro-
gress is shown in terms of opposing triangles divided into twenty-
seven stages (see Figures 9.1 and 9.2).[15] This number becomes
twenty-eight if one counts the unknowable Godhead from which it
all proceeds. As in *A Vision*, the movement of opposed vortices

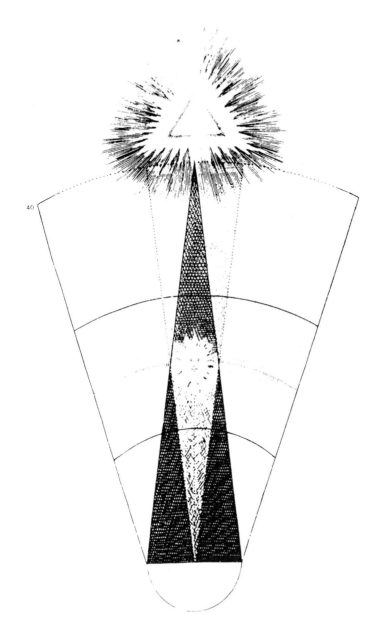

Figure 9.1 From Robert Fludd, *Philosophia sacra et vere Christiana seue Meteorologica Cosmica* (Frankfurt, 1626), p.212.

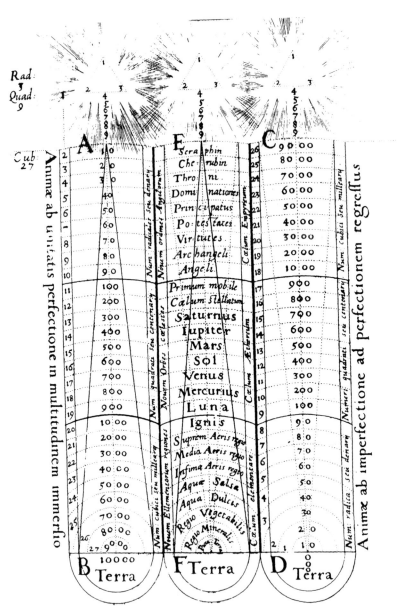

Figure 9.2 From Robert Fludd, *Utriusque Cosmi Maioris scilicet et Minoris Metaphysica, Physica, atque technica Historia*, 2 vols (Oppenheim, 1617–19), vol. II, tractate 1, section 1, p.45.

occurs both in the macrocosm and in the microcosm, according to an unvarying principle of esoteric doctrines. Thus it is applicable to the cosmos and to history, as well as to the life of an individual.

That Yeats also regarded this wisdom as Celtic cannot be proven by any such clear source, but it is suggested by his use of another fiction about the derivation of the system: that the diagrams originating with Kusta ben Luka had ended up in a book called 'Speculum Angelorum et Hominorum [sic]' written 'by Giraldus and printed at Cracow in 1594' (*AVA* xvii).[16] Edmund Dulac, the designer of the fine woodcut of 'Giraldus' which appears in both versions of *A Vision*, asked if Giraldus Cambrensis (?1146–?1220) were the model. Yeats replied that he was not.[17] Giraldus is, in fact, just a name that crops up in the Automatic Script as a communicant with the Control. But Dulac's question is natural, for there is no other historical Giraldus of any note whatsoever. It means nothing to say that Yeats's Giraldus 'is' Cambrensis, especially given his denial. But then it means precious little to say that he 'is' the entity referred to in the Automatic Script. What were the associations of Mrs Yeats and Yeats himself with the name? The allusion to Cambrensis is there, for it seems unlikely they would have thought long about William Allingham's pseudonym, which was Giraldus.

The *Topographia Hibernica* and *Expugnatio Hibernica* of Giraldus Cambrensis were regarded as the source of valuable information about medieval Irish customs, and his *Itinerarium Cambriae* as performing the same service for Welsh ones. He was thus pan-Celtic. His works are cited three times in Thomas Moore's own notes to his *Irish Melodies*. One of these may have held a certain charm for Yeats: in a footnote to 'The Song of O'Ruark, Prince of Breffni' Moore recounts how England was given her first opportunity in Ireland when two princes quarrelled through the adultery of the Princess Dearbhorgil (Dervorgilla). Moore notes: ' "Such," adds Giraldus Cambrensis (as I find him in an old translation), "is the variable and fickle nature of woman, by whom all mischief in the world (for the most part) do happen and come, as may appear by Marcus Antonius, and by the destruction of Troy".'[18] Giraldus is, indeed, the historian of the introduction into Irish history of a Discord all but Trojan; and this, of course, is one of Yeats's favourite metaphors, and one much employed in *A Vision*. There are other ancient Celtic associations Yeats might have entertained with its system. He may

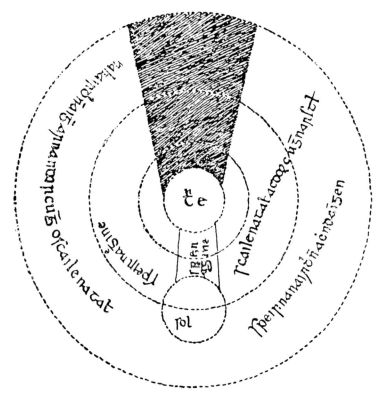

Figure 9.3 P. W. Joyce, *A Smaller Social History of Ancient Ireland*, 2nd
edn (Dublin, 1908), p.192.

have been thinking of a design from a medieval Irish astronomical
treatise which suggests the shape of his vortices. (Figure 9.3).[19]
More likely he had taken a suggestion from Johannes Scotus
Eriugena, the Irish philosopher, who is mentioned in both ver-
sions of *A Vision* (*AVA* 193–4/*AVB* 282–3). Yeats had for some
time been acquainted with Larminie's labours on Eriugena, and
notes that friends who have looked at the manuscript will occa-
sionally tell him what they find (*AVA* 54–5). They may have told
him a good deal, since, as we have already noted, Eriugena's own
version of neo-Platonic emanation and return could be figured as
intersecting triangles, and encompassed the Great Year.

But perhaps the most complex and interesting piece of inter-
textuality is not ancient, but modern, Celtic, or perhaps one should
say Irish. From December 1833, Samuel Ferguson began

publishing in *The Dublin University Magazine* a series of pieces called 'A Hibernian Nights' Entertainment'. The allusion to the *Arabian Nights* was patent, but now the tale-tellers were young Irish princes imprisoned in Dublin Castle in the winter of 1592. They tell their stories to while away the time until they can escape. The escape, though successful, was ultimately followed by the utter defeat of the old Gaelic order, and by the diaspora of the 'wild geese'. The stories they tell are drawn from the Red Branch cycle, and the first night is devoted to 'The Death of the Children of Usnach'.[20] Ferguson's framing devices are highly self-conscious: outside are the Castle guards who discuss the character of the princes within; we then hear the princes' own account of their position and plans; then we have the saga tale. Such self-consciousness is in itself a prompt to scrutiny, since it foregrounds the cultural differences embodied in the texts.

W. J. McCormack has these words to say about the significance of this collocation in the context of *The Dublin University Magazine*:

> the life, not so much of a privileged individual, but of a social elite, is endangered, and the elaboration of a cultural narrative is seen as a means of postponing, perhaps preventing, the threatened end. The magazine itself, at a level above that of the individual contribution, effects a postponement, perhaps even a transvaluation, of extinction. In this sense, Ferguson's choice of material takes on an additional resonance, and his use of the story of Deirdre and the sons of Usnach is highly (but positively) ironic.[21]

At least by analogy, we might do well to consider what Gould calls Yeats's 'time-gaining' in *A Vision* as conducted in view of the probable extinction of his caste: to look, that is, at 'time-gaining' in the light of the apocalypticism of the last words of 'Dove or Swan' or of a poem such as 'The Second Coming'. This would mean that the whole of *A Vision* fulfilled that desideratum of Yeats's maturity, of being written in the face of death, and not least in the sense of facing the death of all the traditions that constitute it.

For the 'measures' and outlines of Yeats's haunted temple are drawn by ghostly 'master-masons' as Yeats calls the 'dream martens' who cause the 'living martens' to build 'elaborate nests' in *Anima Mundi* (M 359). Those dream martens are images and spirits in the Great Mind, who draw the living through the world of time, and the elaborate nests are a prefiguring of the phases, or twenty-six 'cradles', and of everything that, in a life, comes out of them. The character of Yeats's temple is Oriental and Celtic, in that Masonic fashion he could associate with his own caste and ancestry. That loyalty had not changed: yet again his Anglo-Irish background is at the root of what it means to him to codify and measure. But there are changes, at least when Yeats's 'moods' bear him in a certain direction. The quaint figure of the would-be aristocratic magus is also a relatively stern one, espousing an assertively conservative and authoritarian political philosophy. His acceptance of, and indeed enthusiasm for, the mathematical aspects of the system sometimes seemed to him cognate with the firm political lines he wished to draw. But sometimes it seemed like a satanic bargain in which he had sold his loyalty to love and passion in return for a mess of gyres.

IV

The question, how far Yeats felt that he might have made a sinister bargain with abstraction, is chiefly interesting to us for the light it may shed on the extent to which he associated the system with qualities elsewhere described as 'external'. These two points are closely related in the Automatic Script.

The system outlined in the script was said to have developed from the ideas contained in an earlier piece of automatic writing produced by Lady Edith Lyttelton, in which she alludes to the horses of Phaeton.[22] With the guidance of his friend W. T. Horton, Yeats took the allusion to be specifically to the dark and light horses drawing Phaeton's chariot, and this certainly echoes the principles of the dark and light of the moon which were to govern *A Vision*.[23] The original communication from Lady Lyttelton had been cast in the form of an obscure warning. She had been told that Yeats was 'a prince with an evil counsellor'; that he was to think about 'the adverse principle' in relation to Phaeton; and finally, 'In the midst of death we are in life – the inversion is what I *mean*' (*AVA* Editors' Intro. xiii–xiv). Horton explained that Yeats had to conquer and subordinate the dark horse which he had paired with the white one to pull his chariot. (*AVA* Editors' Intro. xiv–xv). Possibly, it was also he who informed Yeats that ' "The inversion" is a technical mystic term for the evil power' (*AVA*

Editors' Intro. xv). It is not hard to see the dark horse, following Plato's *Phaedrus*, as an evil power, but Yeats was not sure what sort of evil was meant, and ignoring the obvious culprit of 'the passions' was inclined to think that Horton might be identifying the dark horse as 'spiritism which he dislikes' (*AVA* Editors' Intro. xv). He would not have been so surprised, though, at the term 'the inversion', assuming he did not already know it, for it refers to the concept embodied in his Golden Dawn name: 'Demon est Deus Inversus'. The adverse principle is 'antithetical', in Yeats's terminology. The demonic aspect of his system partakes of the Urizenic, that abstracted and measuring quality Yeats had long before associated with 'personality'.

There is reason to suspect that for Mrs Yeats, the automatic writing offered a means of weaning the poet from prior devotions. In any case, the Lyttelton and Horton scripts were soon to be glossed by her own communicators, who were already dealing with the grand polarities of Sun (objectivity) and Moon (subjectivity) which were to support the system: Yeats was warned that the sun 'is too little emphasised', and they continued (using the astrological planetary symbols for which I substitute the words in square brackets):

> [sun] in [moon] is the most important & comes before [moon] in [sun] working from outer to inner & afterwards inner outwards Too much [moon] & is to be influenced by [sun] so you must invoke [sun] very forcibly.[24]

While the same script makes clear that white and black horses are 'both winged both necessary to you', it is warning Yeats that he had been under the spell of a subjectivity divorced from objectivity. He had not been working in the right direction (first 'from outer to inner'): hence 'the inversion'. The result is evil: the Lyttelton script, with its inversion of the Book of Common Prayer, suggests a satanic type of Death-in-Life. The particular manifestation of this evil in Yeats's case is chiefly in the willed assumption of the Mask: this results in what the script calls the 'Evil Persona', which arises from the clash of the two principles. The Instructor goes on to clarify:

> It is the purely instinctive & cosmic quality in man which seeks completion in its opposite which is sought by the subconscious self in anima mundi to use your own term

while it is the conscious mind that makes the Ep [Evil Persona] in consciously seeking its opposite and then emulating it.[25]

The way to harmonious reconciliation of opposites is indicated by the following script:

> yes but with gradual growth
> yes – one white one black both winged
> both winged both necessary to you
> one you have the other found
> the one you have by seeking is –
> you find by seeking it in the one you have (*AVA* Editors' Intro. xvi)

This is ambiguous, not to say cryptic, but if the last line is read in conjunction with the very first communication about Iseult, it can be seen as implying that Yeats will find unforced harmony in his relationship with his wife, George.

The work of interpreting and ordering the system took much of Yeats's willing labour. But it is enlightening to note that just as the Instructors warned him against the willed assumption of a Mask, they also warned him against his conscious ordering of the knowledge they were imparting: 'the Guide emphasized that the System was "not from reading" but intuition: "dont deliberately read", he warned in parting.'[26] But as with the warnings about the need to cultivate the primary, and not to seek the Mask consciously, Yeats could not always respond to the spirit of this injunction. He knew from the Kabbalah that the Demons (the *qlippoth*) are the husks or outlines of the Tree of Life, and he knew that Blake drew on this notion for the 'mistaken Demon of Heaven', Urizen. But Blake paints a sublime as well as an erring figure; and Yeats's ambivalence was even greater than his. The symbol of the Covering Cherub which Blake took from Ezekiel was identified with the twenty-seven Christian churches and their errors (*Milton*, plate 37). These churches are to be found in 'the Mundane Shell': that is to say, in the concavity of the sky as symbolising an obstruction between humanity and the infinite. When they are destroyed, Jerusalem will at last be free. Blake thus conflates the ideas of history, deferral, obstruction and the phases of the moon, providing an important source for *A Vision*. But this is Yeats's account of the Covering Cherub:

[Blake] praises or denounces this Covering Cherub according to whether he considers it as a means whereby things, too far above us to be seen as they are, can be made visible in symbol and representative form, or as a satanic hindrance keeping our eager wills away from the freedom and truth of the Divine world. It has both aspects for every man.[27]

But as Harold Bloom tartly remarks of this passage, 'Blake never praises the Covering Cherub.'[28] The fact is that Yeats responded antithetically to his Instructors' warning, sometimes relishing the sense of ghostly mathematics, sometimes reacting against his own reaction, belittling the adequacy of diagrams: 'the forms of geometry can have but a symbolic relation to spaceless reality' (*AVB* 69). In various shapes, regarded in different aspects, this sharpened antinomy of Life and Form recurs throughout his maturity.

V

The topics of geometry, measure, stern outline, husks, lead on to questions about their working in Yeats's occult writings. 'Anima Hominis' begins by broaching the topic of humanity's pursuit of its opposite. Yeats knows, he says, when reading the work of a great poet, that it is 'the man's flight from his entire horoscope' (*M* 328). But this rejection of the given, to which he was later to fix the word 'antithetical', is throughout most of the essay seen in terms not of mere reaction, but of positive pursuit and desire. He recalls the phrase 'a hollow image of fulfilled desire', and asserts that all happy art seems to be that hollow image (*M* 329). It is the anti-self which thus starves us, as perhaps he later, in 'Among School Children', felt that it had starved Maud Gonne: 'Hollow of cheek as though it drank the wind.' As we have seen, hunger and desire are near allied in Yeats's figurings, and this proximity suggests the spirits that feed on our life, bringing us nearer to the condition of death, as they approach life parasitically, 'for man and Daimon feed the hunger in one another's hearts' (*M* 335). It is indeed the death of our given selves to which the anti-self summons us: 'I shall find the dark grow luminous, the void fruitful when I understand I have nothing, that the ringers in the tower have appointed for the hymen of the soul a passing bell' (*M* 332). The hymen here is both marriage-hymn

153

(because of the musical reference) and membrane: the music or poetry of the soul's truest expression is given shape through a partly obstructive tissue: it is not self-present expression.[29] Across this tissue occurs an exchange whereby the soul renounces its own substantial heart or core, and assumes instead the deferred pursuit of images which are antithetical to its own nature: defining itself, making its statement, signifying itself in these apparently inimical terms. That we may speak of signification seems clear: not only does the system obviously allude to the spheres of the Kabbalistic Tree, but, in line with the tradition by which these could be 'Names', each phase (and therefore each component of each phase) is accorded a tag, such as 'The Forerunner' (Phase 12) or 'The Fool' (Phase 28). These Names, or human existence under their signs, embody another property of signification: they represent partial interpretations, and repress what is left in the dark by the partial shape of their light: thus, after death, memory is gathered 'from the *Record* of all those things which have been seen but have not been noticed or accepted by the intellect' (*AVA* 222). The names of our being also represent deferred signification, for not only is humanity defined as part of a gyring, transmigratory process, but even a single incarnation travels, after its fashion, through all the phases of the moon (*AVB* 81).

The outlines of the shape of the moon in its different phases are emblems of tissues such as those described above, converted in *A Vision* into the vehicles or outlines of versions of the self. Yeats's system consists of a series of concavities, more or less full of a shape of energy which can only be differentially defined in terms of some other shape elsewhere in the system. The human existence itself is a differing series of tissues or vehicles, wherein, as we learn from 'Anima Mundi', even what we call 'soul' possesses a subtle material embodiment: 'The vehicle of the human soul is what used to be called the animal spirits . . .' (*M* 349). Thus, while in *A Vision* only one of the Four Principles, *Husk*, 'is symbolically the human body', and the other principles, *Passionate Body, Spirit* and *Celestial Body* are subtler principles, they all have a vehicular aspect. In the first version of *A Vision* we are told how the Four Principles separate at death:

> The *Spirit* first floats horizontally within the man's dead body, but then rises until it stands at his head. The *Celestial Body* is also horizontal at first but lies in the opposite

position, its feet where the *Spirit*'s head is, and then rising, as does the *Spirit*, stands up at last at the feet of the man's body. (*AVA* 222)

And so on. Thus, although *Husk* is the grossest form of envelope, precisely for that reason it also best represents the condition of all the envelopes that compose human existence. It will be recalled that the husks of the spheres of the Kabbalistic Tree were also called Demons. Yeats's *A Vision* is a demonology. Even his spiritualism is antithetical to what he sees as the anti-physicalism of Christianity, as indeed to what he sees as its essentialism. But this must not obscure the fact that for Yeats, our instinctual life is bound up with the sign: 'The dead living in their memories are, I am persuaded, the source of all that we call instinct, and it is their love and their desire . . . that make us drive beyond our reason . . .' (*M* 359). One does not have to be convinced by Yeats's spiritualism to recognise that for him, the agency of the dead is exercised through images and the signs we attach to them, and, most radically, that it is our recognition of these signs that is the source of 'instinct'.

VI

The whole picture, with aspects of a decentered humanity described in terms of a shell-like moon revolving around a void, is grandiose, but chillingly anti-organic in some of its connotations: for although Yeats evinces an eccentrically materialist bent here (and elsewhere in different ways: for instance, in the case of the Steinach rejuvenating operation) organism is reliant for its aims and desires, and even for its conception of them and of itself, on signs and images consciously conceived as founded in radical division, and differentially defined. It will readily be seen that this is the detailed theoretical version of what I have elsewhere called 'measured difference', and as with the operation of that concept in the poems, so here in the case of the occult theorist, we are shown woman being beaten at her own game of masks and moon. The occult theorist, like the antithetical man, enters into a universe dominated by Isis, and rides the lunar tide with masculine skill and measure, which is directly analogous to the relationship of the Anglo-Irish occultist to Ireland.

'And there is hatred in it.' Hatred, that is, of woman, as well as love. This hatred is suggested by the famous description of the feminine *Daimon* from the first version of *A Vision*: 'man and *Daimon* face each other in a perpetual conflict or embrace . . . do one another good and evil . . . every woman is, in the right of her sex, a wheel which reverses the masculine wheel' (*AVA* 27). And the title of 'Ego Dominus Tuus' radiates associations which may shed light on this topic. It is a quotation from the third section of Dante's *La vita nuova*, and is spoken by Love in a vision in which Love shows Dante his own bleeding heart and makes Beatrice eat it. This evacuation of the core inspires what Yeats, in the poem (*P* 160–2/*M* 321–4), calls Dante's 'hunger', associating it with his 'hollow face'. Spivak has pointed to the 'thin disguise' of the phallus in Dante's vision.[30] It would be hard to argue that this was a reductionist point, at least with respect to Yeats, considering the palpable links he makes between desire and writing. Spivak observes that the woman is only enabled to eat the heart through Love's enforcement.[31] Both man and woman are subject to desire, and in claiming to be Dante's lord, he might have claimed as much to Beatrice as well. The woman becomes phallic not in her own right but in virtue of the ceremony of Love. The event instigates writing, a writing that is, as Spivak observes, full of reminders of 'its inadequacy as a transcription of what really happened', and which employs the framing device.[32] We are back with the perspective offered by the *Arabian Nights*: deferrals around a void, which is also what the image of the lunar phases represents.

Spivak also claims that the eating of the heart inaugurates a war against the female in *La vita nuova*.[33] Whatever one may think of this as an interpretation of Dante, it certainly constitutes at least half the truth in the case of Yeats. To return to a point near that at which we began: if the 'gyres and cubes' are but the expression of the 'bitter-sweetness' of a youthful woman's body, they are also its phases and aspects codified and geometrified: provisional interpretations again. But the whole system, at least in so far as it requires the interpreter, may be compared to woman's body submitted to a Cubist or Vorticist analytic reduction. As Yeats says of the historical gyres, 'I regard them as stylistic arrangements of experience comparable to the cubes in the drawing of Wyndham Lewis and to the ovoids in the sculpture of Brancusi' (*AVB* 25). Yeats must have known that for both Lewis and Pound, Vorticism possessed overtly phallic associations, quite apart from other less direct evidences of masculinity. By the same token they regarded it as opposed to the 'blurry, messy' organicism of the nineteenth century, with its 'painted adjectives', as Pound put it in 'Credo'. Even Yeats's artistic metaphor for *A Vision* is steeped in aggression towards woman.

The Rose was a displacement of the Virgin Mary. *A Vision* is a contrary of the Rose, which removes it from its central position at the heart of the Tree of Life, and asserts the importance of what in the Lurianic Kabbalah had seemed like the mere husk or rind of the tree, and gives to this the name of 'measure'. Indeed, it was in 1927, not long after the publication of the first version of *A Vision*, that a revised edition of *Poems* (1895) appeared in which Yeats is seen to have been 'stitching and unstitching' at the rosy hem. For in the version of 'To Ireland in the Coming Times' (*P* 50–1) included here we find for the first time the idea of the 'elemental creatures' hurrying from 'unmeasured mind', and the idea of the poet as 'he who treads in measured ways'. Most suggestive of the influence of *A Vision* is the phrase 'measurer Time' (see *VP* 137–9).

But if the Rose was in some sense Ireland, is the female principle still in some sense Ireland? Yes and no. The ancient, antithetical wisdom of *A Vision* is still seen as something which in its broad outlines was possessed by the Celts before our era began ('And ancient Ireland knew it all'). But Ireland, like an individual woman, though she may express the truth in her fiery temperament, or speak like a learned man in her sleep, requires the Ascendancy occultist to explain her message. In other ways, *A Vision* includes by implication a critique of modern Ireland in offering an ambitious rebuke to Catholicism, and a contemptuous dismissal of the primary-minded opinion to be found in modern politics, including nationalist politics. Only such a general answer may be given, but at that level these conclusions seem reasonable. And there is one other general remark that seems reasonable, too: the whole project of *A Vision* is witness to a painful division of identity which is bound up with strong feelings of ambivalence towards Ireland.

Part Three

Cracked Masonry

10

WALLS OF *THE TOWER*

I THE EMBLEM OF THE TOWER AND 'MEDITATIONS IN TIME
OF CIVIL WAR'

Contemplating the volume *The Tower* when it was completed, Yeats, in letters to Olivia Shakespear, professed astonishment at its 'bitterness' and looked forward to leaving for Italy in a phrase tellingly reminiscent of one in the first poem, 'Sailing to Byzantium': 'Once out of Irish bitterness I can find some measure of sweetness and light' (*L* 737). The bitterness, then, characterises both Ireland and his response to it: it is a feature of the relationship, so to speak. And just as the image of the Tower is the leading one in the book, so it is a very important clue to the source and nature of the bitterness.

The name of the Norman keep Yeats bought was Ballylee Castle at the time of buying. Charles Altieri and Daniel Harris have both recognised that in changing the name to 'Thoor Ballylee' Yeats was engaged in a species of 'Adamic' naming.[1] Harris connects this idea to that of a return to pastoral innocence, and there is much in this. But since for Yeats there is no escaping the effects of Adam's fall, one should be equally alive to the antithetical bitterness and assertiveness involved in the gesture. But is this, perhaps, to be captious about the notorious mutability of Irish names? Not at all: Yeats's decision to change the name of his house is not a typical instance of the normal process by which place-names are generated, but more akin to my private decision to give the name 'Arden' to my house in the woods of the English Midlands, and from this one can clearly perceive the important point that it signifies the poet's assumption of an 'original relation' to Ireland, his marriage to 'rock and hill'.[2]

Ballylee was one of a group of castles or towers built by the Norman family of de Burgo or Burke in the district of Kilmac-duagh, on the borders of Counties Clare and Galway, during the thirteenth and fourteenth centuries.[3] In *The Booke of Connaught* (1585) Ballylee is listed as 'Islandmore Castle'.[4] This suggests that the original Gaelic was very probably 'Caislean Oilean Mór' or more probably 'Caislean Oileáin Mhóir': 'castle of the great island'. At any rate, it was nothing like Thoor Ballylee. In the nineteenth century the keep was known as Ballylee Castle, and so it appeared on the maps and on Yeats's own letters from his new home for a period of nearly two years after his moving in. Thus his first hopeful letter about the place, to John Quinn (23 July 1918), is headed 'Ballylee Castle' (*L* 651). He speaks of plans for furniture, quotes his famous poetic inscription, and asserts, 'I am making a setting for my old age, a place to influence lawless youth, with its severity and antiquity.' The symbol was already a powerful one, but despite this the famous name did not arrive until April 1922, when a letter to Olivia Shakespear is headed 'Thoor Ballylee'. Yeats adverts to it thus: 'What do you think of our address – Thoor Ballylee? Thoor is Irish for tower and it will keep people from suspecting us of modern gothic and a deer park' (*L* 680).

Yet 'Thoor' is not the Irish for a tower, but a clumsy transliteration of the word 'tur', which is. It could hardly look more English, with its 'oo', and use of 'th' to render the dental *t* which occurs in Irish before certain vowel qualities. This last is an error into which many who are ignorant of the Irish language fall. Yet both the Elizabethan transliterators and their successors in the Ordnance Survey (commemorated by Brian Friel in *Translations*) tended to avoid this error. Nevertheless, it does seem that Yeats is deliberately claiming these anglicisers as forebears, and in no apologetic or passive spirit. If this claim seems outrageous to some, it will be worth asking them to consider just how they think this locution of Yeats's would have been regarded by a nationalist Irish speaker of this period. The point will perhaps be taken. The name is, in fact, a compromise. Of course, it is neither 'anglicising' nor 'de-anglicising'; but more to the point it is 'quoted' and thus somehow self-conscious and picturesque.

Yeats was creating his own 'Big House', but in a very particular sense, and one that again conveys compromise. This may seem an unlikely assertion, for many have come to associate the appellation with the somewhat grander domicile of an Anglo-Irish gentleman, such as that of the Gregorys at Coole Park a few miles away. Yet a Norman keep could be, and was, regarded as a Big House by an impoverished peasantry, however small the gentleman. But perhaps more significant, that phrase is a translation of the Gaelic one that had been used for the houses of the native aristocracy and gentry, before they were expropriated by the English – or destroyed, or neglected. Of course, Yeats would have known that the tower had, until the seventeenth century, been occupied by Gaelic-speaking members of the de Burgo family.[5] But he would also have known to what a late date the Gaelic order sometimes persisted. Daniel Corkery, in his book *The Hidden Ireland: A Study of Gaelic Munster in the Eighteenth Century* (1924), devotes a chapter to 'The Big House', meaning a place occupied by a native Gaelic landowner.[6] He shows the remnants of the Gaelic-speaking upper classes still clinging, in the Penal Age, to their old lands and dwellings in certain remote western parts of Ireland. And he records how the still very impressive poets of the learned tradition – such as Aodhagán O Rathaille (Egan O'Rahilly, 1670–1726); or Eoghan Ruadh Ó Súilleabháin (Owen Roe O'Sullivan 'the Red', 1748–84), Yeats's prototype for Red Hanrahan – were visitors to these last outposts, enacting for a few final years the ancient relation of nobleman and bard.[7] Indeed, even the immemorial and arduous institution of the bardic schools ('singing schools' which spent much time studying 'monuments' of their own 'magnificence') seems to have staggered on into the eighteenth century.[8] Yet bred or living among the people, these poets exhibited 'a common culture flowing up and down between hut and Big House in Irish Ireland'.[9]

As the eighteenth century proceeded, more and more such houses passed out of the hands of the Gaels. Corkery quotes a poem of O'Rahilly about Castle Tochar, a house of the great Mac-Carthy family, which had ended up in the possession of a man named Warner; and he comments: 'The structure of life in such districts as West Cork was still so firm and self-contained that the change of ownership in a big house, like Castle Tochar, from Gael to Planter, did not immediately make much difference in what its ancient walls looked upon, day in, day out.'[10] These remarks also make plain what should be clear in any case: that many of these 'big houses' were small castles. This fact, obvious to anybody who knows Ireland, is helpfully spelt out in Edward MacLysaght's *Irish Life in the Seventeenth Century*: 'There is little difficulty in picturing that type of gentleman's country house which consisted of little more than one of the old square keeps whose ruins are still to be found throughout Ireland, especially in Munster.'[11] In modern times, restored and extended, they might furnish a comfortable and romantic residence to a gentleman such as Edward Martyn who owned Tullyra Castle in Galway, a few miles north of Ballylee, where Yeats had stayed in the 1890s in the period of planning an Irish Theatre.

What would have pleased Yeats about such knowledge is as much the sense of continuity, however troubled, as the late persistence of cultured Gaeldom. He could look back at an unbroken line of succession: from Anglo-Irish Ascendancy – or at least squirearchy – up to distant Norman-Gaelic lord – or at least lordling. This is the burden of the second part of 'Meditations in Time of Civil War' (*P* 200–6), 'My House', in which he sees himself as a second founder: instructively, not a seventh or a thirteenth: 'Two men have founded here.' The other founder is a 'man-at-arms'. The tower is thus a simple and potent symbol of that unity of culture he wished to forge from such unpromising material. But it also suggests the manner of that forging. For next to the equable and urbane Georgian mansion of Coole Park, Ballylee Castle could be regarded as – in relative terms – primitive. It would therefore make a good symbol of the early, violent stages of aristocracy, as suggested by a reading of Nietzsche, when a 'man-at-arms' could rise to be a leader and build a keep. The associations of the tower are thus proleptic of the coming shock that will initiate a new era of aristocracy: before the Medicis comes the 'rough beast'. 'Rough men-at-arms' are also proudly recalled in the second section of 'The Tower'. In the first section of 'Meditations', 'Ancestral Houses' (*VP* 417), the creation of the great abodes of the aristocracy is described in these terms:

> Some violent bitter man, some powerful man
> Called architect and artist in, that they,
> Bitter and violent men, might rear in stone
> The sweetness that all longed for night and day,
> The gentleness none there had ever known . . .

This describes a later stage than that in which a keep such as Ballylee had been created: the stage at which violent aristocracy has acquired culture. But the danger is that once the sweet and gentle form has been created, the creators will relax in it:

> O what if levelled lawns and gravelled ways
> Where slippered Contemplation finds his ease
> And Childhood a delight for every sense,
> But take our greatness with our violence?

Or 'with our bitterness', as the final stanza puts it. Art, like aristocracy, requires violence and bitterness – or demon and beast – for the creation of a living form. The image of the fountain in the first stanza is a beautiful evocation of the organic idea: it will 'never stoop to a mechanical/Or servile shape, at others' beck and call'. But these terms are redolent of power and command. And without such qualities life and art become mere empty forms: 'some marvellous empty sea-shell'. The phrase also calls to mind the Duke's 'I choose never to stoop' in Browning's 'My Last Duchess'. There was a violent and bitter aristocrat, indeed, and one who appreciated, as Yeats did, that living form in art was a very different thing from life itself, and had to be won by discipline.

Yeats's choice of Ballylee Castle as his Big House expresses an intention to retain violence and bitterness in his character, and among the impulses which are shaped into art. His remarks about Irish 'bitterness' in his letters suggest that he found in contemporary events in Ireland both a reflection of and a subject for these impulses. At a more general level he associates violence and bitterness with the antithetical and demonic. He would have been encouraged in this association by the Tarot pack, with which, as a member of the Golden Dawn, he had acquired a deep familiarity. The Tarot trump card, called 'The Tower', shows a tower with its top struck off by a zig-zag of lightning. Kathleen Raine points out that initiates would have associated this image with the downward path of inspiration which, as we have seen, Yeats thought of as the demonic 'way of the lightning'.[12] The normal path of the initiate was to toil upwards through the spheres of the Tree of Life; but God descending through the Tree was the unasked inspiration. It was also, however, God inverted: Demon est Deus Inversus, Yeats's secret Golden Dawn name. In a sense, then, the Tower had always been Yeats's emblem. And he would always have appreciated its air of demonic blasphemy. In some moods he could simply look on this as a piece of positive Satanism, like Blake's in *The Marriage of Heaven and Hell* – and like Blake's derived partly from the Kabbalistic conception of contraries within the Godhead. But in other moods he welcomed demon and beast with violent and bitter relish. Such a mood colours the conception of the Tower in this volume.

There is another point to bear in mind about the Tarot: each card may be regarded from two closely related aspects, a favourable and an unfavourable. From a favourable point of view the Tower suggests the descent of a dangerous but renovating inspiration, for both individual and society, one that is both 'Destroyer and Preserver', in Shelley's phrase. But unfavourably aspected it suggests destruction merely, God's wrath at the Tower of Babel. From either point of view, this tower is one from which to contemplate the advent of a social crisis. The Golden Dawn initiates, their minds stocked with Kabbalah, would have thought that the card referred to Babel. There the point at issue between God and the descendants of Noah was not only the hubris of building to the skies, but the related facts that enabled them to do this: settling in one place and giving themselves 'a name' in their 'one language' (Genesis 11:1–9). The Tower signifies for Yeats a naming and a settling. And the violence and bitterness with which he does these things are testimony to a Romantic view, which sees the enterprise as resulting from a defiant Promethean act of will, and possibly from a satanic one. So although a reminiscence of Adam is very much to the point, we are still dealing with a fallen Adam, and one who, as with some of Yeats's Romantic forebears, is composed of contraries.

There are, however, some associations with the emblem of the Tower which seem more benign, at least at first sight. In that Rosicrucian *summa*, Fludd's *Utriusque Cosmi*, there is an engraving of a temple in the shape of a tower fronted by two spirals and some concentric circles bearing patterns. It is flanked by solar Apollo and lunar Marsyas (Figure 10.1).[13] The two spirals represent the system of emanations from God downwards, and the return to God through the same stages. This process is elsewhere represented by Fludd, as we saw above, with two opposed triangles each of twenty-seven segments. The circles represent heavenly spheres beyond the empyrean. Apollo and the satyr Marsyas engaged in a contest to see which was the better musician. The loser, who turned out to be Marsyas, was to be flayed. This was taken to

Figure 10.1 From Robert Fludd, *Utriusque Cosmi Maioris scilicet et Minoris Metaphysica, Physica, atque technica Historia*, 2 vols (Oppenheim, 1617–19), vol. I, section 2, p.168.

symbolise a release from the corporeal, enabling one to hear the music of the spheres. Yeats, who had rewritten such esoteric doctrine so that there was no final winner, would see in this myth only the continual contest and alternation of Apollonian and Dionysian; movement of ascent and movement of descent; up or down the scale of Pythagoras, who had assigned a musical note to each of the planetary spheres. And in *The Tower* it was the analogy with Dionysian music which was uppermost in Yeats's mind.

The Tower itself is given profoundly Rosicrucian and Masonic significance by Yeats; and Freemasonry and Rosicrucianism are directly evoked by the cry of 'Vengenace for Jacques Molay', in section VII of 'Meditations' (*P* 205). Molay had been Grand Master of the Templars, who were often regarded as the original

Freemasons. Yeats's note explains his reasons for including this cry in the poem:

> A cry for vengeance because of the murder of the Grand Master of the Templars seems to me fit symbol for those who labour for hatred and so for sterility in various kinds. It is said to have been incorporated in the ritual of certain Masonic societies of the eighteenth century, and to have fed class hatred. (P 596)

Elizabeth Cullingford has shown how Yeats came into contact with ideas that implicated eighteenth-century Freemasonry in the growth of egalitarianism and communism and saw its modern descendants as part of a plot to overthrow civilisation.[14] Christina Stoddart, one of the people who espoused such ideas, was a member of the Golden Dawn, which, however, she claimed was at the centre of the plot.[15] And her acquaintance, Nesta Webster, claimed that the United Irishmen and the IRB (to which Yeats had belonged) were tools of the Illuminati.[16] Yeats did not take these ideas too literally, but judging by the poem, he seems to have thought that there was a kind of insight in them. As Cullingford judiciously puts it,

> In 'Meditations' the poet who was once an ardent nationalist, a socialist in the tradition of William Morris, and an enthusiastic member of an occult secret society, now contemplates the brutality generated by the idealism of his youth.[17]

She also notes that metaphors of building, of 'operative masonry', dominate the poem, and that the original builders or masons are 'prototypes of the "architect" and "artist" of "Ancestral Houses" '.[18] They are indeed prototypes but they are too 'rough', one might note, to imbue with the sweetness of honey the empty stare's nest in the 'loosening masonry' where the 'bees build' ('The Stare's Nest by my Window': P 204–5). That could be done at some point in time between early roughness and the late stage by which aristocracy has become an 'empty sea-shell' and society an empty stare's nest. Filling these husks with sweetness would require not a return to medieval violence, but to a time before the mid-seventeenth century, when 'Il Penseroso's Platonist toiled on'

('My House'), when the violence of aristocracy had been tamed but not yet removed, and when the Rosicrucian temple had not been infected by modern materialism and mechanism.

The whole series is coloured by Yeats's knowledge that everything returns, as 'the very owls in circles move'. In a sense the medieval man-at-arms, with his 'long wars and sudden night alarms', is like the modern irregular soldier of the Irish Civil War. But it is one thing to be in the middle of a gyre and another to be leaving it. The first violence was the violence of 'founding', the second is that of dissolution. Yeats's perplexity, for there is nothing to be done, conditions his final turning away and climbing the stair. Indeed, the last section of 'Meditations' is somehow above the immediate business of politics. Yeats, as we have seen, notes that the cry about Jacques Molay was said 'to have fed class-hatred' in the eighteenth century, and this remark reveals a political ambiguity: on the one hand, the cry is Masonic, of medieval origin, and belongs to occult lore; on the other, it has become associated with the egalitarian form of Freemasonry for which Yeats would have felt only the most qualified sympathy. The two associations cancel each other out, in terms of Yeats's political sympathies. And thus the rejection of 'hatred', though it is prescribed for the poet himself, is above politics, in the same way that, in 'The Tower', the 'people of Burke and Grattan' are bound 'neither to Cause nor to State,/Neither to slaves that were spat on,/Nor to the tyrants that spat'. It is a Byronic sort of freedom: 'I wish men to be free/As much from mobs as kings – from you as me' (*Don Juan*, IX, st. 25).

Nevertheless, one must distinguish between the rather lofty political stance, appropriate to a tower, and lack of concern. Certainly it would be straining credibility to try to ignore the fact that the series really is a response to the civil war. Nevertheless, readers, understandably perhaps, look for something concrete and direct, such as can be found in the war poetry Yeats so despised. Antony Coleman says of *The Tower*, 'these poems are rather loosely rooted in Irish earth'; and Marjorie Perloff, 'if Yeats does indeed have the political situation of Ireland or the Russian Revolution in mind, as critics such as Harris have supposed, he says nothing meaningful about them.'[19] Well, he says what he thinks is meaningful. For although everything moves in circles, Yeats's turning away cannot conceal the fact that the age in which occurred the great Rosicrucian synthesis of Fludd has been identified as the high point of the history of the British Isles.

II GOLDEN WALL

'Sailing to Byzantium' (*VP* 407–8) offers an extreme version of bitterness towards Ireland: escape. Yet one should beware of a reductionist account of this. The trouble with Ireland in this poem is that it is a country associated with the natural cycle, and thus full of vigorous youth, and the speaker is growing old. The phrase 'and dies' seems almost like a concession to a rounded view of the cycle, for the accent is on youth and sensuality. The irony of Ireland's thus being similar to the immortal Land of the Ever Young is intense, suggesting that Tír na nÓg is an image of eternity that is too like this world. Behind this lurks the notion, unstated but never far from Yeats's mind, that youth and sexuality are bound up with conflict, and one may tire of the bitterness this may occasion. Furthermore, his escape is into a version of the truth that could be understood by Irish Druids as well as by Masons. In P. W. Joyce's *Social History of Ancient Ireland* Yeats could have read about how the art of Irish manuscript illumination found some of its origins in Byzantium. After recording how impressed Giraldus Cambrensis had been by a copy of the Four Gospels he saw in Kildare, Joyce expounds these theories:

> This beautiful art originated in the East – in Byzantium after the fall of the first empire – and was brought to Ireland – no doubt by Irish monks, or by natives of Central Europe who came to Ireland to study – in the early ages of Christianity. . . .
>
> Combining the Byzantine interlacings with the familiar pagan designs at home, they produced a variety of patterns. . . .
>
> In pagan times the Irish practised a sort of ornamentation consisting of zigzags, lozenges, circles both single and in concentric groups, spirals of both single and double lines.[20]

Byzantium has an affinity with Ireland, but belongs more at the geometrical end of a continuum they both share. And when Yeats's speaker reaches Byzantium, he may encounter some very congenial examples of the Platonic philosophy as it had been latterly understood there. It is worth considering what Yeats thought it would have been like. The passage from *A Vision* in which he speaks of Byzantium has often been recalled:

I think if I could be given a month of Antiquity and leave to spend it where I chose, I would spend it in Byzantium a little before Justinian opened St. Sophia and closed the Academy of Plato. I think I could find in some little wine-shop some philosophical worker in mosaic who could answer all my questions, the supernatural descending nearer to him than to Plotinus even. (*AVB* 279)

The important word in the last sentence is 'supernatural', and to understand exactly what Yeats meant we may turn, as he did, to Gibbon (whose works he had bought with some of the Nobel Prize money) at the point where Justinian is about to close the Academy:

The surviving sect of the Platonists, whom Plato would have blushed to acknowledge, extravagantly mingled a sublime theory with the practice of superstition and magic . . . in the intervals of study [Proclus] *personally* conversed with Pan, Aesculapius, and Minerva, in whose mysteries he was secretly initiated, and whose prostrate statues he adored; in the devout persuasion that the philosopher, who is a citizen of the universe, should be the priest of its various deities.[21]

It might have made Plato blush; Yeats it would fill with admiration. The wisdom of the Golden Dawn was the wisdom of Byzantium.

Possibly the temperamental and philosophical affinity of Byzantium and Ireland derives from the fact that both are 'Asiatic' (*AVB* 287). So it is thought-provoking to remember several things about Byron in this context. The verse form in *Don Juan* is *ottava rima*, like that of 'Sailing to Byzantium'; Istanbul is the Eastern term of Juan's voyage; Byron was an eager purveyor of exotic oriental tales; and he was self-exiled from England. Lest this strike the reader as a type of fanciful intertextual web-spinning, it may be worth asking just how far, in terms of detail, one can take the assertion (which we have been invoking) that there is an element of the Byronic in Yeats's attitude to aristocracy, and whether the influence goes further than an attitude. Yeats admired Byron's style. The terms in which the admiration was expressed describe the Yeatsian ideal of the aristocrat who speaks a noble, masculine language, but one which is plain and accessible to the people (*L* 710). And to whom can one compare Yeats, in point of style? Philip Larkin's early indebtedness to him is well known, as is his complaint that Yeats's style was as adhesive as the odour of garlic. But Yeats is not a nonpareil. The sons of Ben have left their mark on his mature work. And one can see the impression that has been made there by a reading of Elizabethan and Jacobean drama – an impression also found in Byron. But if one has to compare Yeats's style to anybody's it is surely most reminiscent of Byron's in his serio-comic mode. Not that Yeats is normally serio-comic. But the *sprezzatura* of Byron's manner possesses a lightness of touch which has imparted itself to many memorable phrases in Yeats. In 'The Tower' the story about Hanrahan is dropped, as Byron will drop a tale, and the narrator intervenes with the admission that he has forgotten the rest of the story: 'O towards I have forgotten what – enough!' In 'Among School Children' there is a stanza reminiscent of Byron's amused contempt for Plato and all philosophers, and of the disrespect he liked to display: 'Solider Aristotle played the taws/Upon the bottom of a king of kings.' These qualities, and with them urbanity, strong rhetorical sinews and a well-judged disposition of long and short periods over the stanza, are all reminiscent of Byron.

What does this mean for 'Sailing to Byzantium'? Not, of course, that it is similar to *Don Juan* or any other poem by Byron. It is clear why Yeats admired Byron's style. But Byron as Romantic hero and ideal of a certain type of aristocrat is also part of the web of allusion in a number of Yeats's poems. There should be nothing surprising about the importance accorded to a figure whose shadow stretches over so much nineteenth-century literature.

'Sailing to Byzantium' is a revision of Juan's voyage, and of the one by Byron of which it is a transmutation. Juan innocently discovers life and sexuality, gradually learning that a cynical worldly wisdom is his best guide and protector, so that he approaches asymptotically the disillusioned state the narrator has always professed. Yeats's narrator is also persuaded of a disjunction between the way in which life presents itself and the way in which it should be understood. The line between life and its significance is a point of similarity and debate. The strong version of withdrawal offered by 'Sailing to Byzantium' (though not by every poem in the volume) is at odds with Byron's intent, and is a rebuke to it. And in the context of the volume as a whole, with its emblem of the Tower, the poem can be seen also as a concealed rebuke to Byron's attitude to rootedness. Byron had, in *Childe Harold*, turned an ancient, ruined house into a symbol of himself. Newstead Abbey, like Ballylee Castle, possessed a spiral staircase; at the top of this the poet would choose to have his private chambers, from which he would be able to see the fountain in the courtyard.[22] In 'Ancestral Houses' it is, in part, Byron's 'violence and bitterness' which are recalled. He had preserved those qualities in his rejection of English hypocrisy and an unhappy marriage. But this perception accords with the positive view of Byron's anarchic temper. Yeats could not always feel positive about this, since he also valued permanence. Byron's mode of life had evinced a contempt for the values which would ensure his permanence in Newstead. Viewed in context, 'Sailing to Byzantium' and its revision of Byron support the notion that rootedness in Ireland would be desirable if only that were the proper and appreciative place for such a choice of existence. But since it is not, one may imagine the value of withdrawal into that eternal order which, as we have seen, exhibits the eternal principles of social order. Aristocracy and rootedness are their finest flower, but where they cannot be encouraged, a mental resuscitation of Byzantium may be the only answer.[23]

The west–east direction in which Yeats and Byron took their course is the opposite of that taken in a chief source of the imagery of the first stanza of 'Sailing to Byzantium'. 'The Fair Hills of Ireland' is one of Ferguson's fine translations from the Irish. It is an old song, which paints a picture of Ireland as a land of fecundity. There is a tradition of such poems. This one seems to date from a period when her vast forests had not yet been felled to build the English fleets, and when the hairstyles of the Gaelic aristocracy still conformed to an elaborate pattern which may go back to the Iron Age, although it probably persisted into the Renaissance. The first stanza evokes bursting ears of barley, 'honey in the trees', 'falling waters' and springs.[24] The last contains bird-song:

> Large and profitable are the stacks upon the ground,
>> *Uileacan dubh O!*
> The butter and the cream do wondrously abound,
>> *Uileacan dubh O!*
> The cresses on the water and the sorrels are at hand,
> And the cuckoo's calling daily his note of mimic bland,
> And the bold thrush sings so bravely his song i'the forests
>> grand,
> On the fair hills of holy Ireland.

It is the second stanza which contains matter about sailing and a
vow to travel to Ireland:

> Curl'd he is and ringletted, and plaited to the knee,
> *Uileacan dubh O!*
> Each captain who comes sailing across the Irish sea;
> *Uileacan dubh O!*
> And I will make my journey, if life and health but stand,
> Unto that pleasant country, that fresh and fragrant strand,
> And leave your boasted braveries, your wealth and high
> command,
> For the fair hills of holy Ireland.

Yeats, of course, would have known this poem very well. Noting
the influence of this poem is helpful, for it clarifies the fact that he
is offering a rebuff not only to life and youth but also to a tradition
of poetic praise of Ireland. The fruitfulness of Ireland is a vener-
able *topos*, of course, and goes back to the earliest phases of Irish
literature. In particular it can be traced back to the moment when
the Milesians attempt to take possession of Ireland but are
thwarted by a storm raised by the *Danann* Druids. In response,
Amergin utters his own Druidical oration, which includes praise
of Ireland's fruitfulness, and the storm abates.[25] Yeats's first
stanza can be seen in the light of this as being more repudiation
than rejection. Another point that is clarified is the idea of passing
from one state to another, even though here it is in the opposite
direction to the one Yeats's narrator takes. In the first drafts of
'Sailing to Byzantium' this narrator is very obviously an early
medieval pilgrim: 'But now these pleasant dark-skinned mariners/
Carry me toward that great Byzantium.'[26] Yeats doubtless came
across the travels of early Irish scholars to the Eastern Empire in
the work of Benedict Fitzpatrick, who, in *Ireland and the Making
of Britain* (1922), asserts that 'Irish scholars, missionaries and
pilgrims' formed 'literary colonies' in 'Constantinople'.[27] Nor
were they modest when they reached there: 'In Constantinople in
the ninth century Irish monks told the Greeks that every Irish
monastery possessed a Chrysostom.'[28]

Yeats's mind was stocked with Blakean imagery with which to
embody his ideas about the voyage of the soul from this world to
the next. L. A. G. Strong informs us that when Yeats wrote about
the soul clapping its hands, he had in mind Blake's vision of his

brother Robert's soul departing the dying body, singing and clapping its hands.[29] There is no reason to doubt this information. But it is corroborated by the previous image in the poem: 'An aged man is but a paltry thing,/A tattered coat upon a stick.' The obvious source for this is in one of Blake's favourite emblems, that of the stooped old man with long, windswept, white hair and beard, and body-length garment, leaning on a stick. The easiest place to find this figure is in the illumination to 'London', in *Songs of Experience*. But the version Yeats probably has in mind is to be found in the illustrations to Robert Blair's *The Grave*.[30] These are notable for their bold depiction of the separation of soul from body, as in 'The Soul hovering over the Body reluctantly parting with Life'. In 'Death's Door' the aged man can be seen leaning on his stick (in fact a crutch) and entering the door of the tomb, on the roof of which the youthful figure of the soul, surrounded by the rays of the rising sun, gazes upwards to Heaven. Ellis and Yeats, in their third volume, chose to represent Blake's skill as a commercial engraver with some of the Blair designs. They omitted 'Death's Door', but the old man with a stick can be seen on *America*, plate 12 and *Jerusalem*, plate 84, both of which they included.

Comparisons of Blake with Yeats yield many similarities, but sometimes point a contrast the more starkly, precisely because of the shared vocabulary. In a complex and multivalent image Blake is depicting a harmful belief in the separation of soul and body, and stating that this belief is caused by a decline in the power of vision or imagination. The aged man symbolises this decline; but the youthful 'soul' symbolises the possibility of reversing it, whatever one's literal age. Blake informs us many times in his later work that the death of imagination is caused by the domination of the 'Selfhood'. This abstract and egotistical demon must go 'to Eternal Death'. So another meaning of the 'old man' figure is 'Selfhood', and when it enters Death's door, humanity will cease to be divided and will regain its spiritual energy.

Yeats, on the other hand, returns Blake's imagery to the Behmenist and neo-Platonic context from which it was borrowed, and treats it in a more traditional manner. 'Aged man' is man facing physical death; 'Soul' is the potentially discarnate spirit which, after death, may be assimilated to that discarnate realm of images which Yeats calls 'the artifice of eternity'. This realm is conceived in neo-Platonic fashion: it organises the physical world and motivates its energies. But it belongs to a different order. Yeats makes explicit the neo-Platonic conceptions to which the Romantic tradition is haphazardly indebted, and in this poem takes them to an extreme conclusion. To take another example: the poem obviously alludes to Keats's 'Ode to a Nightingale'.[31] On external grounds this is hardly surprising: the Automatic Script makes clear Yeats's extraordinary conviction that he had received, by supernatural transference, the thought associations and feelings of Keats prior to the composition of the Ode: the Ode had become 'attached' to him.[32] But Keats's poem is yet another object of subtextual criticism. Keats is not clear enough about the eternal and inorganic character of his image. With his golden bird, Yeats effectively implies that the Grecian Urn is a more appropriate emblem of the objects of imagination. It may be significant that the Automatic Script switches to 'Ode on a Grecian Urn' at one point.[33] But even this does not go far enough. For the pain one feels at not sharing the eternity of Keats's lovers may be assuaged, Yeats claims, by entering their very mode of existence. As to the golden bird itself, Kermode's trenchancy cannot be bettered: it is 'out of nature and life'; it 'must absolutely be a bird of artifice'.[34] But from the point of view of the world of generation, the realm of artifice is best seen in terms of the wall in which the sages stand: a beautiful but stiff outline to all things. This is the apotheosis of the hard boundary, the ultimate husk in Yeats's work.

III THE BROKEN WALL

But Yeats finds yet another way of conceiving the relationship between his slippery antinomies of form and matter, eternity and generation, male and female, Anglo-Irish and native Irish. His uncertainty, and toying with opposed points of view, sometimes bring him to undo the oppositions altogether. This is the case with 'Leda and the Swan' (P 214–15), which originally formed part of A Vision, where, as a poem about the 'Annunciation' of the classical pagan era, it helped to illustrate the historical symbolism.

Ian Fletcher observes that 'A sharp feature of "Leda and the Swan" is the modulation of the tenses and the contraction of syntax.'[35] Leo Spitzer has accurately ascribed a sense of time arrested to these features: eternity is irrupting into history.[36] This founding moment of time is a shock, a 'sudden blow' which sets in motion all the other shocks and discords which flesh is heir to, especially the flesh of those who are alive enough to be 'violent and bitter'. Yet difference has already invaded this presence. Time is there, slowed, in the 'beating' of the wings and the 'beating' of 'the strange heart', a repetition which frames the octave. And a sexual act, however bestial, obviously conveys difference: we are in the world of generation. But closer scrutiny reveals that it is hard to assign clear identity and unambiguous roles to the terms in this emblem of the founding of time. Bernard Levine has pointed out that Leda can be seen as the aggressor.[37] This interpretation must not be completely confused with the proposition (which is nevertheless, in the poem's discourse, both rational and relevant) that Leda enjoys her violation, as her 'staggering' while being 'caressed', her 'loosening thighs' and her 'vague' fingers imply. It depends, rather, on the abstract character of the swan, compared with Leda; on specific features of the general uncertainty created by the grammar; and on finding an active sense in some of Leda's responses. Levine sees the girl as 'staggering' the swan, and as ensuring that her nape is caught by his bill, thus in a sense catching the swan. 'Vague' could mean not just passive but active submission. One might add that 'push' and 'feel' impart a sense of activity to her.

The moment of ejaculation is not just a portent of disaster, but, asserts Levine, 'release from the feeling of fear and alienation'. This may be going too far in imparting humanist niceness to the ecstatic shudder, but it is ecstatic and it is not attributed particularly to the swan rather than to Leda. The 'burning roof and tower', indeed, are the mingled orgasms of both female and male. But they are, of course, portents of disaster as well: sexuality and Discord again. But also sexuality involving loss of power, and behind that being 'engendered' as conditioned by the possibility of castration. Further, the 'gendering' is uncertain for it does not, in accordance with traditional expectation, identify the assumption of power only with membership of the male sex. In so far as Leda's sexuality has given birth to Discord it is she, as much as Zeus, who actively brings about the fall of Troy. And the question at the end provides a conundrum. If Leda has 'put on' Zeus's 'knowledge with his power', she is as powerful and knowledgeable as the king of the gods. But how could one say that she had done so? The clues are there. To put on knowledge is here 'to know' sexually, as well as to understand the meaning of history. In knowing and feeling the 'brute blood' in which the god was embodied, she may have

achieved an access to such understanding that bypasses and sur-
passes mere abstraction. Knowledge from 'the blood' has been
prepared for by the 'beating', which, in enacting both the idea of
pulse and that of broken succession, reminds us that the essential
thing worth knowing about this world is difference and deferral. If
that were not enough, we are reminded of the ineradicability of
difference by the difficulty we face in deciding where the best
source of such instinctual knowledge might be found. Zeus is all-
knowing, but as such is not sufficiently animal. As a swan, how-
ever, perhaps he is. A woman might seem more knowledgeable
than a swan, but we have been tempted by much of Yeats's poetry
to think of women as more instinctual than men, and as being
sharply at odds with abstraction and 'opinion'. The metaphor for
meaning in this poem is 'the broken wall', the hymen, in a sense
which can be illuminated by Derrida's concept of the hymen,
which is both *entre* and *antre* ('between' and 'cavern'), creator of
meaning and obstruction to meaning, place where fullness and
brokenness coincide.[38]

Knowing that this is so, we are not so surprised to find Maud
Gonne, in 'Among School Children', blighted by the heroic stig-
mata of imaginative desire. For all is not really so certain, be-
tween the two sexes, as it sometimes seems: a woman may, after
all, be marked by these stigmata as much as any male poet: 'Hol-
low of cheek as though it drank the wind/And took a mess of
shadows for its meat.' The longing of our blood for the tomb is a
longing for fullness which has to be deferred in brokenness. And
in the vigorous exercise of this longing, characteristically figured
as hunger, we may become cadaverous before we reach the grave.
But we also become powerful, and Yeats is ready on occasion to
concede real power to woman even where it has been expended
on folly. And if that is so, then he can concede real power to what
he thinks of as a feminine mode of sensibility, even in himself. In
allowing this, he may also relax the 'masculine' assertiveness of
the Tower as Masonic emblem, and even infect it with feminine
'loosening', for the 'loosening' thighs of Leda look back to the
'loosening masonry' of the Tower in 'The Stare's Nest by my
Window' (*P* 204–5). The honey for which the poet prays in call-
ing to the honey-bees is in a general sense the 'honey of genera-
tion', in so far as that suggests the potential sweetness of natural
life; but more specifically it is the generative honey to be found in
feminine 'crevices'.

11

PROFANE PERFECTION

Y eats's late phase is characterised by the merging of opposite principles, the loosening of the firm boundaries that had been drawn between them, and the acceptance of brokenness. Ultimately, this was to involve a new affirmation of Gaelic culture: not the Gaelic culture of Iron Age Armagh but that of modern centuries. The last voice Yeats gives to Gaelic Ireland is that of Egan O'Rahilly and the anonymous author of 'Kilcash', voices of the final dispossession of the Gaelic order at the hands of his own ancestors. In this notable and ironic turn, Yeats became once again a spokesman for his nation, and might be said at last to have forged for it an image of unity. But this was a development that had to wait for a few years. The first note of this new phase is one of affirmation of life, of a broad reaction against 'bitterness', and we should first turn to this topic to see how it is bound up with 'brokenness'.

I

Yeats is able to impart sweetness to *The Winding Stair and Other Poems* by accepting the implications of the hymen, of 'the broken wall, the burning roof and tower', and applying to these his philosophy of tragic affirmation. 'Blood and the Moon' (*P* 237–9) expressly rewrites the Tower emblem in terms that accept that it is broken at the top, as in the Tarot trump. The Tower represents both the expression ('uttering') of the 'bloody, arrogant power' of the Irish race, and the discipline ('Mastering'), also blood-born, which had the strength and will to give form to this power. The race is preeminently Anglo-Irish, for in declaring that the Tower contains his ancestral stair, it is Goldsmith, Swift, Berkeley and Burke he remembers. Not only they, however, have helped to make the tradition, but also, in the seven centuries since it was built, the generations who followed the first man-at-arms and have given it a bloody history, such as accompanies the early development of an aristocratic society. The compliment to the Gaelic order is scarcely fulsome, and Yeats seems almost deliberately unfair in the implication that Irish culture came closest to organic unity in the Ascendancy of the eighteenth century. Still, those early centuries had their place, and through it all persisted a building and forming process motivated by 'The purity of the unclouded moon'. It remains pure, for it contains, represents and embodies all those eternal Presences, Images and Ideas which pull life after them. It does not matter that the living work itself will never take a perfect shape: nothing on earth ever does, except a few privileged moments of sexual love. The modern period is not the destruction of some lovely form, but rather the exacerbation of a necessary imperfection:

> Is every modern nation like the tower,
> Half dead at the top? No matter what I said,
> For wisdom is the property of the dead,
> A something incompatible with life; and power,
> Like everything that has the stain of blood,
> A property of the living; but no stain
> Can come upon the visage of the moon
> When it has looked in glory from a cloud.
>
> (P 238–9)

So inextricable is imperfection from everything on earth, that acceptance of this fact is necessary to any effective activity whatsoever, for the belief in perfection rests on an inappropriate and disabling assumption. The broken wall and burning roof and tower are the principle of all the creation we will ever know. As Crazy Jane says ('Crazy Jane Talks with the Bishop': P 259–60), 'Fair and foul are near of kin,/And fair needs foul', and in the same poem, 'For nothing can be sole or whole/That has not been rent.' The pun ('soul or hole') recalls Yeats's remark in 'Anima Hominis': 'I shall find the dark grow luminous, the void fruitful when I understand I have nothing, that the ringers in the tower have appointed for the hymen of the soul a passing bell' (*M* 332). Whatever approximation to wholeness this life has to offer is constructed with a view from the edge of the void, an edge which is ruptured and marked by difference. To imagine that one need not be 'rent' is to dream that one can live in eternity in this life. Here Yeats's later insights join with his early Blakean ones about the inseparability of Joy and Woe.

This language is on display in 'Vacillation' (*P* 249–53), a poem that, by working through contrary positions, expounds existence at the hymeneal line between contraries. 'Between extremities/Man runs his course.' Death ends this process. As we approach death we feel remorse, and after it remorsefully unwind the errors of our existence. But then, 'What is joy?' Joy is to be found occasionally as we run between contrary positions, like the butterfly, as heedlessly as we can manage. Part of the implication, of course, is that we cannot always be heedless. Very well: we must bravely accept that we will sometimes be burdened with care, and, without too much forcing, work and hope for a better day. Thus by acceptance and affirmation can we turn the inevitable brokenness of existence into the ground of a resurrection. This is the wisdom conveyed by the justly admired stanza about the tree which is half flame and half green. Though borrowed from the *Mabinogion*, it is still the Tree of Life from the Kabbalah, half stern and half mild:

> And he that Attis' image hangs between
> That staring fury and the blind lush leaf
> May know not what he knows, but knows not grief.
>
> (*P* 250)

Many discussions of this poem have been bedevilled by an almost entire concentration on the idea of the image, at the expense of Attis. Attis stands in for the Nietzschean Dionysus, who represents a transvaluation of Christ. The liberation offered by understanding the meaning of Attis therefore has a superficial similarity with that which is offered by Christ, and, indeed, other religions seen by Yeats as life-denying: escape from the wheel. But this is a Nietzschean escape into affirmation, and it involves the acceptance of brokenness, imperfection and contrariety. The castrated God, risen again and made, if not whole, at least creative, hangs between life's contraries, not expecting the truth to emerge from either: such an expectation would be still to be trapped in 'Lethean foliage' (section III), a bad oscillation between trust in one contrary or trust in the other, or a bad reliance on one only: bad because involving one in a double-bind (the choice between woman's love and a rich estate), bad because submitted to the illusion that there is an escape from the double-bind, which is also to submit to the illusion of wholeness. Attis's castrated image represents the repudiation of that illusion.

But that it is an image is a fact that refers us to art, and by transference it is art. One can deduce a number of aesthetic propositions from this fact: that the highest art affirms life in the face of death and tragic incompleteness; that it inhabits a line or place of interchange between contraries, but is not itself submerged in those contraries; and that art is created in the suspension of the expectation of perfect wholeness, in deferral. Attis's castrated image is the hymen. In section VI we are told that existence and its contraries – 'branches of the night and day' – have sprung from 'man's blood-sodden heart'. But the proximity of 'Attis's image' reminds us that 'blood' is death as well as passion. Our very pulse is emblematic of contrariety, as the image of 'beating' in 'Leda and the Swan' was meant to convey. But in those branches 'the gaudy moon is hung', dragging life in its circular and conflictual voyage around the void. The moon reminds us, by 'hanging' like 'Attis's image' in the tree, that it is very close to being Attis's image itself. The knowledge brought by the moon is similarly of creation across the boundaries that seem to divide opposites, and of deferral.

The ethical content of this post-Nietzschean view, and its transvaluation of Christianity, can be briefly illustrated from 'A Dialogue of Self and Soul' (P 234–6). The Soul offers escape from the Wheel of Existence and its contrarieties, to 'Deliver from the crime of death and birth'. This is not entirely unlike what the Self has to offer, if one looks at this poem in the light of 'Vacillation': delivery from death and birth could be described as escape from 'Lethean foliage'. In fact, the conflict of Self and Soul is of two different responses to contrariety: the Soul recommends dying to this life, the Self dying to the illusion of a rounded perfection in life.

Possessed of such an insight the Self can affirm its own existence, with all its pain, and does so in the second part of the 'Dialogue' in terms which recall Nietzsche's doctrine of Eternal Recurrence. Yeats says, 'I am content to live it all again', specifically evoking the clumsiness, humiliation and discord of existence. Nietzsche's doctrine is properly understood as leading to a similar affirmation, for however he may have toyed with the mathematical probability of a literal return of the same events in infinite time, he was chiefly interested in it as a hypothesis for testing the spirit of acceptance: can you joyfully accept your own particular life? Think of it as returning again and again: does this fill you with joy or depression? In Thomas Common's translation of *Thus Spoke Zarathustra*:

> Said ye ever Yea to one joy? O my friends, then said ye Yea also unto *all* woe. All things are enlinked, enlaced and enamoured, –
> – Wanted ye ever once to come twice; said ye ever 'Thou pleasest me, happiness! Instant! Moment!' then wanted ye *all* to come back again![1]

Motivated by such an affirmation, one is accepting the whole shape of a life. Hence Yeats can 'Measure the lot; forgive myself the lot!' The organic metaphor, so strongly asserted in parts of *The Tower*, is here qualified, or enriched. 'Measure' remains the outline found by a strong joyful life; but the notion of self-sufficient and balanced form is replaced by that of natural imperfection. This is the meaning of the words about the symbol of the tower in 'Blood and the Moon':

> A bloody, arrogant power
> Rose out of the race
> Uttering mastering it. . .
>
> > (*P* 237)

Utterance and mastery arise out of the same 'bloody' (and thus also vulnerable and broken) impulse.

Unlikely as it might seem, there is nothing in 'Byzantium' (*P* 248–9) that is incongruous with the perspective we have been outlining. The poem is an attempt to make clear the non-natural status of the eternal images and spirits, though in no sense bitterly assertive about this. Denis Donoghue can even say that 'there is an impression that transcendence has been achieved too easily, the difficulties have not been allowed to assert themselves.'[2] Yeats is stating, with all the grandeur of the conception, the character of one pole of the endless cycle of birth, death and rebirth: that of the life after death, or the stage between lives. In doing so he is not rejecting the idea that one should live the corporeal life as fully as possible; whereas in 'Sailing to Byzantium' that was at least the emotional bias. The fact is that Yeats's conceptions do not permit one to say whether the bodily or the spiritual 'comes first'. His intention is expressly to undermine such priorities: what one has is a cycle of this world and the next, each dying the other's life and living the other's death. In the last stanza of 'Byzantium' one discovers that 'the golden smithies of the Emperor' are purging the incoming 'blood-begotten' spirits of all taint of the natural. The spirits, however, are riding on the body ('Astraddle on the dolphin's mire and blood'), out of what Blake called The Sea of Time and Space. This sea of natural existence is also the hymen: 'torn' (or 'rent') by the body and by the contrariety imposed by 'blood', but tormented by the drive towards unity which cannot be suspended: the call of the Byzantine gong. The 'images that yet fresh images beget' are not to be simply identified with the 'spirits'. We know from *Per Amica Silentia Lunae* and from *A Vision*, however, that the spirits of the dead and images in the *anima mundi* share the same quasi-material vehicles, composed of 'animal spirits'. A sentence from Yeats's marginalia to Nietzsche is clear about the possibility he entertained: 'Yet the "supernatural life" may be but the soul of the earth out of which man leaps again, when the circle is complete.'[3] Approaching Byzantium the spirits are best called spirits. Once there, and purged, they enter the realm of images. To assert that these beget fresh examples of themselves is to agree with the apostrophe to them in 'Among School Children': 'O self-born mockers of man's enterprise!' But in that poem, with scant attention to philosophical nicety, Yeats goes on to remind us that our truest experience of beauty is when the images and the blood-begotten energies of life coincide. In 'Byzantium' we are left with a sharper juxtaposition and disjunction: on the one hand, images begetting fresh images in the non-natural realm of the *anima mundi*; on the other, the torn Sea of Time and Space, tormented by a yearning for that eternal realm. But Yeats is too dispassionate here to offer this as a hateful contrary; rather, he gives us sublime description.

II

In all of the foregoing we have been assuming the continuing presence of the metaphor of the hymen, and this means that Yeats had adopted what he thinks of as a feminine aesthetic. Or at least, a more feminine aesthetic, for the image of Attis is hermaphroditic, rather, and in line with the deconstruction and merging to be found in 'Leda and the Swan', there are a number of hints that Yeats is concerned to undertake transactions and engage in identifications with the feminine, without destroying the opposition which gives them their energy and impetus.

It is scarcely acute to note that the symbol of the Tower has phallic implications. It never belonged comfortably among emblems of organic form, but was assimilated to them because it represented building out of the blood of the race; the connection of Yeats's ancestors with that race; and finally the poetry that arose out of that connection. The insistence in *The Winding Stair* that the Tower is broken at the top belongs with the revision of the idea of life-affirming form. But there is another change in the deployment of the tower emblem: simply in the fact of its being treated as a 'winding stair'. Where the Tower was phallic, this is feminine and belongs to the category of the hymen: a staged deferral, or labyrinth, ending in the void.[4] Yeats's 'contrary' progression from *The Tower* to this volume is equivalent to the statement that he also possesses a feminine aspect. And so is his writing of the Crazy Jane poems. Yeats was capable of asserting that he had 'a woman' in him, and of celebrating the idea. As he says in a letter to Dorothy Wellesley, written in November 1936: 'My dear – when you crossed the room with that boyish movement, it was no man who looked at you, it was the woman in me. It seems that I can make a woman express herself as never before. I have looked out of her eyes. I have shared her desire' (*L* 868). Perhaps the most intriguing item in these remarks is the idea of making a woman express herself as never before. For while the sharing of desire might seem to imply letting her behave with the intimacy she usually reserves for the girls, the remark about 'that boyish movement' hints rather at a sweet enforcement of role-reversal. Yeats's apprehension of the hymen permits him to see both male and female as potentially powerful and broken, and this perception is congruent with the rich confusion of 'Leda and the Swan'. And he toys with the idea that woman, in being apparently more broken, is really more powerful: as C. L. Innes puts it, Jane 'challenges time not with intellectual sweetness but with passion and energy'.[5] And in terms of time's depredations she has much to challenge: as Barbara Hardy observes, she has 'several disadvantages. She is crazy, she is a woman, she is old, or for most of the poetry she appears to be old, and she is poor.'[6] She has little that would seem to conduce to the ready satisfaction of the desires which so occupy her, and whose value her wisdom celebrates. As the Bishop remarks to her:

> 'Those breasts are flat and fallen now
> Those veins must soon be dry;
> Live in a heavenly mansion,
> Not in some foul sty.'

But in such a condition she can realise desire at its highest pitch: the object is absent, for her lover Jack is dead, and having lived a disreputable life she has learnt the value of sexual love. The denied, vulnerable, broken body itself becomes Yeats's new metaphor for the hymen. And in inverting the Bishop's priorities, Jane makes the body, so conceived, the type of which soul is mere copy and shadow.

III

It would be otiose to discuss at length what is sufficiently widely held, that in 'Lapis Lazuli' (*P* 294–5) the work of art becomes itself the emblem of affirmation in the face of the void, and may be seen as embodying in its shape the beautiful brokenness of this world: 'Every discolouration of the stone,/Every accidental crack or dent.' No masonry can be sole or whole that has not been cracked. Another and related beauty of the lapis lazuli for Yeats is that it seems able to embody something of the process of time in wearing away man's 'monuments', and he is able to make it convey the artist's acceptance of that even in the act of creation, in a way that parallels the tragic hero's acceptance of death and wasted possibility.

As for death and the void, Yeats seems increasingly to find no consolation in the elaborate machinery of after-life expounded in *A Vision*. This has some bearing on the argument, even if not a bearing that could decide the rightness or wrongness of the assertions made here about artistic form. For this book has been pursuing the idea that from the early years of the century Yeats had been thinking more and more in terms of a system of deferrals without a core or essence. But this was chiefly an argument about signification and the role of image and mask. And in *A Vision* Yeats seemed at least to offer the prospect of an after-life amidst that circle of deferrals imaged in the phases of the moon. But now there are suggestions enough in *New Poems* and 'Last Poems' that at death one confronts nothingness, or at best an unwinding of the self that is so radical that it might as well be regarded as extinction. Stark presentations of the first possibility are to be found in that bleak poem, 'Man and the Echo' (*P* 345-6) and in Yeats's 'little poem about nothing' dated 8 May 1938, and first published by Warwick Gould in *Yeats Annual No. 5*, the last line of which is 'From nowhere unto nowhere nothings run.'[7]

But poems that seem to be predicated on the idea of an after-life turn out to offer little consolation either. In 'The Gyres' (*P* 293) we are granted an apocalyptic perspective: modern times increasingly offer a reminder of the fall of Troy and the sense of an old order coming to an anarchic and violent end. The artist, as if mirroring the confusion, is becoming coarse and insensitive. But, 'What matter?' It is of no account in the long glass of Time. The aristocratic order will return, 'The workman, noble and saint, and all things run/On that unfashionable gyre again.' It is this return which is offered as consolation, not personal survival or even, as in 'Vacillation', self- acceptance and affirmation. And the return of aristocracy is out of nothing:

> From marble of a broken sepulchre
> Or dark betwixt the polecat and the owl,
> Or any rich, dark nothing . . .
>
> (*P* 293)

Although the first image might seem to allude to reincarnation, the last phrase gives the general category subsuming the other two. It is indeed the void which is 'fruitful' here. And as for the gyres themselves, though there is no denying their past implication in supernatural machinery, they are here glossed only by the lines, 'Things thought too long can be no longer thought/For beauty dies of beauty, worth of worth.' Humanity gets tired. As in 'Meru' (*P* 289), the last poem in the preceding book, opposing gyres can be conceived in this-worldly terms as the historical tendency to action and reaction, patterned by the opposition of subjective and objective tinctures, and fuelled by the ravenousness of a desire that outruns all satiety, 'Ravening through century after century,/ Ravening, raging, and uprooting . . .'

187

The chill of the void afflicts even a poem which offers us a precise vision of existence after death, 'Cuchulain Comforted' (*P* 332). The action depicted follows on from the last moments of Yeats's play, *The Death of Cuchulain*, but this is of no special help in interpretation. It is more useful to be reminded by F. A. C. Wilson that the dead (the 'Shrouds') talk in terms that are reminiscent of the instructors in *A Vision*:[8] 'We have no power except to purify our intention, of complexity. We do nothing singly. Every act is done by a number at the same time' (*AVB* 233). And the reader will recall, from other poems, that threading 'the needles' eyes' is a symbol of the cycle of death and rebirth. So Cuchulain is being guided through the unwinding of his earthly existence by these spirits. And appropriate guides they are, for they are Cuchulain's opposites, having been executed or exiled as 'convicted cowards'. They are, then, his Daimons, in the sense explained in *Per Amica Silentia Lunae*. But no explanation in terms of Yeats's symbolic system can palliate the cold shock the poem imparts. After death, bravery and cowardice are as one; and it matters not if one has died heroically or been rejected and killed as a coward by one's humiliated kindred. 'What matter?' These principles apply even to Yeats's iconic hero, Cuchulain, his Achilles. Yet the shock is not chiefly a moral one. Cuchulain would have scorned to sort with cowards when alive, and his identity was bound up with his heroism. Indeed, he had paid with nothing less than his life in the service of that code. Now he must submit to the communal and amorphous, and in doing so surrender every specific trait and belief that had made him what he was. What price resurrection if the unwinding we then experience is that of our very identity? To read the final note of bird-song as merely an allusion to the purged sweetness of spirits is to betray Yeats's persistent ambivalence and more especially the sombre and sinister character of this poem. It is, in any case, an allusion also to the sound of old men's voices, and expresses Yeats's own immediate fears.

IV

The brokenness admired in some works of art does not absolve the artist from the labour of artifice, from 'measurement'.[9] This is firmly asserted in 'The Statues' (*P* 336-7). The mathematical exactitude of Pythagoras is the foundation for the precision of

Greek statuary. But the sculptors who made the statues are 'Greater than Pythagoras', for they use the skills of number and measure to model 'Calculations that look but casual flesh'. So they may incite the desire of 'boys and girls' or the 'dreams' of women, just as Michael Angelo's Adam enters the thoughts of 'girls at puberty' in 'Long-legged Fly' (*P* 339), or in 'Under Ben Bulben' (*P* 325–8). In the latter the 'purpose' of the artist is described as 'Profane perfection of mankind'. This line is a clue to what is shared by works of art that embody profane perfection and those that bear the stigmata of brokenness: both are expressions of what Yeats sometimes calls 'the blood', as well as being products of artifice. The 'beating' of the blood is itself an image of difference, of brokenness. 'Profane perfection', then, comprises more than a fine eliciting of desire. In recalling the 'crime' of generation it bears witness to the fact that it is perfection won from imperfection. The European urge to concrete embodiment is at odds with 'All Asiatic vague immensities'. Though Europe has bred its own Asiatic tendencies, in the mysticism of 'a fat/ Dreamer of the Middle Ages', its genius is with form and particularity. Ireland, as much as any nation, embodies that genius, for whatever wisdom Yeats may have felt she shared with the East he now saw as given an opposing antithetical cast by measurement. 'When Pearse summoned Cuchulain to his side' in the Post Office, he was summoning an image which would later be sculpted and placed there in memory of the Easter Rising. That he was able to do so to give heart to his cause is witness to the fact that the Irish tradition of the distinct 'bounding line' (Blake's phrase) had already given definition to the image of Cuchulain in the mind's eye. The Irish have been ruined by the modern objective temper (this is 'The Curse of Cromwell') but they may still climb into 'their proper dark' to create a living work of art. The 'dark' is theirs partly because of the institution of the bardic school, which involved the novice poet spending days lying in the darkness composing poems in intricate Gaelic metres, and then emerging to recite them from memory.[10] But it is also theirs because it stands for creation in the face of death, the condition of all good art.

Along with Irish art, Gaelic society returns to its former place in Yeats's heart, as if approaching death were concentrating his mind on his true affiliations and on the ultimate significance and posthumous influence of his poetry. Indeed, Yeats has never been more sympathetic to the Gaelic order. It is one thing to laud the

long-lost Iron Age world of Cuchulain as he once did, quite another-
to do as he does now and erect as his ideal the Gaelic aristocracy of
the 'seven heroic centuries' who were dispossessed by his own Prot-
estant forebears. Yeats's image of this aristocracy and its dispposses-
sion is founded in his reading of Frank O'Connor's translations of
Egan O'Rahilly and the anonymous poem 'Cad a dhéanfaimid feasta
gan adhmad?', known as 'Kilcash'. In 'The Curse of Cromwell' (P
304–5) pride in a society that stretches back, as O'Rahilly reminds
us, to an era 'before Christ was crucified', is mingled with images of
its dissolution drawn from 'Kilcash', which is a poem that refers to
deforestation ('What shall we do for timber?/The last of the woods is
down') and the recent destruction of a whole society ('The earls, the
lady, the people/Beaten into the clay').[11] This is the line Yeats
quotes here and in 'Under Ben Bulben'.

Yeats needed some image of Irish tradition which could hold all
the positive associations he had with Ireland. Better than either the
court of King Conchobar or the ruined house of Coole was a
period which stretched between them both, had links with both,
and some of the virtues of both. As for that vehement wildness
which he was unable to detach from his image of the Gaelic poet, it
now seemed more than ever a virtue, however patronising and
inaccurate his view. Ireland becomes like the work of art: wild,
bloody, broken, but dedicated to measurement. And his ability to
accept it as such is an index of the relaxation of some of the old
boundaries. Yeats had been drawing a stern outline of Anglo-Irish
hue around his conception of Ireland and of experience. This out-
line has relaxed and allowed Gaelic Ireland to relegate the people
of Burke and Grattan, who do not appear as such in 'Under Ben
Bulben', being replaced by a less grandiose formula, and one with
rather different implications, 'Hard-riding country gentlemen'.

And there was another claim this tradition had on his imagina-
tion: there was nothing left of it. After the wreck of Coole Yeats
was capable of thinking of himself as O'Rahilly lamenting his lost
patrons, or as the speaker of his own poem, waking in the ruin of 'a
great house'. The end of the Gaelic Big House offered him a
dramatic intensification of his own plight and that of contemporary
Ireland. So yet again we see a factitious tradition. But though
Gaeldom is dead and the Ascendancy dying, things 'both can and
cannot be' in 'The Curse of Cromwell'. The poet can still serve the
swordsmen and the ladies 'though all are underground'. He can do
so simply by imagining them. Thus he may keep faith with what

has been borne away by the 'filthy modern tide' and help to create a future Ireland. For when Pearse stood in the Post Office neither an independent Ireland nor the image of Cuchulain existed, except in his mind. When the poet climbs into the dark to measure his idea, what he creates may come to pass, or bring things to pass, as Yeats had known many years before when he imagined 'A man who does not exist', and promised to write for him.

Gaelic Ireland, then, is like a female Daimon, an image from the dead which has offered enticement and conflict. In Yeats's last years she finally feeds full on Yeats's substance. This is one reason why he is able to write 'Under Ben Bulben' as if posthumously. Indeed, that poem offers us a dead speaker and an Ireland always already composed in his absence. In fact, this is another of Yeats's revisions of the 'Grecian Urn', with eternal pictures of human life and art and, in section IV, a miniature historical gyre, circling around the absence of the speaker: an absence which is seen in relation to Ben Bulben. This is, so to speak, the centre from which he is absent, 'the scene' where 'horsemen' and women of the *sidhe* ride by, and also the 'country gentlemen', but where not the poet but his gravestone is visible. His first inscription poem at Thoor Ballylee (*P* 190) had been associated with (even if it was not in itself) a bitter assertion on the Irish landscape. This, by contrast, is a proud acceptance and affirmation of the whole matter of Ireland in a place that returns Yeats to childhood associations. It also returns Gaelic tradition to its centrality, not only in the reference to the *sidhe* and to the Gaelic aristocracy but in the deliberate evocation of those tales of the Fenian cycle that are associated with the region of Ben Bulben, in particular that of the death of Diarmuid, who, having been gored by a wild boar, becomes in allusion a type of Attis, considering that the context denies the reality of death. The demonic and the supernatural here make what appears to be a confident reappearance partly in the reassertion of the avocations of a lifetime, and partly in tacit recognition of what was always bound up with the supernatural for Yeats: the mutual vampirism of the dead and the living, where, as we have seen, the agency of the dead is exercised through images. This recognition, along with the inscription and the posthumous quality of the poem, show him proudly revealing that he has exchanged the fullness of life for an artifice of Hibernia, conscious that he could never have helped to forge an Irish Revival if he had really belonged in some belated way to the tradition of Georgian Ireland. What moved him had always been an exchange of life with the Gaelic tradition. And the poem, for all that it asserts about reincarnation, really offers the return of the same. That is to say, it does not look forward to some state of affairs which might bear a broad similarity to elements of the Irish tradition; it looks rather to the recurrence of Ireland. And if Ireland is to recur, so must the poet. But if the poet should return, it would only be to the same vampiric relationship. The circle is closed: we are shown the fair and lively image of Ireland and the idea of the poet's death. The poem accepts and affirms that he would always have both imagined and pursued that image and always have expended his life in doing so. These are reasons why it is a fitting epitaph. The final lines which constitute the inscription evoke the idea of the speaker's both disappearing and persisting in their very manner, for as Helen Vendler has pointed out, they seem to have a 'missing line', in that one might half expect a fourth and final line rhyming with 'death'.[12] The air of suspense suggests both a slow evaporation into the air, and on the other hand, that the speaker is about to speak again. But if he did speak again, it would only be to say the same thing. In that case the poem would be like a Möbius strip, eternally recurring. The poem alludes to the idea of eternal recurrence as the acceptance of a life and what has been made of it; and what has been made of it has been made by 'Measurement', which 'began our might', of course, but which also allowed Pearse as it were to create something out of nothing in the Post Office. This might make one think again about the 'superhuman' horsemen in section I: are they really spirits, after all, or are they images that permit self-measuring and self-transcendence 'in the human mind', in a way that alludes to Nietzschean self-overcoming? And is the poem not a testimony to Yeats's achievement of that? In that case even the blunt imperatives ('learn', 'Sing', 'scorn', and so on) are not only the prerogative of a last will and testament read from beyond the grave, but testimony to the achievement that has turned him into a superhuman artefact from which others may draw strength and desirable images. 'Under Ben Bulben' is really Yeats's most confident circling round the void; but, while it insists on measurement, it qualifies the insistence with an acceptance of profanity and of Gaelic Ireland that shows form and calculation to be an aspect of energetic and imaginative existence and one in which he has taken instruction from (among other places) the whole Gaelic tradition to pass on to others as a wisdom tried and proved.

In this sense Yeats both is and is not offering yet another version of the husk, for while there is again no transcendent principle at the heart of things, it is not emptiness that is shown to us, but completion, in the sense that the truest measurement or outline is the most lively, and has created both the art and the life that are most admirable. This is an interpretation supported also by 'The Circus Animals' Desertion' (P 346–8). For although admittedly the tone is rather different, the underlying concepts are not. Yeats's life has been expended in exfoliations of the 'heart' which take place in a 'show' which is somehow above the 'heart' and has to be reached by ladder. This place is like the stage as interpreted by Derrida in 'The double session': a 'between' of difference and deferral: these are conditions that have to be imposed on a 'heart' in the world of time. Yet there had been too much of what Yeats elsewhere calls 'externality': 'Players and painted stage took all my love,/And not those things that they were emblems of.' The alternative, however, is not a descent into essential meaning, for the image offered of the heart is emphatically one of disjunction rather than essence: 'Old kettles, old bottles, and a broken can,/Old iron, old bones, old rags . . .' What we are offered is the heart's expression as encompassing the almost unspeakable brokenness and profanity of life, and it is thus a truer expression in that sense, but we are no closer to some 'core' of value: the foul rag-and-bone shop is merely a different 'scene'. There is triumph here, as well as bitterness. And there is even more triumph in Yeats's setting the 'scene' by Ben Bulben ('Where Ben Bulben sets the scene') for there he makes the Irish tradition the occasion of the liveliest husk or outline, fed by the most energetic and measured exfoliations of the heart.

NOTES

1 INTRODUCTION: MATTER AND METHODOLOGY

1. Okifumi Komesu, *The Double Perspective of Yeats's Aesthetic* (Gerrards Cross, 1984).
2. Seamus Deane, *Celtic Revivals: Essays in modern Irish literature, 1880–1980* (London, 1987), p.48.
3. W. J. McCormack, *Ascendancy and Tradition in Anglo-Irish Literary History, 1789–1939* (Oxford, 1985), p.244.
4. Michèle Barrett, 'Some different meanings of the concept of "difference": feminist theory and the concept of ideology', in Elizabeth Meese and Alice Parker (eds), *The Difference Within: Feminism and critical theory* (Amsterdam and Philadelphia, 1989), p.37.
5. *Ibid.*, pp.38–44.
6. *Ibid.*
7. Edward Larrissy, *William Blake* (Oxford, 1985).
8. Theodor Wolpers, 'Motif and theme as structural content units and "concrete universals" ', in Werner Sollors (ed.), *The Return of Thematic Criticism: Harvard English studies*, 18 (Cambridge, Mass. and London, 1993), p.91.
9. Hazard Adams, *The Book of Yeats's Poems* (Tallahassee, Fa, 1990); Hugh Kenner, 'The Sacred Book of the Arts' (1955), reprinted in William H. Pritchard (ed.), *W. B. Yeats: A critical anthology* (Harmondsworth, 1972).
10. Adams, *The Book*, pp.18–26.
11. Warwick Gould, ' "A lesson for the circumspect": W. B. Yeats's two versions of *A Vision* and the *Arabian Nights*', in Peter L. Caracciolo (ed.), *The Arabian Nights in English Literature: Studies in the reception of The Thousand and One Nights into British culture* (London and Basingstoke, 1988), pp.248–50, 261.

12. Stan Smith, 'Porphyry's cup: Yeats, forgetfulness and the narrative order', in Warwick Gould (ed.), *Yeats Annual No. 5* (1987), pp.15–45.

13. *Ibid.*, p.16.

14. See Frank Kinahan, *Yeats, Folklore and Occultism: Contexts of the early work and thought* (Boston, 1988), p.110.

15. See Diana Basham, *The Trial of Woman: Feminism and the occult sciences in Victorian literature and society* (London and Basingstoke, 1992), p.187.

16. Joseph Adams, *Yeats and the Masks of Syntax* (London and Basingstoke, 1984), p.1.

17. David Pierce, *W. B. Yeats: A guide through the critical maze* (Bristol, 1989), p.118.

18. Robin Skelton, *Celtic Contraries* (Syracuse, N.Y., 1991), p.155.

19. R. B. Kershner, 'Yeats/Bakhtin/orality/dyslexia', *Yeats and Postmodernism*, ed. Leonard Orr (Syracuse, N.Y., 1991), p.185.

20. Elizabeth Cullingford, 'How Jacques Molay got up the tower: Yeats and the Irish civil war', *ELH* 50:4 (1983), pp.763–89; R. F. Foster, 'Protestant magic: W. B. Yeats and the spell of Irish history' (Chatterton Lecture, 1989), *Proceedings of the British Academy* 75 (1989), pp.243–66.

21. Foster, 'Protestant magic', pp.247–50. That mediation might be temporal or historical, in the sense of preparing the ground for a new age in which Celtic qualities would be more to the fore, is suggested by a reading of Marjorie Reeves and Warwick Gould, *Joachim of Fiore and the Myth of the Eternal Evangel in the Nineteenth Century* (Oxford, 1987), pp.142–51, 202–15.

22. *Ibid.*, p.260.

23. Joseph Th. Leerssen, 'On the edge of Europe: Ireland in search of oriental roots, 1650–1850', *Comparative Criticism: An annual journal* 8, ed. E. S. Shaffer (1986), pp.91–112; Norman Vance, 'Celts, Carthaginians and constitutions: Anglo-Irish literary relations, 1780–1820', *Irish Historical Studies*, 22 (March 1981), pp.216–38.

24. e.g., S. B. Bushrui, 'Yeats's Arabic interests', in A. N. Jeffares and K. G. W. Cross (eds.), *In Excited Reverie: A centenary tribute to William Butler Yeats, 1865–1939* (London, 1965), pp.280–314.

25. Edward W. Said, *Orientalism: Western conceptions of the Orient* (London, 1978), p.102.

26. *Ibid.*, p.139.

27. John Barrell, *The Infection of Thomas De Quincey: A psychopathology of imperialism* (New Haven and London, 1991).

28. *Ibid.*, pp.7, 8.

29. *Ibid.*, pp.11–12.

30. *Ibid.*, pp.12–13.

31. *Ibid.*, p.13.

32. See David Cairns and Shaun Richards, *Writing Ireland: Colonialism, nationalism and culture* (Manchester, 1988), pp.42–57.

33. Basham, *Trial of Woman*, pp.178–214.

2 MATRIX AND MEAN

1. Sir James O'Connor, *History of Ireland, 1798–1924*, 2 vols (London, 1925), I, pp.82–3.
2. E. M. Johnston, 'Problems common to both Protestant and Catholic Churches in eighteenth-century Ireland', in Oliver MacDonagh, W. F. Mandle and Pauric Travers (eds.), *Irish Culture and Nationalism, 1750–1950* (London and Basingstoke, 1983), p.34.
3. William M. Murphy, *The Yeats Family and the Pollexfens of Sligo*, with drawings by Jack Butler Yeats (Dublin, 1971), p.44.
4. Ian Fletcher, 'The white rose rebudded: neo-Jacobitism in the 1890's', *W. B. Yeats and his Contemporaries* (Brighton, 1987) pp.83ff.
5. F. McLynn, *The Jacobites* (London, 1985), p.140.
6. John Daly and Edward Walsh, *Reliques of Irish Jacobite Poetry* (Dublin, 1844).
7. *The Penguin Book of Irish Verse*, ed. Brendan Kennelly (Harmondsworth, 1970), p.264.
8. The lack of evidence is pointed out by George Mills Harper, in *Yeats's Golden Dawn* (London, 1974), p.199, n.13.
9. These words are applied to the case of Rudolf Steiner, in Ellic Howe, *The Magicians of the Golden Dawn: A documentary history of a magical order 1887–1923* (London, 1972), p.263.
10. See George Mills Harper, *Yeats's Golden Dawn* (London, 1974), p.199, n.13.
11. For the Golden Dawn, see Harper, *Yeats's Golden Dawn*; Howe, *The Magicians of the Golden Dawn*; and R. A. Gilbert, *The Golden Dawn: Twilight of the Magicians* (Wellingborough, 1983). On the Golden Dawn and Freemasonry see Harper, *Golden Dawn*, and Howe, *Magicians*, pp.7, 11, 56, 71, 256, 263.
12. Elizabeth Cullingford, 'How Jacques Molay got up the Tower; Yeats and the Irish civil war', *ELH*, 50 (1983), p.777.
13. Maud Gonne MacBride, *A Servant of the Queen: Reminiscences* (London, 1974), p.259.
14. *Ibid.*, p.37
15. *Ibid.*, p.259.
16. Howe, *Magicians*, p.2.
17. Richard Ellmann, *Oscar Wilde* (London, 1987), p.39.
18. *Ibid.*, p.65.
19. *Ibid.*
20. *Ibid.*, p.134.
21. W. J. McCormack, *Sheridan Le Fanu and Victorian Ireland* (Oxford, 1980), p.247.
22. Quoted in Malcolm Brown, *Sir Samuel Ferguson* (Lewisburg, 1973), p.43.
23. Thomas Crofton Croker, *Popular Songs of Ireland* (London [1887]), pp.146–7. 'Bad cess' means 'heavy taxation'.
24. *Poems of Sir Samuel Ferguson*, with an introduction by Alfred Perceval Graves (Dublin and London, n.d. [1916?]), p.132.

25. Vivian Mercier, 'Victorian evangelicalism and the Anglo-Irish literary revival', *Literature and the Changing Ireland*, ed. Peter Connolly (Gerrards Cross and Totowa, N.J., 1982), p.88. For links with the so-called 'Celtic Church', see pp.88–90. For Irish language scholarship, see pp.91–2. Mercier is summarising points already made by Greene and McDowell (below). For a conspectus on recent thoughts about the Church of Ireland as an influence on the Revival, see Terence Brown, 'The Church of Ireland and the climax of the ages', *Ireland's Literature: selected essays* (Mullingar and Totowa, N.J., 1988), pp.49–64.

26. MacDonagh, Mandle and Travers, *Irish Culture*, pp.20–1.

27. David Greene, 'The Irish language movement', *Irish Anglicanism 1869–1969*, ed. Michael Hurley, S.J. (Dublin, 1970), pp.110–11.

28. *Ibid.*, p.111.

29. *Ibid.*, pp.112, 113.

30. R. B. McDowell, *The Church of Ireland 1869–1969* (London and Boston, 1975), p.102.

31. *Ibid.*, p.101.

32. *A Book of Irish Verse selected from Modern Writers with an Introduction and Notes*, ed., rev., W. B. Yeats (London, 1900), p.170.

33. Quoted in Fergal Grannell, 'Early Irish ecclesiastical studies', in Hurley, *Irish Anglicanism*, p.44.

34. See Kathleen Raine, 'Yeats and the creed of St. Patrick', *Yeats the Initiate: essays on certain themes in the work of W. B. Yeats* (Mountrath and Dublin, 1986), pp.379–99.

35. *James Clarence Mangan, His Selected Poems*, ed., with a study, Louise Imogen Guiney (London, Boston and New York, 1897), pp.123, 125.

36. *Lyra Celtica: an anthology of representative Celtic poetry*, ed. E. A. Sharp and J. Matthay, intro. and notes W. Sharp, repr. (Edinburgh, 1932), p.3.

37. *Ibid.*, p.xxxvii.

38. Kuno Meyer and Alfred Nutt, *The Voyage of Bran Son of Febal to the Land of the Living*, 2 vols (London, 1895, 1987), II, p.86.

39. John Rhys, *Lectures on the Origin and Growth of Religion as Illustrated by Celtic Heathendom* (London, 1888), p.224.

40. Meyer and Nutt, *The Voyage*, II, p.104.

41. Brooke F. Westcott, 'Dionysius the Areopagite', *Contemporary Review* 5 (1867), pp.5, 6, 25.

42. J. -K. Huysmans, *Là-Bas* (Paris, 1908), p.280.

43. Alice Gardner, *Studies in John the Scot (Erigena): A philosopher of the Dark Ages* (London, 1900).

44. John J. O'Meara, *Eriugena* (Oxford, 1988), p.137.

45. See Israel Regardie, *The Golden Dawn: An account of the teachings, rites and ceremonies*, 4 vols, bound in one (St Paul, Minn., 1978), III, pp.20–36; IV, p.240.

46. Eugene O'Curry, *Manners and Customs of the Ancient Irish*, 3 vols (Dublin, 1873), II, p.179.

47. *Ibid.*

48. P. W. Joyce, *Old Celtic Romances* (London, 1879), p.403, n.3.

49. Douglas Hyde, *A Literary History of Ireland From Earliest Times to the Present Day* (London, 1899), p.89.

3 THE HAPPY SHELL AND THE SAD SHELL

1. Edward W. Said, *Orientalism* (London, 1978), p.74.
2. See 'The manuscript of "Leo Africanus" ', ed. Steve L. Adams and George Mills Harper, *Yeats Annual No. 1*, ed. Richard J. Finneran (1982), pp.3–47.
3. *Ibid.*, p.22.
4. Ireland was traditionally divided into a northern and southern half. The northern, *Leth Cuinn*, 'the portion of Conn', contained Ulster and Connacht (in which was Sligo); the southern, *Leth Moga*, Leinster and Munster. See Alwyn Rees and Brinley Rees, *Celtic Heritage: Ancient tradition in Ireland and Wales* (London, 1961), pp.101, 103.
5. T. W. Moody, F. X. Martin and F. J. Byrne (eds.), *A New History of Ireland*, 9 vols (Oxford, 1974–7), IX (1984), p.81, map 98. The copy of this map in Roy Foster's *Modern Ireland 1600–1972* (London, 1988), p.464, fails to reproduce the important detail of Sligo. *A New History* gives the Protestant population of Sligo as 75 per cent 'and over!'. It must therefore have comprised some of the working population, including the stable-boy who sang 'Orange rhymes' to Yeats (*Au* 14).
6. Cf. Michael Ivens, 'Yeats: the Faustian quest', *Books and Bookmen* 17:3 (December 1971), pp.20–2.
7. 'Erionnach', *The Poets and Poetry of Munster: A selection of Irish songs by the poets of the last century*, second series (Dublin, 1860), p.141, note to 'Sile Bheag Ni Chonnolain', another personification of Ireland.
8. *Ibid.*, pp.141, 145.
9. John Daly and Edward Walsh, *Reliques of Irish Jacobite Poetry* (Dublin, 1844), pp.45–7.
10. Maud Gonne MacBride, *A Servant of the Queen* (London, 1974), p.134.
11. See M. Barry Delaney's poem, 'Maud Gonne', in *The Shan Van Vocht* 1 (7 February 1896), p.33. Quoted by C. L. Innes, in ' "A voice in directing the affairs of Ireland": *L'Irlande Libre*, *The Shan Van Vocht* and *Bean na h-Eireann*', *Irish Writing: exile and subversion*, ed. Paul Hyland and Neil Sammels (Basingstoke, 1991), p.152. Compare Yeats's Journal for May 1910: 'Thinking of [Maud Gonne], as I do, as in a sense Ireland . . .' (*Mem* 247).
12. Gonne MacBride, *Servant of the Queen*, pp.226–46.
13. *Ibid.*, p.240.
14. *Ibid.*, p.241.
15. *Ibid.*, pp.230–1.
16. Quoted in Bram Stoker, *Dracula*, ed. Maurice Hindle (Harmondsworth, 1993), pp.500–1, 503.
17. Edmund Spenser, *The Works of Edmund Spenser: a variorum edition*, ed. Edwin Greenlaw, Charles Grosvenor Osgood, Frederick Morgan Padelford and Ray Heffner, 10 vols (London and Baltimore, 1932–49); *The Prose Works*, ed. Rudolf Gottfried (Baltimore, 1949), p.158.
18. Quoted in Phyllis A. Roth, *Bram Stoker* (Boston, 1982), p.56.

19. In *The Shan Van Vocht* 3:3 (7 March 1898), p.1. Quoted in C. L. Innes, 'A voice in directing', p.158.
20. See Deborah Dorfman, *Blake in the Nineteenth Century* (New Haven and London, 1969), pp.136–9.
21. *The Complete Poetry and Prose of William Blake*, newly rev. edn, ed. David V. Erdman (New York, 1988), p.491.
22. David Erdman, *Complete Poetry and Prose of William Blake* (New York, 1988), p.71.
23. For useful general thoughts on the influence of Browning on Yeats, see Harold Bloom, *Yeats* (London, Oxford and New York, 1970), pp.18–22; and George Bornstein, 'Last Romantic or last Victorian: Yeats, Tennyson and Browning', *Yeats Annual No. 1* (1982), ed. Richard J. Finneran, pp.114–32.
24. W. B. Yeats, *Letters to the New Island: A new edition*, ed. George Bornstein and Hugh Witemeyer (Basingstoke and London, 1989), p.28.
25. Cf. Frank Kinahan, *Yeats, Folklore, and Occultism: contexts of the early work and thought* (Boston and London, 1988), p.110. Kinahan makes the connection with *The Wanderings of Oisin*.
26. James Hardiman, *Irish Minstrelsy, or Bardic Remains of Ireland; with English poetical translations*, 2 vols (London, 1831), I, p.viii, n. on 'Scotland's pretensions to Ossian'.
27. For all these matters, and especially Yeats's sources, see Russel K. Alspach, 'Some sources of Yeats's *The Wanderings of Oisin*', *PMLA*, 58 (1943), pp.849–66.
28. Kinahan, *Yeats, Folklore and Occultism*, pp.87–8, discusses Yeats's innovations with the Oisin story.
29. Freud's essay on 'The Uncanny' (1919) is in volume XVII of the *Standard Edition*, 24 vols (London, 1953–74), pp.217–56.
30. The terms can be seen in relation to Lacan's 'Imaginary' and 'Symbolic', also interwoven.
31. For Lacan on art, see Jacques Lacan, 'What is a picture?' *The Four Fundamental Concepts of Psycho-Analysis*, ed. Jacques-Alain Miller, trans. Alan Sheridan (Harmondsworth, 1979), pp.105–19.
32. For reflections on Anglo-Irish alienation and its effects in Yeats's early life and work, see Declan Kiberd, 'Yeats, childhood and exile', *Irish Writing: exile and subversion*, ed. Paul Hyland and Neil Sammels (Basingstoke and London, 1991), pp.126–45.
33. *Ibid.*, p.141.
34. W. B. Yeats, *Writings on Irish Folklore, Legend and Myth*, ed. Robert Welch (Harmondsworth, 1993), pp.39–43.
35. Subject of an uncollected poem by Yeats: *VP* 720–2.
36. Anon., 'Early Irish history – the O'Briens', *The Gentlemen's Magazine* (August 1860), p.114: 'passing over two centuries, during which the descendants of the mighty Con reigned supreme, though not without many hard battles with their fellow kings . . .'
37.   O Goat-Foot God of Arcady!
      This modern world is grey and old
      And what remains to us of thee?

(Oscar Wilde, *Poems*, 12th edn (London, 1913), p.243). This poem was discovered in MS. by Robert Ross, and added to the edition, subsequent to the publication of the Uniform Edition of 1908.

4 HUSKS, WANDERING AND THE NATION

1. *The Works of William Blake*, ed. Edwin John Ellis and William Butler Yeats, 3 vols (London, 1893), II, p.120.
2. *Ibid.*, I, p.241.
3. *Ibid.*, III, 'Four Zoas', Night IX, line 648.
4. Desirée Hirst, *Hidden Riches: Traditional symbolism from the Renaissance to Blake* (London, 1964), p.63.
5. Gershom G. Scholem, *Major Trends in Jewish Mysticism*, 3rd revd edn (New York, 1973), pp.265–6.
6. Christian Ginsburg, quoted in Hirst, *Hidden Riches*, p.63.
7. Scholem, *Major Trends*, p.260.
8. *Ibid.*, p.261.
9. *Ibid.*, p.265.
10. *Ibid.*, pp.237, 239.
11. *Ibid.*, p.266.
12. Kathleen Raine, 'Yeats, the Tarot and the Golden Dawn', *Yeats the Initiate*, p.191.
13. [W. B. Yeats], 'Is the Order of the R.R. and A.C. to remain a magical order?' Quoted by Kathleen Raine in *Yeats the Initiate*, p.245.
14. Allen R. Grossman, *Poetic Knowledge in the Early Yeats: A study of* The Wind Among the Reeds (Charlottesville, N.C., 1969), pp.129–30.
15. *Ibid.*, p.130.
16. *Ibid.*
17. *Ibid.*
18. *Druid Craft: the writing of* The Shadowy Waters, ed. Michael J. Sidnell, George P. Mayhew and David R. Clark (Amherst, Mass., 1971), p.38.

5 ROSE, MIRROR AND HEM

1. John Unterecker, *A Reader's Guide to W. B. Yeats* (London, 1975), p.72.
2. A. E. Waite, *The Real History of the Rosicrucians* (London, 1887), p.434.
3. Isidore Epstein, *Judaism* (Harmondsworth, 1959), p.137.
4. *Ibid.*, p.238.
5. Waite, *The Real History*, p.24.
6. Leon Surette, *A Light from Eleusis: A study of Ezra Pound's* Cantos (Oxford, 1979), pp.40–1.
7. Robert Macoy, *A General History, Cyclopaedia, and Dictionary of Freemasonry* (New York, 1869), pp.133–7.

8. Colin Wilson, *Aleister Crowley: The nature of the beast* (Wellingborough, 1987), pp.118–34.
9. *Ibid.*, p.41.
10. Macoy, *A General History*, p.170.
11. *c.*1874. Reproduced in Bram Dijkstra, *Idols of Perversity: Fantasies of feminine evil in fin-de-siècle culture* (New York and Oxford, 1986), p.152.
12. Richard Ellmann, *Oscar Wilde* (London, 1987), pp.66–73.
13. *Ibid.*, pp.70–1.
14. Oscar Wilde, *Poems*, 12th edn (London, 1913), p.45.
15. *Ibid.*, p.54.
16. *Ibid.*, pp.55–9, p.55.
17. *Ibid.*, p.59.
18. Reproduced in Dijkstra, *Idols*, p.15.
19. See Diana Basham, *Trial of Woman* (London and Basingstoke, 1992), pp.209–10, 270–8.
20. Donald Masterman and Edward O'Shea, 'Code breaking and myth making: the Ellis–Yeats edition of Blake's *Works*', in Warwick Gould (ed.), *Yeats Annual No. 3* (1985), p.75.

6 *FIN-DE-SIÈCLE* FENIANISM: *THE WIND AMONG THE REEDS*

1. For up-to-date research on the biographical background to the poems, see John Harwood, *Olivia Shakespear and W. B. Yeats* (Basingstoke and London, 1989).
2. See Peter Kuch, *Yeats and A.E.: 'The antagonism that unites dear friends'* (Gerrards Cross and Totowa, N.J., 1986), pp.128–71.
3. W. B. Yeats, *The Wind Among the Reeds*, 6th edn (London, 1911), corrected reprint of 1st or 1899 edn, pp.61–2; future references to this volume will be given as page numbers in the text following the quotation.
4. Henri d'Arbois de Jubainville, *The Irish Mythological Cycle and Celtic Mythology*, trans. Richard Irvine Best (Dublin, 1903), p.190. Originally published as *Cours de littérature celtique*, vol. II (Paris, 1883).
5. *Ibid.*, p.191.
6. K. Meyer and A. Nutt, *Voyage of Bran* (London, 1895), I, p.52.
7. See Dáithí O hOgáin, *Fionn mac Cumhaill: Images of the Gaelic hero* (Dublin, 1988), p.21.
8. Meyer and Nutt, *Voyage of Bran*, I, p.139.
9. Allen R. Grossman, *Poetic Knowledge in the Early Yeats: A study of* The Wind Among the Reeds (Charlottesville, N.C., 1969).
10. *Silva Gadelica: A collection of tales in Irish*, ed. and trans. Standish Hayes O'Grady, 2 vols (London and Edinburgh, 1892), II, pp.172–3.
11. Grossman, *Poetic Knowledge*, pp.51–62.
12. *Ibid.*, pp.52–3.
13. T. W. Rolleston, *The Adventures of Finn Mac Cumhal and Other Stories of Ancient Ireland* (Dublin and Cork, 1979), p.15.

7 THE MASKS OF DIFFERENCE

1. Cf. Joseph Adams, *Yeats and the Masks of Syntax* (London and Basingstoke, 1984), p.4.
2. Donald Davie, *Purity of Diction in English Verse*, 2nd edn (London, 1967), p.59.
3. T. R. Henn, 'The rhetoric of Yeats', *In Excited Reverie: A centenary tribute to W. B. Yeats 1865–1939*, ed. A. Norman Jeffares and K. W. G. Cross (London and New York, 1965), pp.102–22.
4. *Literary Essays of Ezra Pound*, ed. and intro. T. S. Eliot (London, 1954), p.379.
5. Richard Ellmann, *Eminent Domain: Yeats among Wilde, Joyce, Pound, Eliot and Auden* (London, Oxford and New York, 1970), p.66.
6. Adelyn Dougherty, *A Study of Rhythmic Structure in the Verse of William Butler Yeats* (The Hague and Paris, 1973), p.41.
7. *Ibid.*
8. *Ibid.*, p.27.
9. William Morris, *The Earthly Paradise: A poem* (London, 1903), p.427. First edn 1868–70.
10. Dougherty, *Study*, p.22.
11. Derek Attridge, *The Rhythms of English Poetry* (London and New York, 1982), pp.9–17. Casts doubt on the usefulness of the term 'foot'. And see Richard Taylor, 'Metrical variation in Yeats's verse', in Warwick Gould (ed.), *Yeats Annual No. 8* (1991), pp.21–38; this attempts to apply the Attridge model to Yeats, but the results (if that is the word for them) are completely inconclusive (pp.37–8).
12. Dougherty, *Study*, p.94. See Steven Putzel, *Reconstructing Yeats: The Secret Rose and The Wind Among the Reeds* (Dublin and Totowa, N.J., 1986), pp.147–66 for a detailed discussion of metre in *The Wind*.
13. Allen Grossman, *Poetic Knowledge in the Early Yeats* (Charlottesville, N.C., 1969), p.14.
14. *Ibid.*, p.15.
15. Dougherty, *Study*, p.59.
16. Davie, *Purity of Diction*, p.59.
17. Dougherty, *Study*, p.94.
18. Marjorie Perloff, *Rhyme and Meaning in the Poetry of Yeats* (The Hague and Paris, 1970), p.19.
19. Austin Clarke, *Selected Poems*, ed. Thomas Kinsella (Mountrath, 1984), p.5.
20. Perloff, *Rhyme*, p.35.
21. Cf. Ronald Schuchard, 'The minstrel in the theatre: Arnold, Chaucer, and Yeats's new spiritual democracy', in R. Finneran (ed.), *Yeats Annual No. 2* (1983), pp.3–24.
22. 1895 saw the republication of Thomas Taylor's translation of *Selected Works* of Plotinus, and also of his translation of Plotinus's *An Essay on the Beautiful*. Yeats refers to Plotinus in a review of A.E.'s poems published in *The Sketch* in 1898 (*UP*, II, p.112).

23. Plotinus, *An Essay on the Beautiful*, trans. Thomas Taylor (London, 1794), p.ix.
24. *Ibid.*, pp.42–3.
25. R. T. Wallis, *Neoplatonism* (London, 1972), p.6.
26. For a discussion of these aspects of Blake's thought, see Edward Larrissy, *William Blake*, (Oxford, 1985), pp.70–95.
27. Quoted in Otto Bohlman, *Yeats and Nietzsche: An exploration of major Nietzschean echoes in the writings of William Butler Yeats* (London and Basingstoke, 1982), p.84.
28. Nicholas Flammel, *His Exposition of the Hieroglyphical Figures Which he caused to be Painted* (1624), ed. W. Westcott (London, 1889), p.vi.
29. Harwood, *Yeats and Olivia Shakespear*, p.65.
30. Flammel, *His Exposition*, p.vi.

8 FRAMING IRELAND

1. Ezra Pound and Ernest Fenollosa, *The Classic Noh Theatre of Japan* (New York, 1959), p.64. See also Akhtar Qamber, *Yeats and the Noh* (New York and Tokyo), p.46; and Steven Putzel, 'Poetic ritual and audience response: Yeats and the Nō', *Yeats and Postmodernism*, ed. Orr, p.123.
2. Qamber, *Yeats and the Noh*, p.50.
3. Richard Ellmann, *Yeats: The man and the masks*, new rev. edn (Oxford, 1979), p.193.
4. *Ibid.*, pp.194–7.
5. Qamber, *Yeats and the Noh*, p.52.
6. Joseph Hone, *W. B. Yeats 1865–1939*, reprint of 2nd 1962 edn (Harmondsworth, 1971), p.52.
7. See, for instance, James Hardiman, *Irish Minstrelsy, or Bardic Remains of Ireland, with English Poetical Translations*, 2 vols (London, 1831), vol. I, p.xxviii, ref. to Memoirs of Marquis of Clanricarde.
8. Cairns Craig, *Yeats, Eliot, Pound and the Politics of Poetry* (London, 1982), pp.72–111.
9. *Ibid.*, p.36.
10. *Ibid.*, pp.38–9.
11. *Ibid.*, pp.78–82.
12. Terry Eagleton, 'Politics and sexuality in W. B. Yeats', Lecture delivered to the Yeats Summer School, Sligo, 1985, *Crane Bag*, 9:2 (1985), p.139.
13. *Ibid.*, p.138.
14. *Ibid.*
15. *Ibid.*, p.139.
16. Gloria Kline, *The Last Courtly Lover: Yeats and the idea of woman* (Cambridge, Mass., 1983).
17. Cf. Craig, *Yeats, Eliot and Pound*, pp.95–104.
18. Cf. Frank Kermode, *Romantic Image* (London, 1957), p.34.
19. Cf. Stan Smith, 'Porphyry's cup', in W. Gould (ed.), *Yeats Annual No. 5*, pp.15–45.

20. Jahan Ramazani, *Yeats and the Poetry of Death: Elegy, self-elegy and the sublime* (New Haven, CT and London, 1990), p.41.
21. Richard J. Finneran, 'The manuscripts of Yeats's "Reprisals" ', in D. C. Greetham and W. Speed Hill (eds), *Text 2* (1985), pp.69–77.
22. Carmel Jordan, *A Terrible Beauty: The Easter Rebellion and Yeats's 'Great Tapestry'* (Lewisburg, 1987), p.42.
23. *Ibid.*
24. Nina Auerbach, *Woman and the Demon: The life of a Victorian myth* (Cambridge, Mass. and London, 1982), p.23.
25. Cf. Declan Kiberd, 'Yeats, childhood and exile', in Paul Hyland and Neil Sammels (eds), *Irish Writing* (Basingstoke and London, 1991), pp.141–4.

9 REFLECTIONS ON YEATSIAN OCCULTISM

1. Jon Stallworthy, *Between the Lines: W. B. Yeats's poetry in the making* (Oxford, 1963), pp.60–4.
2. Warwick Gould, 'A lesson for the circumspect', in Peter Caracciolo (ed.), *Arabian Nights and English Literature* (Basingstoke and London, 1988), p.244.
3. *Ibid.*, pp.256, 273.
4. *Ibid.*, p.250.
5. Richard Ellmann, *Yeats: the man and the masks*, 2nd edn (Oxford, 1979), p.200.
6. Gayatri Chakravorty Spivak, 'Finding feminist readings: Dante–Yeats', in Ira Konigsberg (ed.), *American Criticism in the Poststructuralist Age* (Michigan, 1981), p.47n.
7. S. B. Bushrui, 'Yeats's Arabic interests', in A. Jeffares and K. G. W. Cross (eds), *In Excited Reverie* (London and Basingstoke, 1965), pp.295, 296–7.
8. *Ibid.*, p.306.
9. *Ibid.*, p.297.
10. C. H. Josten, 'Robert Fludd's theory of geomancy and his experiences at Avignon in the winter of 1601–1602', *Journal of the Warburg and Courtauld Institutes*, 27 (1964), pp.327–35.
11. A. E. Waite, *Real History of Rosicrucians*, (London, 1887), pp.283–307.
12. J. B. Craven, *Dr. Robert Fludd, His Life and Works* (Kirkwall, 1902); Rev. William Wynn Westcott, *In Memory of Robert Fludd* (London, 1907).
13. Isaac D'Israeli, 'The Rosacrusian Fludd', *Amenities of Literature* (London, 1842), pp.642–9.
14. Keith Thomas, *Religion and the Decline of Magic* (London, 1971), p.215.
15. Robert Fludd, *Utriusque Cosmi Maioris scilicet et Minoris Metaphysica, Physica, atque technica Historia*, 2 vols (Oppenheim, 1617–19); and *Philosophia sacra et vere Christiana seue Meteorologica Cosmica* (Frankfurt, 1626).

16. *A Vision* (1925), p.xvii (in *AVA*). 'Hominorum' was later corrected to 'Hominum'.
17. *AVA* Notes, p.1 contains very full information.
18. *The Poetical Works of Thomas Moore*, 2 vols (Paris, 1835), II, p.343.
19. P. W. Joyce, *A Smaller Social History of Ancient Ireland*, 2nd edn (Dublin, 1908), p.192.
20. Seamus Deane (ed.), *The Field Day Anthology of Irish Writing*, 3 vols, assoc. eds. Andrew Carpenter and Jonathan Williams (Derry, 1991), I, pp.1186–1200.
21. *Ibid.*, p.1185.
22. George Mills Harper, *The Making of Yeats's* A Vision: *A study of the Automatic Script*, 2 vols (London and Basingstoke, 1987) I, pp.10–11.
23. *Ibid.*
24. *The Making*, p.12.
25. *Ibid.*, p.16.
26. *Ibid.*, p.144.
27. Edwin Ellis and W. B. Yeats, *The Works of William Blake*, I (London, 1893), p.288.
28. Harold Bloom, *Yeats* (New York, 1970), p.76.
29. Jacques Derrida, 'The double session', *Dissemination*, trans. Barbara Johnson (Chicago, 1981), pp.173–285.
30. Spivak, 'Finding feminist readings', p.50.
31. *Ibid.*
32. *Ibid.*, pp.49, 50.
33. *Ibid.*, p.51.

10 WALLS OF THE TOWER

1. Charles Altieri, 'From a comic to a tragic sense of language in Yeats's mature poetry', *MLQ* 33 (1972), p.156–9; Daniel A. Harris, *Yeats, Coole Parke and Ballylee* (Baltimore and London, 1974), p.95.
2. Harris, *Coole Park*, p.9.
3. Mary Henley and Liam Miller, *Thoor Ballylee, home of William Butler Yeats*, foreword T. R. Henn, 2nd rev. edn (Dublin, 1977), p.9.
4. *Ibid.*, p.10.
5. *Ibid.*
6. Daniel Corkery, *The Hidden Ireland: A study of Gaelic Munster in the eighteenth century*, 2nd edn (Dublin and London, 1967), pp.42–67.
7. *Ibid.*, p.65–6.
8. *Ibid.*, pp.68–94.
9. *Ibid.*, p.66.
10. *Ibid.*, pp.55–6.
11. Edward MacLysaght, *Irish Life in the Seventeenth Century*, 3rd edn (Dublin, 1979), p.94.
12. Kathleen Raine, 'Yeats, the Tarot and the Golden Dawn', *Yeats the Initiate* (Dublin and London, 1986), pp.238–44.

13. Robert Fludd, *Utriusque Cosmi Maioris scilicet et Minoris Metaphysica, Physica, atque technica Historia* (Oppenheim, 1617–19), I, ii, p.168.
14. Elizabeth Cullingford, 'How Jacques Molay got up the Tower', *ELH* 50 (1983), pp.767–8.
15. *Ibid.*, p.767.
16. *Ibid.*, p.768.
17. *Ibid.*, p.771.
18. *Ibid.*, p.772.
19. Antony Coleman, 'The Big House, Yeats, and the Irish context', in Warwick Gould (ed.), *Yeats Annual No. 3* (1985), p.33; Marjorie Perloff, 'Between hatred and desire: sexuality and subterfuge in "A Prayer for My Daughter" ', in Warwick Gould (ed.), *Yeats Annual No. 7* (1990), p.39.
20. P. W. Joyce, *A Smaller Social History of Ancient Ireland*, 2nd edn (Dublin, 1908), pp.242–3.
21. Edward Gibbon, *The Decline and Fall of the Roman Empire*, 6 vols (London, 1910), IV, p.205.
22. Eileen Bigland, *Lord Byron* (London, 1956), p.24.
23. Thomas Docherty relates the theme of rootedness to the question of poetic tradition as it exerts itself through the influence of Keats in this poem: *After Theory: Postmodernism/postmarxism* (London, 1990), p.184.
24. Sir Samuel Ferguson, *Poems* (Dublin and London [1916]), pp.60–1.
25. Eugene O'Curry, *Manners and Customs of the Ancient Irish*, II (Dublin, 1873), p.190. Philip L. Marcus is a critic who has realised the importance of Amergin's poem not just as a source of ideas about Druidic lore, but as contributing to Yeats's conception of what it meant to participate in the Irish bardic tradition; see his *Yeats's Artistic Power* (London and Basingstoke, 1992), pp.50–61.
26. Cited by A. Norman Jeffares in 'The Byzantine poems of W. B. Yeats', *Review of English Studies*, 22 (January 1946), p.45. See also Curtis Bradford, 'Yeats's Byzantium poems: a study of their development', *Yeats: A collection of critical essays*, ed. John Unterecker (Englewood Cliffs, N. J., 1963), pp.129–30; and Jon Stallworthy, *Between the Lines* (Oxford, 1963), pp.95–6. In more general terms, for some useful approaches which often employ a consideration of source material, see Richard Finneran (ed.), *The Byzantium Poems* (Columbus, 1970).
27. Benedict Fitzpatrick, *Ireland and the Making of Britain* (New York and London, 1922), pp.10–11.
28. *Ibid.*, p.18.
29. Cited in A. Norman Jeffares, *A New Commentary on the Poems of W. B. Yeats*, 2nd edn (London and Basingstoke, 1984), p.214.
30. See Robert N. Essick and Morton D. Paley, *Robert Blair's* The Grave *Illustrated by William Blake: A study with facsimile* (London, 1982).
31. Joost Daalder, 'Some possible sources for "Sailing to Byzantium": a reconsideration', *The Yeats–Eliot Review* 9:1 (Fall 1987), pp.11–14.
32. George Mills Harper, ' "Out of a medium's mouth": Yeats's theory of "Transference" and Keats's "Ode to a Nightingale" ', in Richard J. Finneran (ed.), *Yeats: An Annual of Critical and Textual Studies*, 1 (1983), pp.17–32; for 'attached', *see* p.32.

33. *Ibid.*, p.31.
34. Frank Kermode, *Romantic Image* (London, 1957), p.88.
35. Ian Fletcher, 'Yeats's "Leda and the Swan" as iconic poem', *W. B. Yeats and his Contemporaries* (Brighton, 1987), p.227.
36. Leo Spitzer, 'On Yeats's poem "Leda and the Swan" ', *Modern Philology* 51 (1954), pp.271–6.
37. Bernard Levine, *The Dissolving Image: The spiritual-esthetic development of W. B. Yeats* (Detroit, 1970), pp.114–19.
38. As pointed out and expounded by Maud Ellmann, 'Daughters of the Swan', *m/f*, Nos 11 & 12 (1986), pp.49–62; and see Jacques Derrida, 'The double session', *Dissemination*, trans. Barbara Johnson (Chicago, 1981), pp.173–285.

11 PROFANE PERFECTION

1. Friedrich Nietzsche, *Thus Spake Zarathustra: A book for all and none*, trans. Thomas Common (Edinburgh and London, 1914), p.396. Vol. XI of *Complete Works*, ed. O. Levy (1909–13). Reprint of 1909 edn.
2. Denis Donoghue, *Yeats* (Glasgow, 1971), p.65.
3. *Ibid.*, p.57 gives this quotation.
4. See Deirdre Toomey, 'Labyrinths: Yeats and Maud Gonne', in Deirdre Toomey (ed.), *Yeats Annual No. 9* (1992), pp.95–131.
5. C. L. Innes, 'Yeats's female voices: Crazy Jane and other women in *The Winding Stair and Other Poems*', *Text & Context* (Autumn 1988), p.58.
6. Barbara Hardy, 'The wildness of Crazy Jane', *Yeats, Sligo and Ireland: Essays to mark the twenty-first Yeats International Summer School* (Gerrards Cross, 1980), p.31.
7. Warwick Gould, ' "What is the explanation of it all": Yeats's "little poem about nothing" ', in Warwick Gould (ed.), *Yeats Annual No. 5* (1987), pp.212–13.
8. F. A. C. Wilson, *W. B. Yeats and Tradition* (London, 1958), p.248. See the whole discussion for some interesting possible sources: pp.244–52.
9. For a valuable discussion of the idea of art in *New Poems* and [Last Poems], see J. R. Mulryne, 'The "Last Poems" ', in Denis Donoghue and J. R. Mulryne (eds), *An Honoured Guest: New essays on W. B. Yeats* (London, 1965), p.124–42.
10. Brendan Kennelly (ed.), *Penguin Book of Irish Verse* (Harmondsworth, 1970), p.69.
11. Seán O. Tuama (ed.), *An Duanaire: 1600–1900: Poems of the dispossessed*, with trans. by Thomas Kinsella (Mountrath, 1981), p.166. Brendon Kennelly (ed.), *Penguin Book of Irish Verse* (Harmondsworth, 1970), p.75.
12. Helen Vendler, 'Technique in the earlier poems of Yeats', in Warwick Gould (ed.), *Yeats Annual No. 8* (Basingstoke and London, 1991), p.9.

BIBLIOGRAPHY

PRIMARY TEXTS AND WORKS OF REFERENCE

Allt, Peter and Russel K. Alspach (eds), *The Variorum Edition of the Poems of W. B. Yeats* (New York, 1957; rev. 1966).

Alspach, Russel K. (ed.), *The Variorum Edition of the Plays of W. B. Yeats* (London, 1966).

Ellis, Edwin and William Butler Yeats (eds), *The Works of William Blake*, 3 vols (London, 1893).

Frayne, John P. (ed.), *Uncollected Prose by W. B. Yeats*, Vol. I (London, 1970).

Frayne, John P. and Colton Johnson (eds), *Uncollected Prose by W. B. Yeats*, Vol. II (London and Basingstoke, 1975).

Harper, George Mills and Walter Kelly Hood (eds), *A Critical Edition of W. B. Yeats's* A Vision *(1925)* (Basingstoke and London, 1978).

Jeffares, A. Norman, *A New Commentary on the Poems of W. B. Yeats* (London and Basingstoke, 1984).

Kelly, John and Eric Domville (eds), *The Collected Letters of W. B. Yeats*, *Vol. I, 1865–1895* (Oxford, 1986).

Marcus, Phillip L., Warwick Gould and Michael J. Sidnell (eds), *The Secret Rose, Stories by W. B. Yeats: A variorum edition* (Ithaca, N. Y. and London, 1981).

Sidnell, Michael J., George P. Mayhew and David R. Clarke (eds), *Druid Craft: The writing of* The Shadowy Waters (Amherst, Mass., 1971).

Wade, Allan (ed.) *The Letters of W. B. Yeats* (London, 1954).

Yeats, W. B. (ed., rev.), *A Book of Irish Verse Selected from Modern Writers with an Introduction and Notes* (London, 1900).

Yeats, W. B., *The Wind Among the Reeds*, 6th edn (London, 1911).

Yeats, W. B., *A Vision* (London, 1937).

Yeats, W. B., *Autobiographies* (London, 1955, 1970 reprint).

Yeats, W. B., *Mythologies* (London, 1959).

Yeats, W. B., *Essays and Introductions* (London, 1961).

Yeats, W. B., *Explorations*, selected by Mrs W. B. Yeats (London, 1962).

Yeats, W. B., *Memoirs*, ed. Denis Donoghue (London and Basingstoke, 1972).

Yeats, W. B. (ed.), *Fairy and Folk Tales of Ireland*, foreword by Kathleen Raine (London, 1979). First published as *Fairy and Folk Tales of the Irish Peasantry* (London, 1888) and *Irish Fairy Tales* (London, 1892).

Yeats, W. B., *The Early Poetry. Vol.I: 'Mosada' and 'The Island of Statues':*
Manuscript materials including the author's final text, ed. George Bornstein (Ithaca, N. Y., 1981).

Yeats, W. B., *The Poems: A New Edition*, ed. Richard J. Finneran, 2nd edn (London and Basingstoke, 1989).

Yeats, W. B., *Letters to the New Island: A new edition*, ed. George Bornstein and Hugh Witemeyer (Basingstoke and London, 1989).

Yeats, W. B., *Writings on Irish Folklore, Legend and Myth*, ed. Robert Welch (Harmondsworth, 1993).

SELECT BIBLIOGRAPHY OF OTHER WORKS CONSULTED

Adams, Hazard, *The Book of Yeats's Poems* (Tallahasee, Fa, 1990).

Adams, Joseph, *Yeats and the Masks of Syntax* (London and Basingstoke, 1984).

Adams, Steve L. and George Mills Harper, 'The manuscript of "Leo Africanus" ', in Richard J. Finneran, *Yeats Annual No. 1* (1982), pp.3–47.

Alspach, Russel K., 'Some sources of Yeats's *The Wanderings of Oisin*', *PMLA*, 58 (1943), pp.849–66.

Altieri, Charles, 'From a comic to a tragic sense of language in Yeats's mature poetry', *MLQ*, 33 (1972), pp.156–71.

Anon., 'Early Irish history – the O'Briens', *The Gentleman's Magazine* (August 1860), pp.111–18.

Arbois de Jubainville, Henri d', *The Irish Mythological Cycle and Celtic Mythology*, trans. Richard Irvine Best (Dublin, 1903). Originally Vol. II (Paris, 1883) of *Cours de Littérature Celtique*.

Arnold, Matthew, *The Study of Celtic Literature* (London, 1905).

Attridge, Derek, *The Rhythms of English Poetry* (London and New York, 1982).

Auerbach, Nina, *Woman and the Demon: The life of a Victorian myth* (Cambridge, Mass. and London, 1982).

Barrell, John, *The Infection of Thomas De Quincey: A psychopathology of imperialism* (New Haven and London, 1991).

Barrett, Michèle, 'Some different meanings of the concept of "difference": feminist theory and the concept of ideology', in Elizabeth Meese and Alice Parker (eds), *The Difference Within: Feminism and critical theory* (Amsterdam and Philadelphia, 1989), pp.37–48.

Basham, Diana, *The Trial of Woman: Feminism and the occult sciences in Victorian literature and society* (London and Basingstoke, 1992).

Bigland, Eileen, *Lord Byron* (London, 1956).

Blake, William: *See* Ellis, Edwin (under Primary Texts above); *see also* Erdman, David V., below.

Blavatsky, H. P., *The Secret Doctrine*, 2 vols (London, 1888).

Bloom, Harold, *Yeats* (New York, 1970).

Bohlmann, Otto, *Yeats and Nietzsche: An exploration of major Nietzschean echoes in the writings of William Butler Yeats* (London and Basingstoke, 1982).

Bradford, Curtis, 'Yeats's Byzantium poems: a study of their development', in John Unterecker (ed.), *Yeats: A Collection of Critical Essays* (Englewood Cliffs, N.J., 1963), pp.93–130.

Brown, Malcolm, *Sir Samuel Ferguson* (Lewisburg, 1973).

Brown, Terence, *Ireland's Literature: Selected essays* (Mullingar and Totowa, N.J., 1978).

Bushrui, S. B., 'Yeats's Arabic interests' in A. Norman Jeffares and K. G. W. Cross (eds.), *In Excited Reverie* (London and Basingstoke, 1965), pp.280–314.

Cairns, David and Shaun Richards, *Writing Ireland: Colonialism, nationalism and culture* (Manchester, 1988).

Clarke, Austin, *Selected Poems*, ed. Thomas Kinsella (Mountrath, 1984).

Coleman, Antony, 'The Big House, Yeats, and the Irish context', in Warwick Gould, *Yeats Annual No. 3* (1985), pp.33–52.

Corkery, Daniel, *The Hidden Ireland: A study of Gaelic Munster in the eighteenth century*, 2nd edn (Dublin and London, 1967).

Cowley, Abraham, *Essays, Plays and Sundry Verses* (Cambridge, 1906).

Craig, Cairns, *Yeats, Eliot, Pound and the Politics of Poetry* (London, 1981).

Craven, J. B., *Dr. Robert Fludd, His Life and Works* (Kirkwall, 1902).

Croker, Thomas Crofton, *Popular Songs of Ireland* (London, [1887]).

Cullingford, Elizabeth, 'How Jacques Molay got up the Tower: Yeats and the Irish civil war', *ELH*, 50 (1983), pp.763–89.

Cullingford, Elizabeth, *Yeats, Ireland and Fascism* (London and Basingstoke, 1981).

Daalder, Joost, 'Some possible sources for "Sailing to Byzantium": a reconsideration', *The Yeats–Eliot Review*, vol. IX, no. 1 (Fall 1987), pp.1–16.

Daly, John and Edward Walsh, *Reliques of Irish Jacobite Poetry* (Dublin, 1844).

Davie, Donald, *Purity of Diction in English Verse*, 2nd edn (London, 1967).

Deane, Seamus, *Celtic Revivals: Essays in modern Irish literature 1880–1980* (London, 1987).

Deane, Seamus (ed.) *The Field Day Anthology of Irish Writing*, assoc. eds Andrew Carpenter and Jonathan Williams, 3 vols (Derry, 1991).

Derrida, Jacques, *Dissemination*, trans. Barbara Johnson (Chicago, 1981).

Dijkstra, Bram, *Idols of Perversity: Fantasies of feminine evil in fin-de-siècle culture* (New York and Oxford, 1986).

D'Israeli, Isaac, 'The Rosacrusian Fludd', *Amenities of Literature* (London, 1842), pp.642–9.

Docherty, Thomas, *After Theory: Postmodernism/postmarxism* (London and New York, 1990).

Donoghue, Denis and J. R. Mulryne (eds), *An Honoured Guest: New essays on W. B. Yeats* (London, 1965).

Donoghue, Denis, *Yeats* (Glasgow, 1971).

Dorfman, Deborah, *Blake in the Nineteenth Century* (New Haven, CT and London, 1969).

Dougherty, Adelyn, *A Study of Rhythmic Structure in the Verse of William Butler Yeats* (The Hague and Paris, 1973).

Eagleton, Terry, 'Politics and sexuality in W. B. Yeats', *Crane Bag*, 9:2 (1985), pp.138–42.

Eliot, T. S. (ed.), *Literary Essays of Ezra Pound* (London, 1954).

Ellmann, Maud, 'Daughters of the swan', *m/f*, nos 11 and 12 (1986), pp.119–62.

Ellmann, Richard, *Eminent Domain: Yeats among Wilde, Joyce, Pound, Eliot and Auden* (London and New York, 1970).

Ellmann, Richard, *Yeats: The man and the masks*, 2nd edn (Oxford, 1979).

Ellmann, Richard, *Oscar Wilde* (London, 1987).

Epstein, Isidore, *Judaism* (Harmondsworth, 1959).

Erdman, David V. (ed.), *The Complete Poetry and Prose of William Blake*, newly revd (New York, 1988).

'Erionnach' [G. Sigerson], *The Poets and Poetry of Munster: A selection of Irish songs by the poets of the last century*, 2nd series (Dublin, 1860).

Essick, Robert N. and Morton D. Paley, *Robert Blair's* The Grave *Illustrated by William Blake: A study with facsimile* (London, 1982).

Ferguson, Sir Samuel, *Poems of Sir Samuel Ferguson*, intro. by Alfred Perceval Graves (Dublin and London, n.d. [1916?]).

Finneran, Richard J. (ed.), *The Byzantium Poems* (Columbus, Ohio, 1970).

Finneran, Richard J. (ed.), *Yeats Annual No. 1* (1982).

Finneran, Richard J. (ed.), *Yeats Annual No. 2* (1983).

Finneran, Richard J. (ed.), *Yeats: An annual of critical and textual studies*, 1 (1983).

Finneran, Richard J. (ed.), *Yeats: An annual of critical and textual studies*, 8 (1990).

Finneran, Richard J., 'The manuscripts of W. B. Yeats's "Reprisals" ', *Text: Transactions of the Society for Textual Scholarship*, 2 (1990), ed. D. C. Greetham and W. Speed Hill, pp.269–77.

Fitzpatrick, Benedict, *Ireland and the Making of Britain* (New York and London, 1922).

Fletcher, Ian, *W. B. Yeats and His Contemporaries* (Brighton, 1987).

Fludd, Robert, *Philosophia sacra et vere Christiana seue Meteorologica Cosmica* (Frankfurt, 1626).

Fludd, Robert, *Utriusque Cosmi Maioris scilicet et Minoris Metaphysica, Physica, atque technica Historia*, 2 vols (Oppenheim, 1617–19).

Foster, Roy, *Modern Ireland, 1600–1972* (London, 1988).

Foster, R. F. 'Protestant magic: W. B. Yeats and the spell of Irish history' (Chatterton Lecture 1989), *Proceedings of the British Academy*, 75 (1989), pp.243–66.

Freud, Sigmund, *Standard Edition of the Complete Psychological Works of Sigmund Freud*, trans. under general ed. James Strachey, 24 vols (London, 1953–74).

Gardner, Alice, *Studies in John the Scot (Erigena): A philosopher of the Dark Ages* (London, 1900).

Gibbon, Edward, *The Decline and Fall of the Roman Empire*, 6 vols (London, 1910).

Gilbert, R. A., *The Golden Dawn: Twilight of the magicians* (Wellingborough, 1983).

Gonne, Maud. *See* MacBride, Maud Gonne.

Gould, Warwick (ed.), *Yeats Annual No. 3* (1985).

Gould, Warwick (ed.), *Yeats Annual No. 5* (1987).

Gould, Warwick, ' "What is the explanation of it all?": Yeats's "little poem about nothing" ', in Gould (1987), pp.212–13.

Gould, Warwick, ' "A lesson for the circumspect": W. B. Yeats's two versions of *A Vision* and the *Arabian Nights*', in Peter L. Caracciolo (ed.), *The Arabian Nights in English Literature: Studies in the reception of The Thousand and One Nights into British culture* (Basingstoke and London, 1988), pp.244–80.

Gould, Warwick (ed.), *Yeats Annual No. 7* (1990).

Gould, Warwick (ed.), *Yeats Annual No. 8* (1991).

Gould, Warwick, *see also* Reeves, Marjorie.

Grannell, Fergal, 'Early Irish ecclesiastical studies', in Hurley, pp.39–50.

Greene, David, 'The Irish language movement', in Hurley, pp.110–19.

Grossman, Allan R., *Poetic Knowledge in the Early Yeats: A study of* The Wind Among the Reeds (Charlottesville, N.C., 1969).

Guiney, Louise Imogen (ed.), with a study, *James Clarence Mangan, His Selected Poems* (London, Boston and New York, 1897).

Hanley, Mary and Liam Miller, *Thoor Ballylee, Home of William Butler Yeats*, foreword T. R. Henn, 2nd revd edn (Dublin, 1977).

Hardiman, James, *Irish Minstrelsy, or Bardic Remains of Ireland, with English Poetical Translations*, 2 vols (London, 1831).

Hardy, Barbara, 'The wildness of Crazy Jane', *Yeats, Sligo and Ireland: Essays to mark the twenty-first Yeats International Summer School* (Gerrards Cross, 1980), pp.31–55.

Harper, George Mills, *Yeats's Golden Dawn* (London and Basingstoke, 1974).

Harper, George Mills, ' "Out of a medium's mouth": Yeats's theory of "transference" and Keats's "Ode to a Nightingale" ', *Yeats: An annual of critical and textual studies*, ed. Richard J. Finneran, vol. I (1983), pp.17–32.

Harper, George Mills, *The Making of Yeats's* A Vision: *A study of the Automatic Script*, 2 vols (London and Basingstoke, 1987).

Harper, George Mills, *see also* Adams, Steve L.

Harris, Daniel A., *Yeats, Coole Park and Ballylee* (Baltimore and London, 1974).

Harwood, John, *Olivia Shakespear and W. B. Yeats* (Basingstoke and London, 1989).

Henn, T. R., 'The rhetoric of Yeats', in A. Norman Jeffares and K. G. W. Cross (eds), *In Excited Reverie* (London and Basingstoke, 1965), pp.102–22.

Hirst, Désirée, *Hidden Riches: Traditional symbolism from the Renaissance to Blake* (London, 1964).

Hone, Joseph, *W. B. Yeats, 1865–1939*, reprint of 2nd or 1962 edn (Harmondsworth, 1971).

Howe, Ellic, *The Magicians of the Golden Dawn: A documentary history of a magical order, 1887–1923* (London, 1972).

Hurley, Michael, S. J. (ed.), *Irish Anglicanism, 1869–1969* (Dublin, 1970).

Hutchinson, Thomas (ed.), *Shelley: Poetical works*, new edn, corrected by G. M. Matthews (London, 1970).

Huysmans, J. -K., *Là-Bas* (Paris, 1908).

Hyde, Douglas, *The Story of Early Gaelic Literature* (London, Dublin and New York, 1895).

Hyde, Douglas, *A Literary History of Ireland from Earliest Times to the Present Day* (London, 1899).

Hyland, Paul and Neil Sammels (eds), *Irish Writing: Exile and subversion* (Basingstoke and London, 1991).

Innes, C. L., 'Yeats's female voices: Crazy Jane and other women in *The Winding Stair and Other Poems*', *Text and Context* (Autumn 1988), pp.55–70.

Innes, C. L., ' "A voice in directing the affairs of Ireland": *L'Irlande libre, The Shan Van Vocht*, and *Bean na h-Eireann*', in Paul Hyland and Neil Sammels, *Irish Writing* (Basingstoke and London, 1991), pp.146–58.

Ivens, Michael, 'Yeats: the Faustian quest', *Books and Bookmen*, 17:3 (December 1971), pp.20–1.

Jeffares, A. Norman, 'The Byzantine poems of W. B. Yeats', *Review of English Studies*, 22 (January 1946), pp.44–52.

Jeffares, A. Norman, *W. B. Yeats: A new biography* (London, 1988).

Jeffares, A. Norman and Cross, K. G. W. (eds), *In Excited Reverie: A Centenary Tribute to William Butler Yeats 1865–1939* (London and Basingstoke, 1965).

Johnston, E. M., 'Problems common to both Protestant and Catholic Churches in eighteenth-century Ireland', in O. MacDonagh, W. F. Mandle and P. Travers (eds), *Irish Culture and Nationalism, 1750–1950* (London and Basingstoke, 1983), pp.14–39.

Jordan, Carmel, *A Terrible Beauty: The Easter Rebellion and Yeats's 'Great Tapestry'* (Lewisburg, 1987).

Josten, C. H., 'Robert Fludd's theory of geomancy and his experiences at Avignon in the winter of 1601–1602', *Journal of the Warburg and Courtauld Institutes*, 27 (1964), pp.327–35.

Joyce, P. W., *Old Celtic Romances* (London, 1879).

Joyce, P. W., *A Smaller Social History of Ireland*, 2nd edn (Dublin, 1908).

Jubainville, de. *See* Arbois de Jubainville Henri d'.

Kennelly, Brendan (ed.), *The Penguin Book of Irish Verse* (Harmondsworth, 1970).

Kermode, Frank, *Romantic Image* (London, 1957).

Kershner, R. B., 'Yeats/Bakhtin/orality/dyslexia', in Orr, pp.167–88.

Kiberd, Declan, 'Yeats, childhood and exile' in Paul Hyland and Neil Sammels (eds), *Irish Writing* (Basingstoke and London, 1991), pp.126–45.

Kinahan, Frank, *Yeats, Folklore, and Occultism: Contexts of the early work and thought* (Boston and London, 1988).

Kline, Gloria, *The Last Courtly Lover: Yeats and the idea of woman* (Cambridge, Mass., 1983).

Komesu, Okifumi, *The Double Perspective of Yeats's Aesthetic* (Gerrards Cross, 1984).

Larrissy, Edward, *William Blake* (Oxford, 1985).

Leerssen, Joseph Th., 'On the edge of Europe: Ireland in search of oriental roots, 1650–1850', *Comparative Criticism: An annual journal*, 8, ed. E. S. Shaffer (1986), pp.91–112.

Levine, Bernard, *The Dissolving Image: The spiritual–esthetic development of W. B. Yeats* (Detroit, 1970).

MacBride, Maud Gonne, *A Servant of the Queen: Reminiscences*, 2nd edn (London, 1974).

MacDonagh, Oliver, W. F. Mandle and Pauric Travers (eds), *Irish Culture and Nationalism, 1750–1950* (London and Basingstoke, 1983).

MacLysaght, Edward, *Irish Life in the Seventeenth Century*, 3rd edn (Dublin, 1979).

Macoy, Robert, *A General History, Cyclopaedia and Dictionary of Freemasonry* (New York, 1869).

Macpherson, James, *Introduction to the History of Great Britain and Ireland* (Dublin, 1771).

Mangan, James Clarence. *See* Guiney, Louise Imogen.

McCormack, W. J., *Sheridan Le Fanu and Victorian Ireland* (Oxford, 1980).

McCormack, W.J., *Ascendancy and Tradition in Anglo-Irish Literary History from 1789 to 1939* (Oxford, 1985).

McDowell, R. B., *The Church of Ireland, 1869–1969* (London and Boston, 1975).

McLynn, F. *The Jacobites* (London, 1985).

Mercier, Vivian, 'Victorian evangelicalism and the Anglo-Irish literary revival', in Peter Connolly (ed.) *Literature and the Changing Ireland* (Gerrards Cross and Totowa, N.J., 1982), pp.59–101.

Meyer, Kuno and Alfred Nutt, *The Voyage of Bran Son of Febal to the Land of the Living*, 2 vols (London, 1895, 1897).

Moore, Thomas, *The Poetical Works of Thomas Moore*, 2 vols (Paris, 1835).

Morris, William, *The Earthly Paradise: A poem* (London, 1903); first edn 1868–70.

Mulryne, J. R., 'The "Last Poems" ', in D. Donoghue and J. R. Mulryne (eds), *An Honoured Guest* (London, 1965), pp.124–42.

Murphy, William M., *The Yeats Family and the Pollexfens of Sligo*, with drawings by Jack Butler Yeats (Dublin, 1971).

Nietzsche, Friedrich, *Thus Spake Zarathustra: A book for all and none*, trans. Thomas Common (Edinburgh and London, 1914), vol. XI of *Complete Works*, ed. O. Levy (1909–13); reprint of 1st or 1909 edn.

O'Brien, Conor Cruise, 'Passion and cunning: an essay on the politics of W. B. Yeats', in A. Norman Jeffares and K. G. W. Cross (eds), *In Excited Reverie* (London and Basingstoke, 1965), pp.207–78.

O'Connor, Sir James, *History of Ireland, 1798–1924*, 2 vols (London, 1925).

O'Curry, Eugene, *Manners and Customs of the Ancient Irish*, 3 vols (Dublin, 1873).

215

O'Grady, Standish Hayes (ed. and trans.), *Silva Gadelica: A collection of tales in Irish*, 2 vols (London and Edinburgh, 1892).

O hOgáin, Dáithí, *Fionn mac Cumhaill: Images of the Gaelic hero* (Dublin, 1988).

O'Meara, John J., *Eriugena* (Oxford, 1988).

O Tuama, Seán (ed.), *An Duanaire: Poems of the dispossessed*, trans. Thomas Kinsella (Mountrath, 1981).

Orr, Leonard (ed.) *Yeats and Postmodernism* (Syracuse, N.Y., 1991).

Owen, A. L., *The Famous Druids: A survey of three centuries of English literature on the Druids* (Oxford, 1962).

Perloff, Marjorie, *Rhyme and Meaning in the Poetry of Yeats* (The Hague and Paris, 1970).

Perloff, Marjorie, 'Between hatred and desire: sexuality and subterfuge in "A Prayer for my Daughter" ', in Warwick Gould, *Yeats Annual No. 7* (1990), pp.29–50.

Pierce, David, *W. B. Yeats: A guide through the critical maze* (Bristol, 1989).

Plotinus, *An Essay on the Beautiful*, trans. Thomas Taylor (London, 1794).

Pound, Ezra. For *Literary Essays*, see Eliot, T.S.

Pound, Ezra and Ernest Fenollosa, *The Classic Noh Theatre of Japan* (New York, 1959).

Putzel, Steven, *Reconstructing Yeats*: The Secret Rose and The Wind Among the Reeds (Dublin and Totowa, N.J., 1986).

Putzel, Steven, 'Poetic ritual and audience response: Yeats and the Nō', in Orr, pp. 105–25.

Qamber, Akhtar, *Yeats and the Noh* (New York and Tokyo, 1974).

Raine, Kathleen, *Yeats the Initiate: Essays on certain themes in the work of W. B. Yeats* (Dublin and London, 1986).

Ramazani, Jahan, *Yeats and the Poetry of Death: Elegy, self-elegy and the sublime* (New Haven, CT and London, 1990).

Rees, Alwyn and Brinley Rees, *Celtic Heritage: Ancient tradition in Ireland and Wales* (London, 1961).

Reeves, Marjorie and Warwick Gould, *Joachim of Fiore and the Myth of the Eternal Evangel in the Nineteenth Century* (Oxford, 1987).

Regardie, Israel, *The Golden Dawn: An account of the teachings, rites and ceremonies*, 4 vols bound in one (St Paul, Minn., 1978).

Rhys, John, *Lectures on the Origin and Growth of Religion as Illustrated by Celtic Heathendom* (London, 1888).

Richards, Shaun. *See* Cairns, David.

Rolleston. T. W., *The Adventures of Finn Mac Cumhal and Other Stories of Ancient Ireland* (Dublin and Cork, 1979); reprinted from *The High Deeds of Finn* (London, 1910).

Roth, Phyllis A., *Bram Stoker* (Boston, 1982).

Rudd, Margaret, *Divided Image: A study of William Blake and W. B. Yeats* (London, 1953).

Said, Edward, *Orientalism: Western conceptions of the Orient* (London and Henley, 1978).

Sammels, Neil. *See* Hyland, Paul.

Scholem, Gershom G., *Major Trends in Jewish Mysticism*, 3rd revd edn (New York, 1973).

Schuchard, Ronald, 'The minstrel in the theatre: Arnold, Chaucer, and Yeats's new spiritual democracy', in Richard Finneran, *Yeats Annual No. 2* (1983), pp.3–24.

Sharp, E. A. and Matthay J. (eds), intro. and notes by William Sharp ['Fiona Macleod'], *Lyra Celtica: An anthology of representative Celtic poetry*, reprint of 2nd or 1924 edn (Edinburgh, 1932). First edn, 1896.

Skelton, Robin, *Celtic Contraries* (Syracuse, N.Y., 1991).

Smith, Stan, 'Porphyry's cup: Yeats, forgetfulness and the narrative order', in Warwick Gould, *Yeats Annual No. 5* (1987), pp.15–45.

Spenser, Edmund, *The Works of Edmund Spenser: A variorum edition*, ed. Edwin Greenlaw *et al.*, 10 vols (London and Baltimore, 1932–49).

Spitzer, Leo, 'On Yeats's poem "Leda and the Swan" ', *Modern Philology* 51 (1954), pp.271–6.

Spivak, Gayatri Chakravorty, 'Finding feminist readings: Dante-Yeats', in *American Criticism in the Poststructuralist Age*, ed. Ira Konigsberg (Michigan, 1981), pp.42–65.

Stallworthy, Jon, *Between the Lines: Yeats's poetry in the making* (Oxford, 1963).

Stoker, Bram, *Dracula*, ed. Maurice Hindle (Harmondsworth, 1993).

Surette, Leon, *A Light from Eleusis: A study of Ezra Pound's Cantos* (Oxford, 1979).

Symons, Arthur, *The Symbolist Movement in Literature* (London, 1899).

Taylor, Richard, 'Metrical variation in Yeats's verse', in Warwick Gould, *Yeats Annual No. 8* (1991), pp.21–38.

Thomas, Keith, *Religion and the Decline of Magic* (London, 1971).

Torchiana, Donald T., *W. B. Yeats and Georgian Ireland* (Evanston, Ill., 1968).

Unterecker, John (ed.), *Yeats: A collection of critical essays* (Englewood Cliffs, N.J., 1963).

Unterecker, John, *A Reader's Guide to W. B. Yeats* (London, 1965).

Vance, Norman, 'Celts and Carthaginians: Anglo-Irish literary relations, 1780–1820', *Irish Historical Studies* 22 (1981), pp.216–38.

Vendler, Helen, 'Technique in the earlier poems of Yeats', in Warwick Gould, *Yeats Annual No. 8* (1991), pp.3–20.

Waite, A. E., *The Real History of the Rosicrucians* (London, 1887).

Wallis, R. T. *Neoplatonism* (London, 1972).

Walsh, Edward. *See* Daly, John.

Westcott, Brooke F., 'Dionysius the Areopagite', *Contemporary Review*, 5 (May–August 1867), pp.1–28.

Westcott, Rev. William Wynn, *In Memory of Robert Fludd* (London, 1907).

Westcott, Rev. William Wynn (ed.), *Nicholas Flammel, His Exposition of the Hieroglyphical Figures Which he Caused to be Painted* (London, 1889).

Wilde, Oscar, *Poems*, 12th rev edn (London, 1913).

Wilson, F. A. C., *W. B. Yeats and Tradition* (London, 1958).

Wilson, Colin, *Aleister Crowley* (Wellingborough, 1987).

Wolpers, Theodor, 'Motif and theme as structural content units and "Concrete universals" ', in Werner Sollors (ed.), *The Return of Thematic Criticism: Harvard English studies*, 18 (Cambridge, Mass. and London, 1993), pp.80–91.

INDEX

Lightning Source UK Ltd.
Milton Keynes UK
UKOW041500210612

194838UK00012B/83/P